Blueprint for Space

Blueprint

Edited by Frederick I. Ordway III and Randy Liebermann

Prologue by Michael Collins

Epilogue by Arthur C. Clarke

Smithsonian Institution Press
Washington and London

for Space

SCIENCE FICTION
TO SCIENCE FACT

Contributors

Ben Bova

Edward O. Buckbee

Arthur C. Clarke

Michael Collins

Peter H. Diamandis

R. Cargill Hall

William K. Hartmann

Gerald S. Hawkins

Todd B. Hawley

Alan Ladwig

Randy Liebermann

John M. Logsdon

Ron Miller

Sam Moskowitz

Frederick I. Ordway III

Thomas O. Paine

Robert D. Richards

Sally K. Ride

Ernst Stuhlinger

Wernher von Braun

Charles Walker

Fred L. Whipple

Frank H. Winter

Editor: Matthew Abbate
Production Editor: Eileen D'Araujo
Designer: Alan Carter

Library of Congress Cataloging-in-Publication Data

Blueprint for space : science fiction to science fact /
edited by Frederick I. Ordway III and Randy
Liebermann.
p.   cm.
Includes bibliographical references and index.
ISBN 1-56098-072-9 (alk. paper). — ISBN 1-56098-
073-7 (pbk.)
1. Astronautics.   2. Astronautics and state—United
States.   I. Ordway, Frederick Ira, 1927–
II. Liebermann, Randy, 1956–
TL790.B64   1991
629.4—dc20   91-3160

British Library Cataloguing-in-Publication Data is
available

99 98 97 96 95 94 93 92 5 4 3 2 1

♾ The paper used in this publication meets the
minimum requirements of the American National
Standard for Permanence of Paper for Printed
Library Materials Z39.48–1984

The photographic assistance of J. Patrick Gardner
and Carol Bishop Hipps is gratefully acknowledged.

For permission to reproduce illustrations appearing
in this book, please correspond directly with the
owners of the works, as listed in the individual cap-
tions. The Smithsonian Institution Press does not
retain reproduction rights for these illustrations
individually, nor maintain a file of addresses for
photo sources.

Printed in Singapore by Toppan Printing Company

Contents

Preface

Blueprints for the human exploration of space are found in both fictional and nonfictional writings, some centuries old. Mark Siegel, the biographer of Hugo Gernsback, this century's most influential advocate of speculative literature, subtitles one of his chapters "Science Fiction Is the Blueprint of the Future." On the occasion of 20th-anniversary celebrations of the first manned landing on the Moon, the aerospace trade magazine *Aviation Week & Space Technology* published an editorial (17 July 1989) on "The Legacy of Apollo 11." Reminding its readers that the late Wernher von Braun's "genius and determination" had been "primary drivers" in realizing the lunar expeditions, the magazine added that years earlier he had drawn up "a blueprint . . . that charted the direction the U.S. should take following the lunar landings." The editorial went on to report that the space agency's administrator Admiral Richard H. Truly had "recently reviewed von Braun's plan and found that if NASA's budget had been maintained at Apollo-level funding over the last 20 years, the U.S. already would be operating a lunar base, would have manned crews en route to Mars and would be developing a second-generation space station." The editorial then asked, "Where are the U.S. space visionaries of comparable stature today?"

Recently the same magazine reported (17 December 1990) that "The Augustine committee's valiant effort has produced a solid blueprint which U.S. space planners should seize upon." This referred to the report of the White House/NASA Advisory Committee on the Future of the U.S. Space Program chaired by Norman R. Augustine. Among its 15 recommendations, no. 7 proposed that "technology be pursued which will enable a permanent, possibly man-tended outpost to be established on the Moon for the purposes of exploration and for the development of the experience base required for the eventual human exploration of Mars." Words like these, as this book will reveal, echo those uttered decades ago that not only influenced the decision to go to the Moon in the first place but recommended an ambitious post-Apollo surge into space.

This volume's 23 contributors represent an impressive array of interdisciplinary talent. We find three professional writers of science and science fiction; three astronomers, one of whom also happens to be an artist; an artist-author; an art historian; two aerospace historians; an authority on science, technology, and public policy specializing in space; three former astronauts who have gone on to occupy important positions in the aerospace field; three heads of large space organizations; three individuals with broad professional experience; and three educators.

The book is divided into four parts. The five chapters of Part One offer several perspectives on spaceflight's progression from dream to reality. In the first chapter, Ben Bova argues that space development is "desirable, important, even vital to humanity's continued existence and success"; that "the human species needs all that space has to offer us, all the knowledge, all the wealth, all the spiritual exaltation that comes with our expansion into this new realm."

Only recently have we come to appreciate the validity of this perspective. It took untold generations for an awareness of space to coalesce in the mass consciousness of mankind. As Gerald Hawkins writes in his chapter, what he calls a "mindstep" is a phenomenon that "takes hold slowly but relentlessly. Ideas pass from brain to brain, changing the whole thought pattern. . . . Just as a species requires a favorable environment to propagate, a mindstep takes hold and spreads when the conditions are right." For the idea of spaceflight, these conditions began to appear at the end of the nineteenth century and matured during the first half of the twentieth. "The new idea," continues Hawkins, "began to spread irreversibly sometime during the last 50 or 100 years; by the mid-twentieth century, leaving the Earth and its atmosphere had become a reality. Life on our ancestral world could not be the same again."

Long before flight into and beyond our atmosphere became a reality, it was the subject of dreams and aspirations. In the third chapter, Frederick Ordway follows the evolution of the spaceflight concept from ancient writings to the publication of Jules Verne's lunar tales during the last third of the nineteenth century. Imaginative flights into the skies, according to Ordway, "occurred long before Galileo Galilei's early-seventeenth-century telescopic observations of the Moon and planets." In fact, they can be found back in the second century after Christ. The heroes of Lukian of Samosata's *True History* reach "a large tract of land, like an island, round, shining, and remarkably full of light"—in short, they've reached the fictional Moon 1,800 years before Apollo astronauts Armstrong and Aldrin stood on the real one. The chapter continues to explore the rich and diversified literature built up over the centuries in response to man's ponderings of worlds beyond his own.

Ron Miller takes up the story during the last third of the nineteenth century, by which time modern notions of the spaceship were taking shape. It had become apparent that astronauts traveling through airless space would have to be as protected from the outside environment as crew members in a submarine. Not surprisingly, therefore, spaceship and submarine designs share many common features. In both, air has to be provided as well as temperature control and food and water. Moreover, if a spaceship is to land on an airless body, something akin to an aquatic diving suit becomes indispensable. Despite improved awareness of what a real space vehicle might one day become, progress did not follow a straight line from fantasy to reality. But with the arrival of the twentieth century, such fantastic

schemes as the "anti-gravity ship" had largely disappeared; by then, most writers understood that on the rocket and the rocket alone rested man's destiny as a spacefaring creature.

Miller devotes the latter portion of his chapter to the space artist, his own specialty. "The late nineteenth century saw the visual arts finally catch up with the breadth of vision in fiction and scientific speculation," he explains. "If the authors of scientific romances were creating more and more imaginative—and increasingly plausible—schemes for leaving the Earth, artists were beginning to illustrate the reasons we had for wanting to leave." Miller draws an analogy with the penetration of the American West by colonists from the eastern seaboard, accompanied and partly instigated by artists' visions of the lands being opened. As this book demonstrates at several points, the collaboration of the space artist and the space engineer helped sensitize the public to the wonders and promise of space and to galvanize nations to seek its exploration.

During the first half of the twentieth century, an explosion of interest in what came to be known as science fiction occurred in the magazine literature. The better part of this literature appeared in the "pulp" variety, so named because of the nature of the paper used in its manufacture. Many prominent scientists and engineers pursued careers in rocketry and astronautics as a result of reading about space travel in the pulps. The astonishing growth of science fiction in the magazine literature is chronicled in the final chapter of Part One. Sam Moskowitz begins his story at the end of the nineteenth century with the appearance of science fiction particularly in London and San Francisco. We learn that H. G. Wells's famed *The War of the Worlds* first appeared as a serial in *Pearson's Magazine* in England and in *The Cosmopolitan* in the United States. At about the same time, André Laurie's *A Month in the Moon* came out as an eight-part serial. Science fiction got a boost in 1912 with the publication of Edgar Rice Burroughs's delightful *Under the Moons of Mars*. Influenced by the late-nineteenth-century discoveries of *canali* (channels or grooves) on Mars by Italian astronomer Giovanni Virginio Schiaparelli and their interpretation as artificially constructed canals by the American astronomer Percival Lowell, Burroughs painted an intriguing image of Martian peoples, animals, and flora. As Moskowitz writes, "Burroughs brought into being and made immensely popular a form of science fiction frequently called the 'scientific romance.' It stressed imaginative, colorful, and romantic adventures set on other worlds, in other dimensions, and in otherwise remote locales."

Pulp magazines continued to be the mainstay of science fiction throughout the 1930s and 1940s, only to die out by the mid-1950s. Henceforth, readers would find their science fiction in digest-format magazines, paperbacks, and hardcover books. Meanwhile, much of what they had been reading in the old pulps was about to become the stuff of reality.

Two quite distinct paths led to the reality of space travel: man's expanding knowledge of the universe coupled with a growing appetite to explore it; and, until the end of the nineteenth century, the completely unrelated evolution of the rocket that eventually would make exploration possible. Part Two tells the story of the rocket from its origin to the eve of its first tentative probings into space. Frederick Ordway relates how the rocket got its start in eleventh-century China and gradually made its way into western Europe carried by Mongolian invaders. By the second half of the thirteenth century rockets were being described in European manuscripts, and during the next couple of hundred years they became increasingly commonplace in festive pyrotechnic displays and to a much lesser extent in warfare.

A surge of interest in the latter aspect of rocketry resulted from the experiences of British troops in India. There, rockets were being employed by local armies to such an extent that they came to the attention of William Congreve, a brilliant ordnance engineer. Early in the nineteenth century, at his laboratory at Woolwich Arsenal near London, he studied and then improved upon captured Indian designs. Soon, the English were using rockets in campaigns on the Continent and in naval engagements throughout their colonial empire. Other European powers followed suit as the first golden age of rocketry flourished during much of the century. By the end of the same century, the rocket was being eclipsed by vastly improved artillery and gradually phased out of military service. It briefly reemerged during the First World War, only to languish following the armistice.

Events that followed are picked up by Frank Winter. In his first chapter, he explores the work of the American rocket pioneer Robert H. Goddard, who, in 1926, launched the world's first liquid-propellant rocket. (All earlier rockets had relied on solid pro-

pellants that had been in use, in one form or another, for centuries.) Other early experimenters with liquid propellants were the members of the American Interplanetary (later, Rocket) Society and its German equivalent, the Verein für Raumschiffahrt (Society for Spaceship Travel, VfR) whose members were inspired by another pioneer, Hermann Oberth.

Building on work undertaken by the VfR, German army ordnance and artillery experts stepped into the picture beginning in 1932. At the urging of Captain Walter R. Dornberger, young Wernher von Braun and a few associates from the VfR accepted contracts to work for the army; in 10 short years this would result in the first successful test firing of the long-range A-4 ballistic missile that toward the end of World War II became known to the world as the V-2. It was not only "one of the war's most awesome weapons" but also, Winter adds, "the direct ancestor of the spaceship."

In the next chapter, Winter regresses to the 1880s to examine how the scientific underpinnings of spaceflight were conceived and developed. The first man to demonstrate rigorously the reaction principle's relationship to interplanetary travel was the Russian schoolteacher Konstantin Eduardovich Tsiolkovsky. Concluding that he was "the first spaceflight planner," Winter recalls Tsiolkovsky's early deliberations as to the role of rockets in spaceflight: "For a long time I regarded rockets, in the same way as others did, as diversions of limited practical use."

Once the seed had been planted, the idea blossomed. Working quite independently of Tsiolkovsky, Robert Esnault-Pelterie in France, Goddard in the United States, and Hermann Oberth in German-speaking Transylvania all came to recognize the indispensable role of the rocket and to varying extents sought to promote its development. Of the three, Goddard focused most of his energies on the practical development of liquid-propellant rockets. For their parts, Esnault-Pelterie and Oberth concentrated on the theoretical aspects of astronautics through fundamental—and now classic—writings on the subject. The work of all four pioneers, Tsiolkovsky, Esnault-Pelterie, Goddard, and Oberth, led to a proliferation of efforts by colleagues and followers in their respective countries. As it turned out, many space enthusiasts banded together in rocket and space travel societies that sprang up in the late 1920s and early 1930s.

The final chapter in Part Two is by Ernst Stuhlinger, a former collaborator of von Braun's whose career in rocketry began at Peenemünde during World War II and continued in the United States through the Apollo expeditions to the Moon, the launching of America's Skylab space station, and the beginning of the development of the space shuttle Earth-to-orbit transportation system. Stuhlinger's story begins at the end of the 1930s; carrying us through World War II, he relates how the A-4 (V-2) came into being as one of the great technological triumphs of the age. At the end of hostilities, von Braun and a team of well over a hundred engineers and scientists transferred to the United States. Cooperating closely with erstwhile enemies, the Germans helped their new American colleagues convert the V-2 from a weapon of war to a device of peace. Newly modified rockets were pressed into service to explore the upper reaches of the atmosphere and fringes of space. The assault on the "third dimension" had begun in earnest.

During its first five years in America, the von Braun team shuttled between their home base at Fort Bliss, Texas, and the V-2 launching range at White Sands, New Mexico. Then, beginning in the spring of 1950, team members and their families moved from the southwest to Huntsville, Alabama, site of the sprawling Redstone Arsenal complex. There, von Braun began to reach out directly to the American public with a message that was at once compelling and intriguing: we can reach the Moon and planets sooner than we think. "From then on," remembers Stuhlinger, "and for the next 25 years, von Braun grasped every opportunity, private and public, to talk and write about rockets and spaceflight. He addressed writers and publishers, educators and politicians, engineers and industrialists, scientists, economists, generals, and statesmen—the more prominent, the better!"

The next five chapters cover what many consider to be the golden age of space travel: the period from the end of World War II in 1945 to the landing of Apollo 11 astronauts on the Moon in mid-1969. During this period, many war-derived technological wonders penetrated society, the civilian use of atomic energy being the most obvious. It was also a time when the public began to think of space travel in terms other than those of science fiction. The prospect of travel beyond the Earth came to hold such a grip on the public that it provided a constant

theme in advertising, television, motion pictures, consumer goods, books, and magazines.

Fred L. Whipple summarizes the heady days following World War II when the idea of Earth satellites began to be considered in sober scientific terms. He introduces us to some key personalities who helped propel America into space, and to the role of the German V-2s brought to the United States after the war to undertake scientific investigations of the upper atmosphere and borders of space. Once the space frontier had been penetrated by the modified wartime missiles, Whipple notes, it was only a matter of time until rocket-lofted payloads would be sent into Earth orbit.

That achievement, it turned out, required political as well as scientific and engineering acumen. In the case of the United States, to sell a viable space program to the executive and legislative branches of government, one first had to convince the public that the concept was feasible. A major effort to reach out to the public was a series of articles published in the popular weekly magazine *Collier's*. As Randy Liebermann relates in his chapter, these articles were inspired in part by a space travel symposium held in New York's Hayden Planetarium in October 1951 and in part by another symposium held in San Antonio, Texas, the same year. *Collier's* soon called together Wernher von Braun, Fred L. Whipple, and other experts to lay out a blueprint for manned flight into orbit, to the Moon, and eventually to Mars. So brilliantly illustrated were the *Collier's* articles that likenesses of von Braun's space vehicle designs soon appeared in movies, books, posters, even children's lunch boxes. His designs also came to life in three films produced by Walt Disney for the "Tomorrowland" segment of the "Disneyland" television series, which was viewed by millions during the latter half of the 1950s.

Once the United States had launched Explorer I, its first artificial satellite, in late January 1958, it was no easy matter to maintain support for further activities in space. John Logsdon reviews the national and international political climate that influenced President Kennedy's decision to approve the Apollo effort to land an American on the Moon. After eight years of but modest interest in space exhibited by the Eisenhower administration, the new president felt space offered an ideal vehicle to demonstrate America's prowess to the world. Kennedy also wanted to counteract a humiliating series of disappointments growing out of Soviet triumphs that included the first unmanned satellite, the first manned satellite, and the first space walk.

R. Cargill Hall discusses some of the political hurdles that had to be negotiated as well as the technological challenges that had to be met once the Apollo program was under way. Momentum had to be maintained during a period when America was engaged in an Asian war, was suffering social unrest at home, and was beginning to become concerned with environmental issues. As it turned out, Apollo was the result of political expediency rather than a discrete, well-planned step in a long-term process of space exploration. In fact, Apollo came to an abrupt end: before the program was over, three missions were canceled, leaving Apollo 17 to culminate man's exploration of the Moon for decades to come.

Following the Apollo 11 triumph in July 1969, Wernher von Braun looked forward to a long-term commitment to space exploration. In a previously unpublished essay that appears here, he outlined many of the practical benefits of space while calling for the continued study of the Moon to be followed by manned missions to Mars. He was convinced that the future viability of his adopted nation lay in its increased presence in space. Von Braun drew a parallel to those nations that took part in the great diaspora of the fifteenth and sixteenth centuries and found themselves transformed to the point that "Europeans and their American offspring have ever since led the world in intellectual dynamism."

Having met President Kennedy's goal of landing men on the Moon by the end of the 1960s, the United States space program began to lose its sense of direction and seemed to some to be floundering. The five chapters that constitute Part Four suggest that the promise of space is as inspiring as ever but may remain unfilled unless drive, purpose, and commitment are rekindled.

Sally K. Ride and Alan Ladwig review selected recommendations of individuals, task groups, and commissions interested in generating such a commitment. Responding to Thomas O. Paine's National Commission on Space 1986 report to President Reagan, NASA Administrator James C. Fletcher stated, "It is our intent that this process [adopting a revised set of goals and objectives] produce a blueprint to guide the United States to a position of leadership among the spacefaring nations of the Earth." NASA also responded to the Paine report by creating a

■

This photograph of crescent-shaped Earth and Moon, the first ever taken by a spacecraft, was made on 18 September 1977 by Voyager 1 when it was 7.25 million miles (11.66 million kilometers) from the Earth. As viewed from the spacecraft, the Moon (top) was beyond the Earth (below). When the picture was taken, Voyager 1 was directly above Mount Everest. NASA.

Long-Range Planning Task Force on which both Ride and Ladwig served. Their conclusion: the United States needs a program that "builds the nation's capabilities to explore and operate in space. . . . The program must feature visible and periodic accomplishments to sustain the necessary long-term commitment and support."

Without presidential—and congressional—support, such a program would inevitably languish. But additional support must be sought elsewhere. In the United States, several approaches are described by Edward O. Buckbee and Charles Walker. In the first part of the chapter, Buckbee addresses the importance of science centers and museums as educational tools, able to raise public awareness of the value of spaceflight and the many disciplines on which it relies. To capture the imagination of youth and develop curiosity toward science, engineering and mathematics are among the goals of the U.S. Space & Rocket Center in Huntsville, Alabama, which opened its doors in 1970, and of the U.S. Space Camp, which offered its first session in 1982. Buckbee, who is Center director, stresses that hands-on experience is essential to the Space Camp process, reinforcing otherwise abstract concepts traditionally taught in formal classroom situations. "A survey has shown," he reports, "that 91 percent of all Space Camp/Academy [for those over 12] attendees have become more interested in mathematics, science, and technology than before their space training experience." By early 1991, the 100,000th trainee had gone through the main camp at Huntsville and its Florida counterpart in Titusville.

Well-organized activists also play an essential role in altering public perceptions on major issues. In the second part of the chapter, former astronaut Charles Walker sketches the history of two grass-roots, membership-based societies dedicated to publicizing the benefits, excitement, and purpose of spaceflight. After operating for many years as independent organizations, in 1986 the L5 Society, which was perceived as being somewhat radical, merged with the National Space Institute, perceived as more mainstream, to form the National Space Society. Since then, under Walker's presidency, it has grown to some 30,000 members and plays an effective liaison role between the public, the aerospace industry, and government.

Assessing space progress makes up the first part of William K. Hartmann's chapter, following which he offers a four-point program for future activities involving lunar bases, asteroid reconnaissance, and the exploration of Mars and its tiny moon Phobos. He is followed by former NASA administrator Thomas O. Paine, who provides a blueprint for the next 25 years in space. Paine sees "six challenging new technology bases and program elements" as forming the cornerstone to set into motion President Bush's Space Exploration Initiative.

In the final chapter, Robert D. Richards, Todd B. Hawley, and Peter H. Diamandis declare that human destiny is to live and work outside cradle Earth. Once this is realized, they say, old social structures will give way to new ones and mankind will become transformed in the process. The three authors suggest that new economic opportunities will emerge in the "off-Earth" environment, eventually creating economies that will compete with terrestrial ones.

Blueprint for Space concludes with an epilogue by Arthur C. Clarke, who revisits a review he wrote in 1950 of Willy Ley's and Chesley Bonestell's seminal *The Conquest of Space*. Clarke feels that it "probably did more than any other book of its time to convey to a whole generation the wonder, romance and sheer *beauty* of space travel."

An exhibition also entitled Blueprint for Space has been developed as a major educational component of the International Space Year 1992. Organized by the Space & Rocket Center under a grant from the IBM Corporation, its pre-ISY five-month run at the Center began in mid-1991 followed by its ISY premiere at the IBM Gallery of Science and Art in New York in January 1992. The exhibit opens for a year-long showing at Smithsonian's National Air and Space Museum in October 1992.

We hope that this book, and the exhibition that parallels it, will help demonstrate the importance of maintaining a vigorous, well-coordinated space program. The Augustine report observed that "the space program produces technology that enhances competitiveness; the largest rise and subsequent decline in the nation's output of much-needed science and engineering talent in recent decades coincided with, and some may say have been motivated by, the build-up and subsequent phase-down in the civil space program."

A thought all actual and potential spacefaring nations should ponder.

Frederick I. Ordway III
Washington, D.C.

Randy Liebermann
New York City

August 1991

Prologue

MICHAEL COLLINS

My key to success in the space program was that—like Neil Armstrong and Buzz Aldrin—I was born in 1930. We three were exactly the right age when flights to the Moon began. My own preparation for a career in astronautics had been oblique and unwitting. As a child, I was a clumsy but persistent model airplane builder and as a young adult I wanted to switch from unmanned to manned investigations. It was just after World War II and I lusted after each sleek new jet fighter. If I was too late for the *Spitfire* and *P-51*, how about the *Shooting Star* or the *Sabre-jet*? Soon I found myself a test pilot at a time when NASA decided that its new space machines should be flown by test pilots. Moltke the elder may be correct in observing that luck in the long run favors only the able, but certainly luck was the main ingredient in introducing me to space flight.

Not so for those whose stories are told in this book. Some of these people were dreamers who saw their dreams come true. Others were meticulous planners who mastered every detail of a machine or orbit. Some were dogged inventors, persisting despite ridicule. Others were brilliant scientists whose minds roamed freely through our solar system. Still others were organizers who understood that motivating teams of people was the first step on the celestial path. But all reached the expert level through skill and perseverance, not luck.

One man combined all these talents. When I knew him, in the 1960s, Wernher von Braun was leading a hectic life overseeing the birth and adolescence of the Saturn V rocket. Despite the mounting pressures of his schedule, he still had time to recall the early days of rocketry and to speculate about what might happen after Apollo. Mars seemed the obvious next step, and it was a familiar one to Wernher. In 1954, he had written a detailed account in *Collier's* magazine: "Can We Get to Mars?" His answer then was yes, but it might take a century. Over the next two decades he became considerably more optimistic. In 1969, he and others convinced Vice-President Spiro Agnew that Mars should be the post-Apollo goal, with two intermediate steps: a space station as a jumping-off point, and a shuttle to relay crew and supplies between Earth and station. Thus the shuttle was born, but the rest of the proposal died after an Agnew speech failed to generate public or congressional support. Wernher died too, in 1977, a cancer victim in middle age.

Since then, things have not gone well for the space program. Just as von Braun's luck ran out, so has NASA endured a series of mishaps and one tragedy, the loss of a shuttle crew. President Bush may be able to reverse this trend and put us back on track. As I look over this book, it all seems so sensible, so inevitable, that we go on to Mars, and now we have a president who agrees. Between the president and the red planet, however, there are a thousand intermediate steps. We need to ponder them, and *Blueprint for Space* is valuable in this process. It allows us to travel in time, to assess what has been done and what remains to be done before we can venture beyond the Moon.

When we do go, to Mars and beyond, all our skill—and I hope a lot of luck—will be riding along with the crew.

Part One

From Dream to Reality

The planet Mercury viewed
by the Mariner 10 spacecraft
on 29 March 1974. NASA.

The Vision of Spaceflight

BEN BOVA

Nothing is too wonderful to be true.
—Michael Faraday

Like all great human endeavors, our expansion into space began with dreams, with a vision of a future in which humankind has spread its seed among the stars. The dreamers always come first.

For me, the vision of spaceflight began when I was a schoolchild, in the 1940s, during a class trip to the Fels Planetarium. Raised in the narrow streets of South Philadelphia, I knew nothing of astronomy. You could hardly see a star in the scant slice of city sky between the rows of houses. We were ushered into a strange round room with the huge, almost eerie planetarium projector in its middle. The lights slowly dimmed, then went out altogether. I had never experienced real darkness before; no street lamps, no night glow of any kind penetrated the utter black.

Then they turned on the stars. And I became turned on, too. For the first time in my young life I got a vision of the real world out there beyond the limits of Earth. The course of my life changed at that moment. The stars drew me to them.

I began to haunt the Fels Planetarium on my own, and the science museum it was part of: the Franklin Institute. Gradually I began to learn some astronomy. I even learned that there were dreamers who believed that one day human explorers might reach out toward the stars.

Today, half a century later, I can recite dozens of very practical reasons why space development is desirable, important, even vital to humanity's continued existence and success. But behind it all is that original thrill, that moment of sheer joyful revelation, that vision of the universe.

We live at the edge of a frontier that begins a

■

Optical effects produced in the atmosphere of Mercury. From Camille Flammarion, Les terres du ciel. *Paris, 1884. Ordway Collection/Space & Rocket Center.*

scant hundred miles from where you are now. Roughly a hundred miles overhead, space begins. It is a frontier in every sense of the word, a new unexplored region that offers knowledge and wealth and adventure beyond our most fantastic dreams. Not since Europe began to expand across the Atlantic Ocean and into the Americas has there been such an adventure.

We desperately need that promise. The human species needs all that space has to offer us, all the knowledge, all the wealth, all the spiritual exaltation that comes with our expansion into this new realm. We need it urgently. For we are engaged in a new space race, like it or not. This race is not merely between two nations jockeying for political prestige and military power, as the USA and USSR did in

■

Viewed from the planet Venus, our Earth shines brightly in the sky. From Camille Flammarion, Les *terres du ciel.* Paris, 1884. *Ordway Collection/Space & Rocket Center.*

the space race of the 1960s. This new race involves the entire human species in a competition against time. All of the people of Earth—indeed, all of the life-forms on Earth—are in a desperate race against global disaster.

Starvation stalks our world in Africa and Asia. Malnutrition is pervasive over more than half the globe. Thousands of species of plant and animal life are being driven into extinction. Pollution chokes the air and fouls the seas. The protective screen of ozone high in our atmosphere, thin as a winter's first gentle dusting of snow, is being eaten away by man-made chemicals. Global temperatures are rising, causing fears of a greenhouse effect that will drastically alter climates all over the world.

While the threat of nuclear confrontation between the superpowers lessens, smaller nations are acquiring nuclear know-how and building rocket boosters to carry weapons of mass annihilation. Chemical and biological weapons, "the poor man's atomic bomb," are available to almost any nation that wants them. Civil wars rage in Afghanistan, Cambodia, and elsewhere, while smaller-scale strife—no less deadly—simmers from Ireland to Israel to India. Terrorism kills innocent men, women, and children almost at random.

All the potential disasters we face, from the possibility of nuclear war to the eventual ecological collapse brought about by the greenhouse warming, have one factor in common: their root cause is population pressure. There are nearly five and a half billion people on Earth today. In the few seconds it takes to read this sentence, nearly twenty more people will be added.

It is fashionable, in some circles, to claim that this swelling tide of humanity is reaching the limits that our planet Earth can support. I doubt that. Properly husbanded, the resources of our planet could support ten or twenty billion people, perhaps more. But we do not husband our resources wisely. Since proto-humans camped at Olduvai Gorge two or three million years ago, we have had a throw-away mentality. We tend to take from our environment what is easiest to get, and then move on when we've plucked the place clean.

The human population of Earth will reach six billion before the end of the century. And it will continue to grow just as rapidly in the next millennium. As we increase our own numbers, we are rapidly destroying the biological resources on which we de-

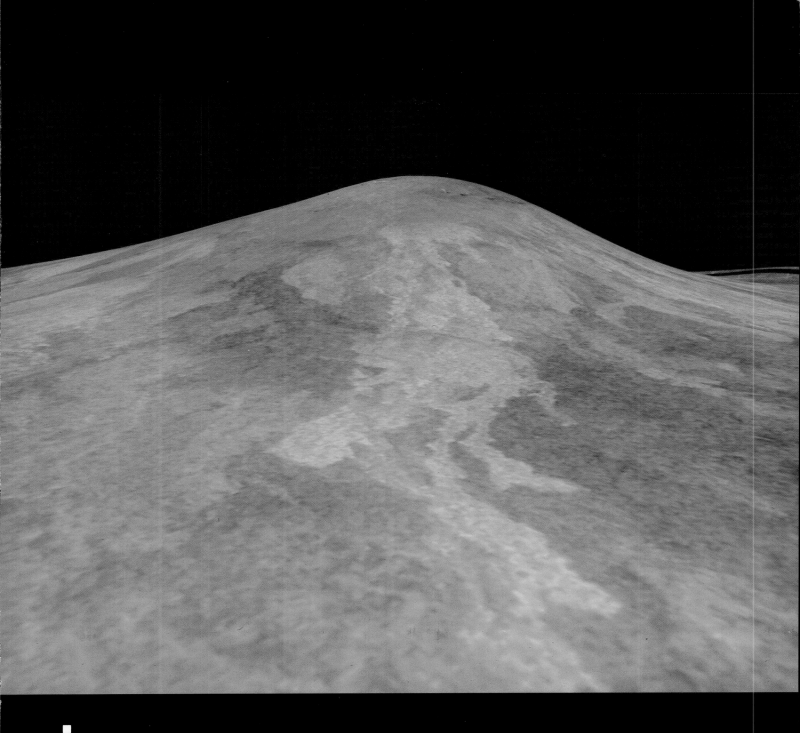

This false color view of the
volcano Sif Mons on Venus
was prepared in December
1990 by superimposing Magellan spacecraft radar image
data on information derived
from topographic measure-
ments. Bright and darker
lava flows are seen in the
central part of the image; the
bright flow is over 70 miles
long. NASA.

and smaller slices. Even with the fairest distribution, however, if population keeps growing eventually the slices will become so slim that everyone faces starvation.

We can try to curb population growth. Easier said than done. While the rich, industrialized nations have largely stabilized their population growth, the poorer nations continue to explode with babies. China achieved some measure of population control under the stern dictates of its government, but once Peking liberalized its economy its population figures began to soar again. India is growing so fast that it will have more people than China within a decade or so. Africa and Latin America are bursting. Even in the richest nation on Earth there are powerful groups who oppose family planning and population control measures.

To control global population growth would require, apparently, a global dictatorship of unprecedented scope and power. Science fiction tales have

This first color picture taken by the Viking 2 Lander on the Martian surface reveals a rocky, reddish panorama. The right edge of the picture is due east of the spacecraft and the Sun is behind the camera in the Martian afternoon. Because Viking 2 was tilted about 8 degrees to the west, the horizon appears tilted though in fact it is nearly level. NASA.

pend. Croplands are turning to desert. Forests are being torn down. Fisheries are being exhausted. Grazing grounds are turning into housing developments and shopping malls. Faster than any of these is the destruction of our social systems. The social fabric of human civilization is unraveling under the unremitting pressure of constant population growth. The narcotics plague that afflicts much of the world today is an obvious symptom of this situation. The wars, the tensions, the terrorism, the ecological threats we face are further symptoms. The people of the world are arguing—sometimes with guns, more often with economic weaponry—over who gets which share of the world's dwindling resources, and at what price.

Think of this planet's supply of resources as a great pie. Every living human wants as large a slice of that pie as he or she can get. The more people there are, the more slices there must be. If the human population grows too far, there will not be enough to go around. Famine, starvation, war are the results. We are *already* in that quandary.

What to do?

We can continue to divide the pie into smaller

Sunrise over the canals of Mars. From Camille Flammarion, Les terres du ciel. *Paris, 1884. Ordway Collection/Space & Rocket Center.*

■

The surface of Jupiter lit by two of its large moons. From Camille Flammarion, Les terres du ciel. *Paris, 1884. Ordway Collection/Space & Rocket Center.*

■

Jupiter and two of its many moons, Europa to the left and Io to the right, imaged by the Voyager 1 spacecraft on 13 February 1979 at a distance of 12.4 million miles (20 million kilometers). The dominant large-scale atmospheric motions are west-to-east. Europa, which exhibits less color variation than Io, is about 375,000 miles (600,000 kilometers) above the Jovian clouds, while dark orange to reddish Io is about 222,000 miles (350,000 kilometers) above Jupiter's famed Great Red Spot. NASA.

warned of governments that can reach into the bedroom and force limits on family size. Is that the only way the human species can save itself from destruction?

There is a possible alternative. Looking at the population growth figures, one is struck by the fact that the richest nations have the lowest growth. Even within the United States, the poorest people have the biggest families. The most effective way to slow population growth is to make poor people rich. Redistributing the world's wealth is ineffective, however. First, the rich resist such redistribution, and the rich usually have the reins of political power firmly in their hands. Second, there are not enough rich! Consider the pie that represents all the Earth's resources. It may not be large enough to make everyone rich enough to slow the population explosion.

The alternative, then, is to make the pie bigger.

That is where spaceflight comes in. No one who has thought about the problem for more than ten minutes seriously advocates exporting the Earth's "excess" population into space. Even if people agreed to such emigration and there were livable habitats to send them to, it would take most of the planet's resources simply to lift those billions off the surface of the Earth.

There is a better way: utilize the wealth to be found in space to make the people of this Earth richer. The first three decades of space exploration have shown that our planet is part of a solar system that is incredibly rich in energy, in natural resources, in all the physical wealth and raw materials we need to build a flourishing, fair, and free global society.

Three antiquated modes of thought stand in the way of utilizing space resources to increase humankind's supply of real wealth. I call these three misconceptions the Flat-Earth Fallacy, the Either/Or Fallacy, and the Mañana Fallacy.

The Flat-Earth Fallacy: Many well-intentioned people believe that spaceflight is an extravagance, a luxury that our increasingly impoverished Earth cannot afford. "Let us solve the problems we face here on Earth," they say, "before we spend any further funds on exploring outer space."

I believe, however, that we will *never* solve the problems we face here on Earth *unless* we draw upon the wealth of space.

■

Voyager 2 obtained this stunning picture of Saturn and its rings from a distance of 2.1 million miles (3.4 million kilometers) on 30 August 1981. The view shows some detail and differences in the complex ring system. NASA.

Saturn's rings seen from the planet's supposed rugged surface through the clouds. Camille Flammarion, Les terres du ciel. *Paris, 1884.* Ordway Collection/Space & Rocket Center.

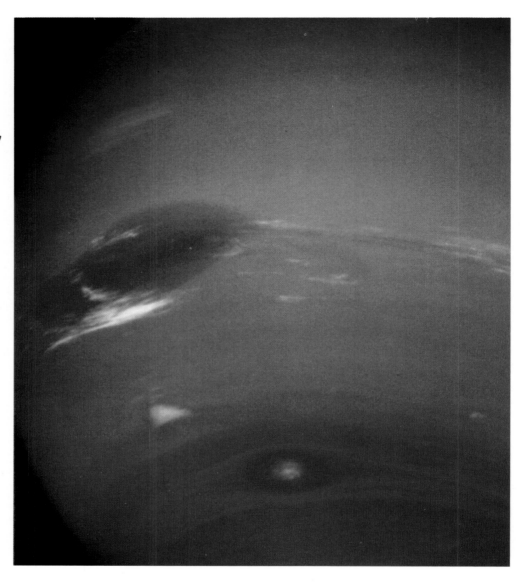

This photograph of Neptune was reconstructed from two images taken on 23 August 1989 by Voyager 2's narrow-angle camera through green and clear filters. At the north (top) is the Great Dark Spot, and in the lower southern hemisphere is a bright feature nicknamed "Scooter." Still farther south is Dark Spot 2 (one of three smaller spots), identified by its bright core. Each of these features moves eastward at a different velocity, with the result that only occasionally do they appear close to each other. NASA.

The Earth is not flat. Our planet exists in the midst of the most gigantic supply of energy and natural resources imaginable. There is no real separation between Earth and space; indeed, physicists and lawyers alike find it difficult to say where "Earth" stops and "space" begins. To solve the problems of Earth we need new wealth. Space can generate new wealth. The natural resources and the energy are there. So are the ideas for constructing new kinds of factories and laboratories in space, capable of producing new knowledge and products for use on the ground.

What makes the rich nations rich? Today, the answer is high technology. For half a century the Soviet Union struggled to become the world's leader in heavy industry. It achieved that enormous feat despite the terrible toll of World War II. Yet the Soviet economy is in a shambles, largely because leading the world in steel and oil production no longer guarantees a powerful economy.

Contrast the Soviet experience with the lowly transistor. Who would have thought that silicon, the stuff of common sand, would be the raw material for an industrial revolution?[1] Yet the industries of Silicon Valley and similar centers are the backbone of virtually every Western nation's economy today. The raw material is lowly, but the ideas that turned silicon into the electronics revolution have generated trillions of dollars in gross national product for the industrialized nations of the West.

Similar opportunities await us in space. Utilizing microgravity, virtually free solar energy, and raw materials from the Moon or asteroids, vast new industries are waiting to be born in space. Yet the pessimists still sing their Malthusian song, and learnedly speak of the tragedy of the commons:

Men seeking gain naturally desire to increase the size of their herds. Since the commons [grazing ground] is finite, the day must come when the total number of cattle reaches the carrying capacity; the addition of more cattle will . . . eventually destroy the resource on which the herdsmen depend.[2]

■

"Neptune appears to symbolize a world of ice." From Camille Flammarion, Les terres du ciel. *Paris, 1884. Ordway Collection / Space & Rocket Center.*

Since the commons is finite. That is the Flat-Earth Fallacy in a nutshell. We are no longer restricted to the resources obtainable from this one planet alone. The solar system is hostile to human habitation, yet incredibly rich in energy and natural resources. It may be generations before large numbers of people can live in space. But we can, today, send a small number of men and women into space to begin to reap the resources waiting there for us. We need not starve to death because we are in the midst of plenty. The Earth is not flat.

The Either/Or Fallacy: Should the major objective of the United States in space be Mars or the Moon? Should we continue manned spaceflight at all, or concentrate on unmanned scientific probes of the solar system?

Those are two prime examples of the Either/Or Fallacy. This fallacy is a frame of mind that falsely assumes two goals to be in conflict with one another. In the hands of a cynical politician, the Either/Or Fallacy can be a potent weapon indeed. Should we fund space exploration at all, or spend the money on social welfare programs? If you say that you want to feed the poor, then you have admitted that we should not push the exploration of space. If you say you want to do more in space, you are showing that you do not care about the needy.

The answer to this conundrum, of course, is this: space feeds the poor. The American investment in space technology has created more jobs and real wealth in the U.S. economy than all the welfare programs since the end of World War II. Studies have shown that space-derived industries such as space transportation and payload processing, satellite communications, satellite remote sensing, and low-gravity materials research and processing have been growing at an average rate of 18 percent per year, and now generate some $50 billion per year for the U.S. gross domestic product. In another decade they will bring more than $70 billion annually into the American economy.

When it is brought out into the open, it is easy to see that the Either/Or Fallacy truly is a fallacy, a false assumption built on false premises. We must reject the either/or thinking that says we cannot fund a vigorous space program at the same time that we fund enlarged programs in other areas. To pit space development against social welfare programs is the cruelest kind of political cynicism, disastrous for the entire world, rich and poor. Without tapping the riches of the solar system, all the world's welfare programs, all

The clearest view ever achieved of outermost planet Pluto and its moon Charon was made possible by the Faint Object Camera of the Hubble Space Telescope. The image is the first long-duration Hubble exposure taken of a moving target. Because Pluto was not discovered until the twentieth century, no nineteenth-century artist's conception of the planet exists. NASA.

the interdependent global economy, will inevitably fall into ruin. To solve the problems of Earth we must look beyond the limits of our one planet.

It is vital to look on space as a necessary area of investment and development, rather than as a luxury. That is the way to break out of the cruel tyranny of the Either/Or Fallacy. Until we do, our efforts in space will always be governed by politics, expediency, and myopia.

The Mañana Fallacy: For an entire generation now, people have watched rocket boosters roar into the heavens. They have seen astronauts and cosmonauts living and working in space. Many have even touched rocks brought back from the Moon. Yet they still say, "Space may be important for my children and grandchildren, but it is not important in my own lifetime."

Mañana. Tomorrow. The fact is that space is already paying off today, with new jobs and new industries that enrich our lives and strengthen our economy. We have already seen that space-derived technologies pump tens of billions of dollars annually into the American economy. The communications satellite industry alone is a multi-billion-dollar market, world-wide. Satellite remote sensing systems, such as France's SPOT, are creating a new international industry before our eyes.

The future belongs to those who build it. The twenty-first century is less than ten years away. In that century human beings will begin to transform the economic and social systems of Earth, thanks to the abundant wealth they will develop in space. Eventually human habitation will expand to the Moon, and then beyond, out to the belt of asteroids that orbit between Mars and Jupiter, and farther still.

The human race will become truly a spacefaring species. No longer bound to the surface of one little world, our species will ultimately ensure its own immortality, able to survive even the death of our home planet, if need be. Like gleaming pearls on an invisible linkage of communications waves, space habitats will spread across the void, carrying the human species to its destiny among the stars, taking us, as Robert Frost wrote in "The Gift Outright,"

To the land vaguely realizing westward,
But still unstoried, artless, unenhanced,
Such as she was, such as she would become.

Notes

1. Actually, a few science fiction writers considered the prospect decades before it actually happened, but practically no one paid any attention to them.
2. Richard J. Barnet, *The Lean Years* (New York, 1980: Simon & Schuster).

For further reading

Boorstin, Daniel J. *The Discoverers.* New York, 1983: Random House.

Bova, Ben. *The High Road.* Boston, 1981: Houghton Mifflin.

Bradbury, Ray. *The Martian Chronicles.* New York, 1950: Doubleday.

Coon, Carlton S. *The Story of Man.* New York, 1971: Alfred A. Knopf (third revised edition).

Dubos, René. *The Wooing of Earth.* New York, 1980: Charles Scribner's Sons.

Mindsteps to the Cosmos

GERALD S. HAWKINS

Humans are unique. There is nothing on Earth gifted with intelligence to equal *Homo sapiens*'s. We are born of the cosmos, but is there a place for us in this glittering jewel box of galaxies and stars? The astronomical clock ticks in measured beats, and life cycles pulse like beacons on our delicate planet. Human minds open and reach out, but is there a cosmic destiny, and will it be fulfilled? Only recently have we been able to trace faintly our first steps as Sapiens, the Intelligent, and those vital threads before that time.

Cave Art and Mindstep 0

In some caves and rock shelters there are circles, some with rays. These might be Sun symbols carefully drawn. Others might be stars. If this is so, the creative Stone Age artists, depictors of earth and animals, were also watching the heavens. Their boundary was not the local environment of the Neanderthals, but the sky above. They went from things within their grasp to something beyond their reach. Perhaps; and if so, it was an important step. They had a sense of wonder about the cosmos.

Cave art is the earliest evidence we have for human cosmic awareness. The act of looking, thinking, and communicating visually is a prerequisite for any connection between humans and the astronomical universe. It is a receptive state, a beginning, an awakening, a cosmic mindstep zero. Without reaching this stage of development there can be no progress in relating humans to the greater cosmos. No answers to the question can be found unless the question is asked.

A mindstep takes hold slowly but relentlessly. Ideas pass from brain to brain, changing the whole thought pattern. A mindstep once established will last indefinitely, like a species of plant or insect, until the next mindstep comes along. Just as a species requires a favorable environment to propagate, a mindstep takes hold and spreads when the conditions are right.

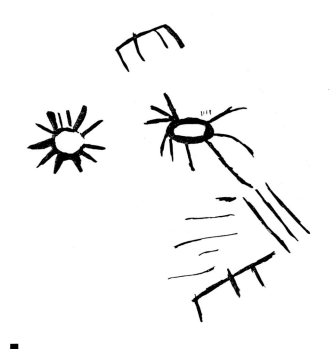

■

Replicas of cave drawings, possibly of the Sun, at La Pileta in Spain. Hawkins Collection.

*Four mindsteps, from the age
of chaos to the age of space.
Hawkins Collection.*

```
                                    ?
                              Age of Space
                           4
                     Age of Revolution
                  3
              Age of Order
           2
     Age of Myth and Legend
        1
  ○──→ Age of Chaos
```

It is interesting to speculate what would have happened if the Earth had been a cloud-shrouded planet. Sapiens the Intelligent would not have seen the stars. Quite possibly those early ancestors of ours would have continued to pick berries and hunt. They would never even have reached the starting point of mindstep 0. They would have become an entirely Earth-oriented species.

Myths, Legends, Stonehenge, and Mindstep 1

Mindstep 1 is linked with the development of myths and legends as explanations for the behavior of the gods of the sky. I tentatively place it at 3000 B.C., at the time of the invention of writing, though it could be earlier, perhaps as early as the paintings of the Moon phases in the rock shelters in Spain about 7000 B.C. One can hypothesize that the pattern is a Moon calendar, and that a legend was told about the changing shape of the Moon, but it is only a hypothesis, and the first hard evidence of astronomical stories comes along only with the appearance of writing.

Around 3500 B.C., the proto-Europeans began to build with large stones—megaliths. What impulse drove them to do this we do not know. The stones, sometimes roughly shaped, sometimes in natural form, were set up in rows, in circles, or alone on bleak hillsides and valleys as single standing menhirs. Tons of dead weight, a challenge to muscle and mind, seemingly impossible to move, these stones have stood through the centuries as a mystery for the civilizations that followed.

Stonehenge, in southern England, is the eighth wonder of the ancient world. In ruins when the Romans conquered Britain, and when King Arthur in fact or legend formed the Round Table at his court, Stonehenge with its air of mystery has inspired poets and story-tellers through the ages. Today more than a million people a year visit the site from all over the world to gaze at the mute standing stones, crusted with lichens and worn by the weathering of the years. One can hear almost every modern language there—German, Spanish, French, Japanese, Estonian, Arabic—yet the language of the original builders is unknown. The circle of stone is a quiet inspiration for the visitor, a symbol, a mindstep monument.

My interest in Stonehenge had begun in grade school when I read that the Sun rose in the avenue on 21 June and that the Druids had built it. But this was folklore tradition, not hard fact. Then I visited the site on Salisbury Plain in 1953 when I was a scientist doing military service with a missile-testing unit 3 miles to the north. At that time, Stonehenge

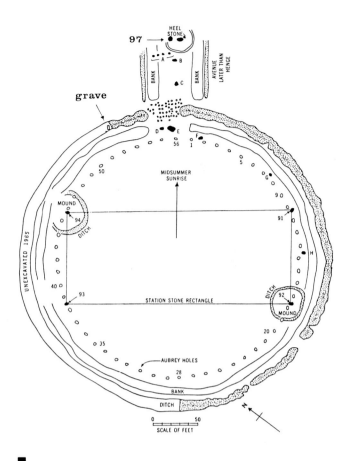

97 →

HEEL STONE

BANK BANK

AVENUE LATER THAN HENGE

grave

MIDSUMMER SUNRISE

UNEXCAVATED 1965

MOUND 94

DITCH

93

40

50

STATION STONE RECTANGLE

DITCH

92 MOUND

H

90

91

20

35

AUBREY HOLES

28

BANK

DITCH

0 50
SCALE OF FEET

■

Plan of the earliest work accomplished at Stonehenge. Hawkins Collection.

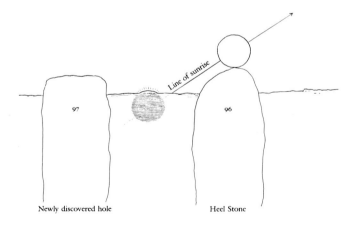

Line of sunrise

97

96

Newly discovered hole

Heel Stone

■

Track of the Sun over the heel stone at Stonehenge on a midsummer's day. Hawkins Collection.

was unfenced and sheep nibbled at the grass. The winter landscape was bleak and forbidding, the stones gray and challenging. Why were the archways so narrow—too narrow to walk through—and why did it have a ring of 56 chalk pits around it?

On paper the folklore claim about sunrise looked reasonable enough, but an accurate measurement at the site was needed to check the theory. Once a calibration point was fixed, then other lines could be investigated.

I returned to Stonehenge in the summer of 1961 to test the sunrise with a telephoto camera. As I stood there at dawn I could see through the viewfinder (and later measurements of the cine frames confirmed) that the Sun *did* stand on the tip of the heel stone as tradition had it. There was no basis for the doubts. Allowing for the tilt of the stone (now 20 degrees), and the passing years (4,500), the disc of the Sun stood precisely on the tip. Armed with this fact, I was able to calculate the azimuths (bearing angle from due north) of all the other lines. I found a good match with the rising and setting of the Sun at midsummer and midwinter. I also found lines and archway pairs that pointed to the Moon. By 1963, I had discovered 24 Sun and Moon alignments; by 1965, 32. Stonehenge was more than a ritual temple, more than a Stone Age architectural wonder; it contained astronomical and mathematical information, and this knowledge was not supposed to have been discovered until the time of the Greeks a full 1,000 years later.

It is natural in mindstep 1 to think of the sky as an enormous dome enclosing the Earth. That's the way the Greeks pictured the cosmos—a celestial sphere on which the stars were hung. The sphere was supposed to rotate once per day on perfect bearings, and this explained how the Sun rose in the east and set in the west. The stars were fixed on the sphere with the zodiac constellations making a wraparound belt. The planets, Sun, and Moon crawled slowly on the sphere. Mother Nature provided a giant planetarium.

The Stonehengers projected the zodiac onto the flat landscape. They watched how the ecliptic track moved along the horizon with the seasons. They joined the Earth to the sky with sight lines and created order from the disorder.

Stonehenge, complete, took about as long to build as the Gothic cathedrals, and was the most intricate and impressive of all the British stone circles. Like those cathedrals, Stonehenge was probably

a place of worship, an area for congregating, and a focus of learning and knowledge. For we who can only look at it as it is and attempt to imagine it as it was, Stonehenge stands as a monument to the concepts of mindstep 1.

Ptolemy and Mindstep 2

An astronomer named Ptolemy made the next step—mindstep 2. Living and working in the library at Alexandria, he had the collected knowledge of the world at his fingertips. We do not know whether he was Egyptian, Greek, or Roman—his Latinized name was Claudius Ptolemaus—but certainly he was influenced by all three cultures.

In Ptolemy's new system, the Earth was at the center and the Sun, Moon, and planets were supposed to revolve around it at spaced distances, the Moon being the nearest and Saturn the farthest away. Uranus, Neptune, and Pluto, of course, were yet to be discovered, and comets and meteors were dismissed as nonastronomical lights at the top of the atmosphere. The stars were hung on the inside of a revolving, crystalline sphere. It was a complicated system; yet, with one creative step, a mortal had brought the planets under mathematical law and created a new concept of space and time and things—at least for that region of outer space containing the Sun, Moon, and planets.

If Ptolemy had been a politician or potentate he could not have done better. The Ptolemaic system was practical, satisfying, and comfortable. The planets could no longer be gods if they followed the scribblings of a pen, yet there was room enough for the transcendental in the space beyond the crystalline sphere. The Earth was at the center of the universe as everyone expected it to be. Earth, air, fire, and water were separated. Heavenly things moved in circles, earthly things stayed put. There was a difference between the shining lights in space and the solid environment of earthlings. Earth did not shine, nor was it a planet. Earth was not balanced on the backs of four turtles in a pool of water; it was fixed, nonrotating, immovable, at the place where no disturbance could ever affect it—at the very heart of the cosmos.

If mindstep 0 depended on drawing and mindstep 1 depended on writing, then mindstep 2 depended on mathematics. Each of these was an aid to thinking and the broadcasting of an idea. They could be classed under the broad heading of communication technologies, because even mathematics is in some ways a language and creates a transmittable record.

Copernicus and Mindstep 3

Nicolaus Copernicus was a man for all seasons. Educated at the universities of Cracow, Bologna, and

Padua, he knew everything there was to know in Renaissance learning, from the Greek classics to medicine. In 1497, he was given the position of canon at Frauenburg cathedral, but he postponed ecclesiastical duties for six years to study astronomy and get a doctorate in canon law. Ptolemy's age of order was now fixed dogma, and Copernicus was expected to believe without question that earthlings lived at the center of the universe, that everything else moved about them in perfect circles, and that the Earth, nonplanet as it was taken to be, stood still.

Canon Copernicus worked at Frauenburg for more than 30 years on things ranging from the practicalities of monetary control and inflation to the finer points of pure theology. Astronomy was a lifelong hobby. Trusting his own mind before the opinions of others, he was aware of the shortcomings of the Ptolemaic system. Finally, after years of pondering, he decided that the movement of the planets could be described more satisfactorily if we took the Sun as fixed and the Earth as moving. With that step, the Earth took its place among the planets.

Copernicus argued that the Sun was a source of light and energy, was larger than the Earth, and was not like the planets, and therefore that it was more natural for the small Earth to travel around this unique object. With the Earth in orbit around the Sun, Copernicus argued for a second motion, a spin of the Earth on its axis. Then, the rising and setting of the Sun and stars would be caused by Earth's rotation. Earthlings were specks on a tiny globe, turning in the rotisserie of sunlight. He argued that the spin could not be felt by earthlings as a wind because the air was carried around with them in the rotation. To check his ideas, Copernicus made observations and did calculations with new equations of spherical trigonometry that had come from Hindu and Arab mathematicians.

Although Copernicus had created mindstep 3, his work was almost lost. He feared for the impact the idea would have and kept it almost a secret, sharing it with only a few. For 30 years he weighed his work carefully as he wrote out his arguments page by page. He realized that those pages if exposed might be destroyed as a heresy, but for him there was no way to escape the pressure of the mindstep.

Ptolemy's mindstep was copied by hand on parchment, but Copernicus's was spread by the new printing press. By 1566, the number of copies of his book

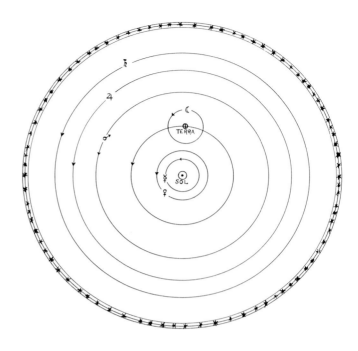

■

Diagram of the Copernican system with the Sun at the center of the solar system. Hawkins Collection.

in circulation had reached 900. Copernicus was by then speaking with 900 voices.

Ptolemy had pulled back the canopy to reveal divine points of light moving in space between us and the crystalline sphere of the immutable stars. In mindstep 2, earthlings were the passive audience and not a part of the show. Copernicus destroyed forever the secure feeling of a fixed, comfortable, central Earth. It spun, it orbited, it moved with the Sun and other planets through vast, unfathomable space. Compared to the greater cosmos, the Earth showed as it truly was—a planet, one of many, an insignificant thing. Bright stars were huge, distant suns, and fainter stars were suns in their thousands, farther away. Nothing lay between us and mysterious infinity. The notion of the crystalline sphere was shattered. "So great, without any question, is the divine handwork of the Almighty Creator!" exclaimed Copernicus in his 900 copies. Those words were ordered deleted by the Vatican censors. It was a disturbing revelation. It would take hundreds of years for greater humanity to adjust to the mindstep.

As the impact of mindstep 3 unfolded, the place of humans shrank to nothing. To passive, earth-bound observers looking out, the physical universe became impossible to comprehend. Nothing in its heritage had prepared the world for such a shock. Seen through a glass darkly at the limits of the telescope, the edge of the universe, filled with explosions and runaway galaxies, was as threatening to the mid-twentieth-century Earth as that awful edge of the Atlantic Ocean had been to Columbus's mutinous crew.

As it happened, mindstep 3 had run its course. Continuation in the role of nonparticipating audience would have produced more revolutionary discoveries, more demeaning facts, but no change of status. Continuing in 3, Sapiens the "wise" would turn inward to the frail ecology of the Earth and try to adjust to a negligible role in the greater cosmos. Without a further step, *Homo sapiens,* the only species known to be aware of the cosmos, to have higher intelligence, would become isolated, marooned on a speck of rock awaiting the red giant phase of the Sun. But a new perspective, even more bewildering and challenging, came along, and we live it today.

The Space Age and Mindstep 4

The old perspective has once again been shattered. We are no longer a passive audience gazing in wonder at the universe, be it a dome or infinitely extending space. We are no longer encapsulated, separated from the cosmic environment. The pod door has opened and human beings, for better or worse, have taken the first steps into the unknown of space. The required mental adjustment is mindstep 4. In all previous mindsteps, humans looked at, up, or out at the universe. From this point on, it is a domain in which to move, to travel, to touch, and to live. The new idea began to spread irreversibly sometime during the last 50 or 100 years; by the mid-twentieth century, leaving the Earth and its atmosphere had become a reality. Life on our ancestral world could not be the same again.

This fourth step gained an irreversible hold on the Earth's collective mind with the launching of Sputnik I on 4 October 1957. The media impact was as great as Orson Welles's radio dramatization of the H. G. Wells novel *War of the Worlds* in 1938, but now the coverage was not limited to the New York area—it was world-wide. I was a staff member of the Harvard-Smithsonian Observatories at the time of Sputnik; hearing the news on a car radio, I drove immediately to the Vanguard tracking center (intended to track the United States' not-yet-launched first satellite), still only half built in the botany building of Harvard University. The place was bedlam. Dozens of press reporters crowded in demanding to know everything there was to know about orbits, space travel, and the outer cosmos. Their first reaction was to denigrate, to disbelieve the Soviet achievement. "It can't be called a moon," they said. But Fred Whipple spoke for the astronomers, responding: "Gentlemen, if it makes one complete orbit, the Earth has a second satellite." Sputnik did. In colloquial Russian the word means "fellow traveler." Radio signals were picked up by a ham operator in New Jersey as the shiny 20-inch globe made its second pass over the United States. The press took Whipple's evaluation and headlines flashed in the world's many languages.

At dawn we got the first pictures. We used a makeshift tracking system—a 10-inch camera timed with a manual shutter. The satellite's rocket casing shone in the sunlight of space and moved silently across the starry background, powered by Earth's gravity. Period: 1 hour 20 minutes. Speed: 18,000 miles per hour plus. Our planet now had a second moon. "I can't believe it," said one technician. "Goodbye Copernicus!" said another.

Now, thousands of spacecraft circle the Earth, dozens circle the Sun, probes have reached every planet except Pluto, four are on their way to the stars, and astronauts have trod the mountains and plains of the Moon.

For further reading

Hawkins, Gerald S. *Beyond Stonehenge.* New York, 1973: Harper & Row.

Hawkins, Gerald S. *Mindsteps to the Cosmos.* New York, 1983: Harper & Row.

Hawkins, Gerald S. *Stonehenge Decoded.* New York, 1965: Doubleday.

Dreams of Space Travel from Antiquity to Verne

FREDERICK I. ORDWAY III

We don't know when the idea of flying into space first occurred to a human being. In the remote past a story-teller may have woven a tale of gods, or god-like men, soaring into the heavens. That they could attain such mysterious realms would surely have awed primitive listeners and set them to wondering about the lights in the skies above.

The concrete beginnings of the cosmic travel theme are not found in legends—though they may be based, in part at least, on legendary materials—but in the written literature. A fictional trip to another world could not be conceived until astronomy had given man some sort of notion of the universe and a tentative feeling for his approximate relationship to it.

Imaginative flights into the skies occurred long before Galileo Galilei's early-seventeenth-century telescopic observations of the Moon and planets. But they were flights of fantasy using the journey itself and the Moon as allegory. And the craft employed were little different from routine contemporary modes of transportation: in one story, someone even walked to the Moon! For centuries, there was no particular reason to suppose that the Moon—or the planets, for that matter—were in any way "real" in the sense the Earth was. There was no more need to invent a special device to visit the lunar sphere than there was to visit Heaven or Mount Olympus. The Moon, like Heaven and Olympus, was suitable only as a setting for allegory.

Allegory or otherwise, a few visionaries suspected that the Moon, and perhaps the planets, might be visited and might even be populated. When this

happened the stage was set for the appearance of the first works of space fiction.

If interpretations of astronomical observations and the development of imaginative literature did not advance along parallel tracks, they were at least distorted reflections of one another. The astronomical relationship between, for example, the Earth and Moon was for centuries believed to be such that a voyage between them would not entail severe hardships. To be sure, the precursors of latter-day space fiction writers had to stretch their sense of reality; but, seen in the context of their intellectual heritage, the solutions they proposed for heavenly travel were more plausible than they appear today.

The Beginnings of an Idea

We know of no pre-Christian-Era work that develops a tale wherein the hero departs from the Earth, makes a voyage, lands on another world, experiences adventures there, and returns—the minimum requirements of a proto–space fiction adventure. The arguments of Aristotle and other philosophers convinced most Greeks that there could be no Earth-like worlds in the universe; however, there were a few who suspected the Moon at least might be something like our planet. One was Plutarch (c. A.D. 46–120), who, in his *De facie in orbe lunae* (*On the Face That Appears in the Orb of the Moon*), countered that the Moon is similar to the Earth, though smaller, and is inhabited by a species of intelligent beings. The seed of space travel is seen in his view

Gustave Doré's depiction of Lukian's True History, *in which a sailing ship carrying Greek athletes is lifted by a "most violent whirlwind" to the Moon. Ordway Collection/Space & Rocket Center.*

that before birth and after death souls may wander off to our satellite and gaze upon its mysteries. Plutarch suggested that the Moon shines by reflected sunlight and that it revolves around the Earth as the Earth revolves around the Sun—an opinion almost unique in his day.

Even before Plutarch, the Latin statesman and orator Marcus Tullius Cicero had written *Somnium Scipionis* (*Scipio's Dream*), in which Scipio ponders the universe and the true insignificance of the Earth. He conjectured, "Below the Moon is nothing that is not mortal and perishable, except the minds given by the gods to the human race, and above the Moon all things are eternal." Such ideas were stirring the imagination, paving the way for cosmic adventures.

Within half a century of Plutarch (around A.D. 165), the Syrian sophist and satirist Lukian (in Greek, Loukianos) of Samosata composed the *Alethes historia,* (commonly known by its Latin title *Vera historia,* in English *True History*). Here we find what is probably the first work of space fiction offering the essential ingredients noted above: the trip, the landing, descriptions of and adventures on the world being visited, and, hopefully, the safe return.

Before commencing this tale of great adventure beyond the Pillars of Hercules, the author warns us that "I shall at least say one thing true, when I tell you that I lie, and shall hope to escape the general censure, by acknowledging that I mean to speak not a word of truth throughout." We are told of bizarre adventures befalling a crew of 50 Greek athletes homeward bound in a sailing vessel. "About noon . . . a most violent whirlwind arose, and carried the ship above three thousand stadia, lifting it up above the water, from whence it did not let us down again into the seas but kept us suspended in mid-air. In this manner we hung for seven days and nights, and on the eighth beheld a large tract of land, like an

island, round, shining, and remarkably full of light; we got on shore, and found on examination that it was cultivated and full of inhabitants, though we could not then see any of them." Called Hippogypi, they ride around on three-headed vultures adorned with feathers "bigger than the mast of a ship."

Hundreds of years pass and there is no repetition of adventures such as this in world literature. People may occasionally dream of going to the Moon; they do not write about it. Then, in 1010, Firdausi's great Persian epic poem *Shāh-Nāma* appeared following 40 years of labor. Among its 60,000 verses covering the legendary history of Persia are lines that tell of a marvelous flight into the heavens. The poem preserves ancient legends of which no earlier records exist:

The soul of that king was full of thought as to how he should rise into the air without wings.
He asked many questions of the learned as to how far it was from this Earth to the sphere of the Moon . . .
Then he fetched four vigorous eagles and bound them firmly to the throne.

Kai-Kā'ūs seated himself on the throne having placed a goblet of wine in front of him.

When the swift eagles grew hungry they each of them hastened toward the meat [legs of lamb suspended from lances fastened to the side of the throne].

They raised up the throne from the face of the Earth; they lifted it up from the plain into the clouds.

During medieval times in Europe there were no true tales of travel to other worlds as such, though dreams and fantasies involving roving spirits were fairly common. In the Italian poet Ludovico Ariosto's *Orlando Furioso* (1532), however, St. John the Evangelist proposes to Astolpho that he "a flight more daring take/To yonder Moon, that in its orbit rolls,/The nearest planet to our earthly poles." So off Astolpho goes to the Moon in a chariot drawn by four red horses in quest of the lost mind of Orlando. The mind turns up in a flask, but that is not all our lunar neighbor offers. "Swell'd like the Earth, and seem'd an Earth in size," not only does it possess most of the natural features of our world but cities, towns, and castles as well.

Statue of the great Persian poet and author of the Shāh-Nāma, *Firdausi* (A.D. 955– 1025), *a gift from the city of Teheran to the city of Rome. Ordway Collection/Space & Rocket Center.*

The Galilean Revolution

Before Galileo, little was known of the Moon, and the planets were merely objects that moved regularly across the skies. In fact, the word "planet" comes from the Greek word for "wanderer," which before Galileo's time did not have the same significance that it has today.

Overnight, Galileo forever changed mankind's view of the universe. The Moon, he explained in *Sidereus nuncius* (1610), "does not possess a smooth and polished surface, but one rough and uneven, and just like the face of the Earth itself, [and] is everywhere full of vast protuberances, deep chasms, and sinuosities." To be sure, many of the ancient Greek philosophers had speculated what the Moon might be like, but Galileo was the first to *know:* he had seen it with his own eyes through a telescope. He then turned his newly invented instrument on the planets. Jupiter, he discovered, was not a point of light like the other stars, but was instead a pale, golden globe with—miracle of miracles!—four tiny planets circling it.

Eventually, Galileo was forced by the Church to recant his discoveries, his interpretations of them, and most important his support of the Copernican Sun-centered solar system. But the damage was done. When men looked skyward, they no longer saw abstract points of light; instead, they saw worlds comparable to their own. Not surprisingly, such discoveries inspired speculation that these new worlds might even be inhabited.

Meanwhile another astronomer, no less a figure than Johannes Kepler, gave to civilization an unusual piece of literature that helped set a new tone to man's yearnings to leave the Earth and explore what is beyond, inspired, he wrote a friend, by his translation of Lukian's *True History* from Greek into

Latin. Mathematician and science adviser to the Habsburg Emperor Rudolph II in Prague, Kepler began to consider voyages beyond the Earth in the very summer of 1609 during which his laws of planetary motion were printed. He communicated his ideas to Galileo in 1610 and talked of "celestial boats with golden sails" manned by "people who will not fear the vastness" of space. Kepler had to be careful about what he said, for his Lutheran church was as adamant about preserving an Earth-centered universe as Galileo's Catholic counterpart. Moreover, Habsburg political sensitivities had to be considered. Accordingly, Kepler wrote what he called his "lunar geography" in the form of fiction.

The *Somnium* (*Dream*) was composed as an allegory in 1609, footnoted between the early 1620s and 1630, and published in 1634 (four years after Kepler's death). It is a strange work not only in itself but because it was written by a renowned astronomer, an unlikely author of such a fantastic tale. *Somnium* is about a voyage to the Moon couched in supernatural terms in which demons can, on occasion, carry humans from Earth (Volva) to the Moon (Levania). Kepler hoped that scholars might recognize in the word *daemon* a supposed relationship to the Greek *daiein* (to know), though philologically the relationship is not, in fact, correct. In any event, *daemon*, more commonly spelled *demon*, retained in *Somnium* its common meaning of evil spirit.

It turns out that demons abhor sunlight but can travel at will during the night. Normally, it is impossible for them to pass between the two worlds; but from time to time, when the shadow of the Earth intersects the Moon, they are able to cross.

And, under seldom-met conditions, these same demons transport humans, who, to prepare them for the journey through the vacuum of space, have been given an anesthetic potion ("sleeping draught") and "moist sponges" held to the nostrils. Since the Moon is so far away (50,000 German miles—1 such mile equaling about 4.6 modern miles), Kepler wrote that "no sedentary persons are accepted into our company; no fat ones; no frail ones; we choose only those who have spent their lives on horseback . . . and are accustomed to eating . . . unpalatable food." In short, a trip to the Moon was only for the well trained and hardy.

Kepler further postulated that voyagers to the Moon "must . . . circulate aloft for several days in the cone of the Earth's shadow in order that . . . [they] be on hand at the moment of the Moon's entry into this shadow." From then on, "The whole journey [to the Moon] is accomplished in

■

The first two notes prepared by Kepler for his Somnium, *which was published posthumously in 1634. In the first note he referred to the name* Duracrotus *(the book's hero) and to the fact that "The sound of this word came to me from a recollection of names of a similar sound in the history of Scotland, a land that looks out over the* Icelandic Ocean." *In the second note he begins by explaining that Iceland,* Duracrotus's *home, "means 'land of ice' in our German language. I saw in this truly remote island a place where I might sleep and dream and thus imitate the philosophers in this kind of writing. . . ."* Ordway Collection/Space & Rocket Center.

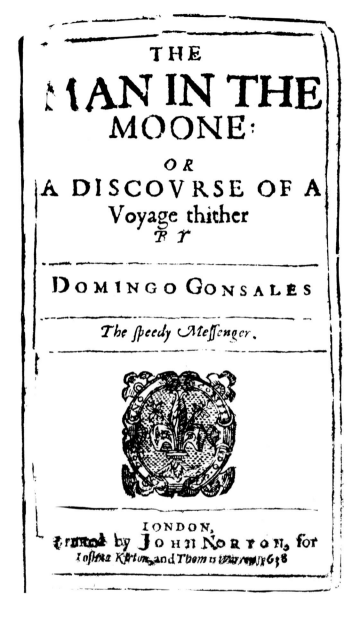

the space of four hours." Explained the allegorical demon, "On such a headlong dash we can take few companions—only those who are most respectful of us."

During the time that Galileo and those who followed him were sighting new worlds in the skies, others were finding new lands on the other side of the Atlantic Ocean. Only a century had passed since Columbus had sailed for China, bumping instead into a new continent. Since then, John and Sebastian Cabot had explored the coasts of North America for Britain while the Portuguese and Spanish had laid the groundwork for a vast empire in the south. Between 1519 and 1522, Ferdinand Magellan and Juan Sebastian del Cano had made their epic voyage around the now undoubtedly spherical Earth. By the time of Galileo, hundreds of ships and thousands of explorers, missionaries, colonists, soldiers, and adventurers had made the journey to amazingly rich and strange new lands. Not only did our planet harbor unsuspected worlds; but, it seemed, skies were full of them, too.

The situation was indeed bizarre. The new worlds of America, which could not be seen from Europe and whose existence relied on travelers' tales and evocative maps, nevertheless *could* be visited by anyone possessing the funds, connections, and courage. But now there were other worlds in the skies visible to anyone. It was tantalizing to imagine that they—like the recently discovered New World on Earth—might contain unknown civilizations and empires. Yet there was no apparent way to reach, explore, and perhaps even conquer them.

Galileo's discoveries, and those of astronomers who followed him (the rings of Saturn, that world's giant moon Titan, the illusive markings on Mars, even a new planet, Uranus), influenced the evolution of the idea of traveling in space. Since the Moon and planets were now known to be real worlds, it was no longer possible to think of them strictly as metaphorical symbols. It was one thing to speak of visiting a shining disk in the skies that, so far as anyone knew, might not possess solid, Earthlike attributes. It was now quite another thing to deal with the Moon or a planet as a tangible world with its own landscapes, scenery, perhaps even flora and fauna. To visit such real places, it was no longer sufficient to propose some miraculous happening like a chance whirlwind. If one were going to visit the Moon or planets, at least somewhat plausible transportation means had to be devised.

Seventeenth-Century Narratives of Space Travel

The shape of things to come is seen in Francis Godwin's charming story of Domingo Gonsales, the "Speedy Messenger," *The Man in the Moone: or a Discourse of a Voyage Thither* (1638). Godwin (later a bishop in the Church of England) relied on bird power while offering such materialistic details as the construction of harnesses, the framework that bound them together, and the velocity of ascent. Gonsales, a Spaniard of good but poor family, leaves his country to seek fortune overseas. Eventually, he ends up in the East Indies, where he does so well that he proudly sets sail for his native land. But on the way home he becomes so sick that he is taken off the ship and left, with his servant Diego, on St. Helena Island. As the adventure unfolds, we are alerted that we shall "have notice of a new world, of many rare and incredible secrets of Nature, that all the Philosophers of former ages could never so much as dreame of."

To escape from the island, our hero trains some young swanlike birds called *gansas* and yokes them to a mechanical device of his invention. After a short test flight, he instructs them to take him to another location on the island, but all does not go according to plan. The birds fly onward, carrying Gonsales to a strange land somewhere between the Earth and the Moon. There, "the *Gansa's* began to bestir themselues, still directing their course toward the Globe or body of the Moone," speeding along at about "Fifty Leagues in every hower." (Godwin estimated the Moon to be about 50,000 miles distant, a figure perhaps taken from Kepler and thus meaning German miles, and stated that the trip took some 11 days. Thus, he traveled about 4,545 miles a day or nearly 190 miles an hour. Since a league ranged from 2.4 to 4.6 statute miles, and since we don't even know what kind of miles Godwin was thinking about, it is impossible to pin down the actual speed in modern terms.)

■

Godwin's Domingo Gonsales en route to the Moon, carried aloft by trained swanlike birds called gansas. *Ordway Collection/Space & Rocket Center.*

As the hard-flying birds carried Domingo Gonsales ever onward the Earth grew smaller, whereas "still on the contrary side the Moone shewed her selfe more and more monstrously huge." Then, "After Eleven daies passage in the violent flight, I perceived that we began to approach neare unto another earth, if I may so call it, being the Globe or very body of that starre which we call the Moone." The rest of the book describes his adventures there and return to Earth.

We cannot be harsh on Domingo Gonsales's creator, Bishop Godwin, from the safe vantage point of a later age, for his was a clear attempt to describe in detail a *mechanical* method of travel. During the years that followed, many writers, great, mediocre, and insignificant, were to imitate, in one way or another, the theme of Domingo Gonsales.

One inspired by Gonsales was the Restoration poet, novelist, and playwright Aphra Behn, often considered to be the first Englishwoman to become a professional writer. Her 1687 play *The Emperor of the Moon: A Farce* enthusiastically brings forth memories of the then half-century-old tale:

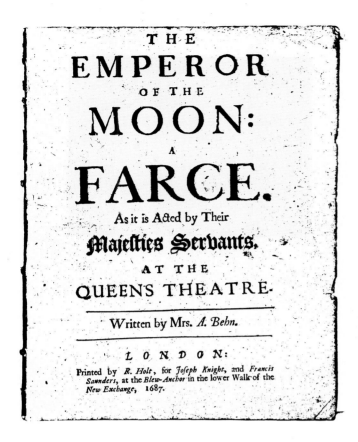

THE
EMPEROR
OF THE
MOON:
A
FARCE.

As it is Acted by Their
Majesties Servants,
AT THE
QUEEN'S THEATRE.

Written by Mrs. A. Behn.

LONDON:

Printed by R. Holt, for Joseph Knight, and Francis
Saunders, at the Blew-Anchor in the lower Walk of the
New Exchange, 1687.

Doct. [Doctor Baliardo] That wondrous Ebula [a magic stone], which *Gonzales* had?

Char. [Don Charmante, one of the suitors to the Doctor's daughter and niece] The same—by Vertue of which, all weight was taken from him, and then with ease the lofty Traveller flew . . . to *Olympus* Top, from whence he had but one step to the Moon. Dizzy he grants he was.

Doct. No wonder, Sir, Oh happy great *Gonzales!*

In the same year as Godwin's tale—1638—another and quite different kind of book was published in London. This one was by John Wilkins—also a future bishop—and, like many works of its era, had a long title: *The Discovery of a World in the Moone; or, A Discourse Tending to Prove, that 'tis probable there may be another habitable World in that Planet.* Unlike Godwin's, Wilkins's work was presented not as fiction but rather as a story based on scientific facts as they were then surmised (a half-century before Newton published his *Principia Mathematica* with its laws of planetary motion).

Wilkins was convinced that the main problem to be resolved for lunar travel was how to loft the flyer to that point between the Earth and Moon where the former's influence ends. This point was believed to be not much farther "than that orb of thick vaporous air, that encompasseth the earth," or about 20 miles. Once that altitude is attained—and Wilkins was convinced it could be quite easily—the rest becomes simple. And since "our bodies will . . . be devoid of gravity," no efforts would be exerted and hence no food would be required en route to the Moon. Wrote Wilkins: "You will say there can be no sailing thither [to the Moon] . . . We have not now any Drake, or Columbus, to undertake this voyage, or any Daedalus to invent a conveyance through the air. I answer, though we have not, yet why may not succeeding times raise up some spirits as eminent for new attempts, and strange inventions, as any that were before them? . . . I do seriously, and upon good grounds affirm it possible to make a flying-chariot."

The next major work of space fiction was by a Frenchman, none other than Savinien Cyrano de Bergerac. Wit, playwright, author, swordsman, philosopher, and satirist, he found time to write two "comical histories": *Histoire comique des États et Empires de la Lune* (1656) and *Histoire comique des États et Empires du Soleil* (1662). The former appeared in English translation by Thomas St. Serf in 1659 and the two books together in 1687 by A. Lovell under the title *The Comical History of the States and Empires of the Worlds of the Moon and Sun.* Both books are parodies on the theme of travels to other worlds, and both enjoyed some credibility because their author was aware of the latest advances in seventeenth-century science. Though his motive was in part to burlesque the concept, Cyrano felt constrained to limit himself to at least somewhat plausible methods of spaceflight. Knowledge of scientific discoveries was becoming increasingly diffused and it was no longer acceptable to rely solely on supernatural means to transport adventurers to the new worlds in the skies.

Cyrano carefully explains his attempts to reach the Moon. Knowing that the Sun "draws" dew upward at dawn, he surrounds his waist with vials filled with the liquid. The idea works: the Sun causes the dew to rise, vials, Cyrano, and all, "above the middle Region of the Air." Lest his speed be so great that he might bypass the Moon altogether, he breaks several vials "until I found my weight exceed the force of the Attraction." But he breaks too many vials, the Earth's attraction dominates that of the Moon, and he ends up in New-France—French-speaking Canada.

So he tries again, constructing a machine "which I fancied might carry me as high as I pleased, so that nothing seeming to be wanting to it, I placed my self within, and from the Top of a Rock threw my self in the Air. But because I had not taken my measures aright, I fell with a sosh in the Valley below." To relieve the bruises resulting from his fall, he anoints himself with beef marrow from head to foot. Meanwhile, some soldiers have attached fireworks to his machine and are about to light them when Cyrano arrives. "I was so transported with Grief," he exclaims, "to find the work of my Hands in so great Peril, that I ran to the Soldier that was giving Fire to it." But he is too late, for "hardly were both my Feet within [the machine], when whip, away went I up in a Cloud." At some point, the firework rockets burn out—"all the combustible Matter being spent"—and the machine falls back to Earth. But Cyrano continues onward, for it seems that when the Moon is in the wane, it sucks up the marrow of animals: "she drank up that wherewith I was annointed, with so much more force, that her Globe was nearer to me, that no interposition of Clouds weakened her Attraction." Soon Cyrano reaches the Moon, landing in a tree.

After a lengthy sojourn on the Moon, Cyrano returns safely to Earth in a day and a half, carried by a whirlwind. Exhilarated by his triumphs, he sets out

to build a flying device to take him to the more distant Sun. Soon, he has fashioned a telephone-booth-shaped device in the roof of which he places a large crystal icosahedron, each facet being a lens. The sunlight focused within the icosahedron by the lenses heats the interior, creating a vacuum. The air that rushes into the bottom of the car, to fill the void, carries the car with Cyrano aboard upward with it. He quickly passes the Moon and other bodies, "sometimes on the right, and sometimes on the left, several Earths like ours." Eventually the air becomes so rarefied that his flying machine starts to fall back toward Earth. But Cyrano continues onward by sheer willpower; 22 months later, "I at length happily arrived at the great plains of Day" whose landscape appeared "like flakes of burning Snow, so luminous it was."

Story after story followed, but most were variations on themes developed earlier. A major event occurred in 1686 when Bernard de Fontenelle published a popular astronomy book called *Entretiens sur la pluralité des mondes* (*Conversations on the Plurality of Worlds*). It was read and translated widely throughout Europe, partly because of its style but largely because of its fascinating speculations on the nature and habitability of the worlds in the solar system. Fontenelle tells us that each known planet has its own race of people and something of their appearance, civilization, and habits. Oddly enough, he was not convinced of the Moon's habitability because the air there was probably too rarefied. Moreover, relatively little attention was given to Mars, compared with such unlikely (to us) abodes of life as Mercury and Jupiter.

Four years after Fontenelle's book came Gabriel Daniel's *Voyage du monde de Descartes* (*A Voyage to the World of Cartesius*), a novel that broke with the incipient trend toward natural methods of attaining the Moon and introduced the idea of soul or thought travel. The hero's soul separates from the body and soars out to the globe of the Moon and the universe beyond, finding, among many myster-

■

In this rendering from a 1710 edition of Cyrano de Bergerac's lunar tale, an attempt is made to use rocket power to reach the Moon. The attempt fails, and the device falls back to Earth. Ordway Collection/ Space & Rocket Center.

ies, the great master "Monsieur Descartes." The Moon is described in some detail and is found to be not unlike the Earth.

In 1698, the renowned scientist Christian Huygens wrote *Cosmotheoros, sive de Terris coelestibus earumque ornatu conjecturae* (translated as *Cosmotheoros: or Conjectures Concerning the Planetary Worlds* and as *The Celestial Worlds Discover'd: or Conjectures Concerning the Inhabitants, Plants, and Productions of the Worlds in the Planets*). No space voyage is described; rather, the author speculates on the habitability of worlds and concludes them to be abodes of rational beings. He sees no hope of visiting other worlds, so "we must be contented with what's in our Power: we must *suppose* ourselves there." Throughout the seventeenth century we find almost universal agreement that the planets are inhabited. The principal variable is the means chosen to visit them, whether birds, wings attached to humans, dew, magnetic attraction, the projection of disembodied thoughts, or "just supposing."

Eighteenth-Century Precursors of Space Fiction

With the publication of David Russen's *Iter Lunare: or Voyage to the Moon* in 1703 we find a curious Moon-spring device being employed. "Since Springiness is a cause of forcible motion, and a Spring will, when bended and let loose, extend itself to its length," Russen speculated that a spring of well-tempered steel could be fashioned "wherein a Man, with other necessaries, could abide with safety, this Spring being with Cords, Pullies, or other Engins bent and then let loose by degrees by those who manage the Pullies, the other end would reach the Moon, where the Person ascended landing, might continue there."

Two years after *Iter Lunare* appeared Daniel Defoe's *The Consolidator*, another tale of lunar travel. In it, we are told how ancient peoples mastered the art of flying to and from the Moon, and how Mira-cho-cho-lasmo came to Earth to visit the emperor of China. Defoe reviews many legends of flights to the

Moon and of several types of what today we would call spaceships. Probably the most intriguing is an engine known as the Consolidator, constructed "in the shape of a Chariot, on the backs of two vast Bodies with extended Wings, which spread about fifty yards in breadth, composed of Feathers so nicely put together, that no air could pass; and as the Bodies were made of lunar earth, which would bear the Fire, the Cavities were filled with an ambient flame, which fed on a certain spirit, deposited in a proper quantity to last out the Voyage; and this Fire so ordered as to move about such springs and wheels as kept the wings in most exact and regular Motion." We cannot fathom what sort of propellant Defoe was thinking of, but he did offer a more technical-sounding approach to space travel than other writers of his time.

Authors are now beginning to provide ever more details: numbers, distances, speeds, construction

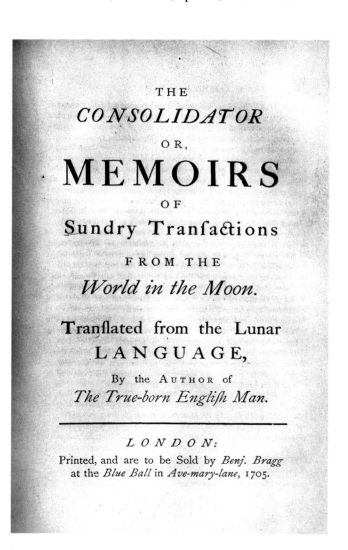

THE

CONSOLIDATOR

OR,

MEMOIRS

OF

Sundry Tranfactions

FROM THE

World in the Moon.

Tranflated from the Lunar LANGUAGE,

By the AUTHOR of
The True-born Englifh Man.

LONDON:
Printed, and are to be Sold by *Benj. Bragg* at the *Blue Ball* in *Ave-mary-lane*, 1705.

Daniel Defoe's anonymously published The Consolidator *describes a strange spaceship propelled by a "certain spirit." Ordway Collection/ Space & Rocket Center.*

methods and materials, and the like. But by the time pseudonymous Samuel Brunt's *A Voyage to Cacklogallinia* (1727) and Murtagh McDermot's *A Trip to the Moon* (1728) appear, we find the lunar world once again, albeit temporarily, being reached by well-tried bird and whirlwind methods. Brunt's tale was inspired in part by Godwin and in part by speculative fever related to the early-eighteenth-century "South Sea Bubble" scandal involving the South Sea Company and English trade with the Spanish West Indies. Brunt decided to invent his own speculative enterprise, one that would offer great economic reward with minimal risk: the hunt for gold on the Moon. After many and varied adventures, Brunt finds himself on a remote island inhabited by an intelligent race of bird people. From there, he and his new Cacklogallinian friend Volatilio set off for the lunar world "with incredible swiftness" in a palanquin lofted by other Cacklogallinians. But the voyage nevertheless takes time: "We were about a Month before we came into the Attraction of the Moon, in all which none of us had the least inclination to Sleep, or Eat, or found our selves any way fatigued, nor, till we reach'd that Planet, did we close our Eyes." While they do find gold on the Moon, the local inhabitants refuse to part with it and the trip is an economic failure.

McDermot's tale tells of a visit to the Canaries during which he ascends the Peak of Teneriffe. While resting at the summit and meditating "on my own corrupt Nature, a sudden Whirlwind came, that rais'd me from the Place I stood on." Up, up, up he is carried, "so that I was quickly remov'd into the Sphere of the *Moon's* Attraction, more than I intended, for two thirds of my Body being attracted by the *Moon,* the rest soon follow'd, so that I was carried with incredible swiftness, which still increas'd in my fall towards that Planet." That fall led McDermot directly into "a Fish-pond, which our sharp-sighted Philosophers mistake for a Part of the Sea, and call it *Sinus Rorum* . . . It is call'd in the Language of the *Moon Brugg Quqns* because it belongs to the King of *Quqns.*" The return required considerable ingenuity on McDermot's part. Convenient whirlwinds will no longer do, so "Gun-Powder" is called into play. Knowing that it "will raise a Ball of any Weight to any Height: Now I design to place myself in the Middle of ten wooden Vessels, placed one within another, with the Outermost strongly hooped with Iron, to prevent its breaking." In the tradition of Godwin and Defoe, details flow: an unspecified amount of gunpowder is not enough; it has to be pointed out that there are exactly 7,000 barrels of it. Nor can McDermot gloss over his landing back on Earth: his fall must be abated by wings during the final descent.

Rather tame compared to McDermot but worked out in almost painful detail is Ralph Morris's 1751 novel *A Narrative of the Life and Astonishing Adventures of John Daniel*. With his son Jacob, the hero finds himself stranded on a faraway island with no way to return home. Together they construct a device from materials salvaged from a shipwreck and made to fly by pump-operated calico cloth wings supported by iron ribs—as the pump goes up and down, so do the wings. So efficiently does the device work that the adventurers land not on some civilized country on Earth but—of course—on the Moon.

In developing his tale of spaceflights, the French *philosophe* François Marie Arouet de Voltaire had a rather different objective in mind. He broke with the trend of offering at least quasi-technical explanations as to how space travelers reach their destinations, using his *Micromégas* (1752) to satirize man's pomposity and the widespread belief of his importance in the universe. First of all, Voltaire does not start his tale here on Earth, as virtually all previous writers had done, or even in the solar system, but on giant Sirius. Because of the star's size, Sirians are logically enormous, our hero Micromégas standing 120,000 royal feet high! A precocious lad only 250 years old, he has mastered geometry and is busily studying and writing about the possibility of life on other worlds. Convicted for heretical beliefs, he is banished for a mere 800 years, a sentence Micromégas puts to good use. Instead of moping in some distant realm of his own world, he decides to explore the universe. Using sunbeams, comets, and a sure knowledge of gravitation, he easily travels from star to star across the Milky Way to our solar system.

Upon arrival, Micromégas strikes up a warm relationship with the Secretary of the Grand Academy of Saturn, and the two argue about, and philosophize on, all manner of subjects. Finally they decide together to visit the rest of the solar system, flying first to the rings and moons of Saturn, then to Jupiter and Mars. Helpful comets are used, an imaginative new transportation means that had not occurred to earlier and more serious space writers. Finally, and inevitably, Earth is reached, a tiny world the Sirian and Saturnian are certain is uninhabited. But events cause Micromégas to peer lazily through one of a chain of diamonds hanging around his neck. The microscopic effect shows a whale to be swimming through an ocean he had considered a mere puddle. Then a ship carrying polar explorers leaps into view. Reluctantly, Micromégas acknowledges

■

Louis Guillaume de La Follie's "electrical" flying device, which was described in his 1775 work Le philosophe sans prétention, ou l'homme rare . . . (The Unpretentious Philosopher, or the Unusual Man). *Ordway Collection/Space & Rocket Center.*

that even so insignificant a world as Earth can harbor intelligent creatures.

A ladder may sound like a particularly absurd way to get to the Moon, but that is how it is done in the mid-eighteenth-century booklet *Man in the Moon,* probably composed by Miles Wilson, an English curate. In a longer book published in 1757, *The History of Israel Jobson, the Wandering Jew,* the hero chooses an easier way: the chariot, a well-proven device of cosmic fiction.

Some of the characteristics of the modern science fiction novel appeared in a 1775 French work by Louis Guillaume de La Follie, *Le philosophe sans prétention.* A strange tale unfolds of a Mercurian who arrives on Earth and relates his adventures to one Nadir, an Oriental. It seems that on the planet Mercury an inventor named Scintilla had created a marvelous flying chariot powered by electricity. Amid scorn and ridicule, he proved that his invention would work in an amazing test flight witnessed by

members of the Academy. This unleashes a series of events that leads to Mercury's first spaceflight. Though doubting the practicality of the invention, a colleague named Ormisais nevertheless tries it out and, to his great surprise, the device functions after all. So he flies away to Earth in Scintilla's electric chariot and, after a fairly standard trip, crash-lands on our world.

Nineteenth-Century Visionaries and Hoaxes

By the time we approach the nineteenth century, scientific knowledge had advanced to the point that fiction writers had to take increasing cognizance of reality. In 1783, the man-carrying balloon was invented by the Montgolfier brothers in France. By then, also, the industrial revolution was getting under way in England. Whether a blessing or a curse, science and engineering were an ever-growing factor in everyday life. Between 1750 and 1810, steam engines, spinning jennys, circular saws, power looms, bicycles, lightning rods, cotton gins, electric batteries, and other inventions had appeared. The changing intellectual environment brought about by such progress understandably influenced writers, resulting in the disappearance of some of the romance of earlier tales of space travel. More and more often, attention was focused on the scientific and technical aspects of lunar and planetary voyages, though once on the target world the hero could do, find, and report whatever pleased the author's fancy.

Take Joseph Atterley's *A Voyage to the Moon with some Account of the Manners and Customs, Science and Philosophy of the People of Morosofia and other Lunarians,* published in 1827. The author (actually University of Virginia professor George Tucker) described a modern-sounding device: "The machine in which we proposed to embark, was a copper vessel, that could have been an exact cube of six feet, if the corners and edges had not been rounded off. It had an opening large enough to receive our bodies, which was closed by double sliding pannels, with quilted cloth between them." A metal called *lunarium* served to "overcome the weight of the machine, as well as its contents, and take us to the moon." We have here the anti-gravity concept that would become popular during the nineteenth and early twentieth centuries, even though it had no more scientific credibility than tethered fowl. Still, it exuded an aura of science, and that had become important.

Eight years later, Edgar Allan Poe—who, incidentally, had been a student under Professor Tucker and was certainly influenced by him—sent the character of "The Unparalleled Adventure of One Hans Pfaall" on a lunar trip in a homemade balloon. The hero's reasons for going to the Moon are neither romantic nor commendable: Hans was heavily in debt, and to him the logical escape from creditors was to hide on the Moon. Poe's description of the Earth as seen from space was surprisingly accurate, evidence of his concern in establishing scientific

■

One of a series of imaginary drawings published by F. Wenzel in Naples in 1836. Inspired by Richard Adams Locke's "Moon Hoax," which had appeared in installments in the New York Sun *in Au-*gust 1835, it purported to describe discoveries of lunar life made at the Cape of Good Hope by astronomer Sir John Herschel. *Ordway Collection/ Space & Rocket Center.*

credibility for his fiction. Interestingly, his balloon and sealed gondola bear striking resemblance to the stratosphere balloons of the 1930s.

At about the same time, Richard Adams Locke was busily populating that same body with all manner of creatures supposedly observed by Sir John Herschel through a telescope mounted in South Africa. What came to be known as the "Moon-Hoax" was published as supposedly serious astronomy in the form of installments in the New York *Sun* during late August 1835. The story enjoyed a large readership and, being presented as fact, was received as fact. Part of the reason it was so accepted was its original title, *Great Astronomical Discoveries Lately Made by Sir John Herschel, LL.D., F.R.S., etc. At the Cape of Good Hope;* it purported to record facts submitted by Sir John to the august, but (unknown to most) defunct, Edinburgh *Journal of Science.* One suspects that the skill of the author had something to do with the success of the hoax, as undoubtedly did the tenor of an epoch when the public was ready to believe almost anything reported as science. In due course the story was found to be a hoax, much to the amusement, or indignation, of the public.

A generation later the Frenchman Achille Eyraud wrote a modest work, *Voyage à Venus* (1865), containing a description of a spaceship powered by the reaction principle. The scheme would not actually have worked, for Eyraud proposed ejecting water as the reaction mass, to be gathered in a container and then recirculated for further use. But the appearance of the book was an important first in that the role of reaction in space travel had finally been recognized in the fictional literature.[1]

With Eyraud and his Venus spaceship we have reached the year of the publication of Jules Verne's seminal *De la Terre à la Lune* (*From the Earth to the Moon*). How this story, along with its 1870 sequel *Autour de la Lune* (*Round the Moon*), influenced the future of space fiction and space fact is the subject of the chapter that follows.

Note

1. The relevant passage states: "There exists, moreover, a motor that borrows no force from the surrounding environment, one that is based on the difference in pressures that act on the interior walls of a body and of which you have frequently been able to observe the results in the air. . . . How many times have you not seen raise themselves into the air, not like balloons because of their relative lightness, but because of an internal impulse, these objects, brilliant signs of popular festivities, that illuminate our holidays in all countries, and for all governments: flying rockets?"

For further reading

Anderson, George K. *The Legend of the Wandering Jew.* Providence, 1965: Brown University Press.

Bailey, J. O. *Pilgrims through Space and Time.* New York, 1947: Argus Books.

Boia, Lucien. *L'Exploration imaginaire de l'espace.* Paris, 1987: Editions La Découverte.

Crowe, Michael J. *The Extraterrestrial Life Debate 1750–1900: The Idea of a Plurality of Worlds from Kant to Lowell.* Cambridge, 1986: Cambridge University Press.

Derleth, August, ed. *Beyond Time and Space.* New York, 1950: Pellegrini & Cudahy.

Dick, Steven J. *Plurality of Worlds: The Origins of the Extraterrestrial Life Debate from Democritus to Kant.* Cambridge, 1982: Cambridge University Press.

Freedman, Russell. *2000 Years of Space Travel.* New York, 1963: Holiday House.

Gunn, James. *Alternate Worlds: The Illustrated History of Science Fiction.* Englewood Cliffs, New Jersey, 1975: Prentice-Hall.

Guthke, Karl S. *The Last Frontier: Imagining Other Worlds, from the Copernican Revolution to Modern Science Fiction.* Ithaca, New York, 1990: Cornell University Press.

Lear, John. *Kepler's Dream.* Trans. Patricia Frueh Kirkwood. Berkeley and Los Angeles, 1965: University of California Press.

Leighton, Peter. *Moon Travellers.* London, 1960: Oldbourne.

Locke, Richard Adams. *The Moon Hoax.* Boston, 1975: Gregg Press.

Meadows, A. J. *The High Firmament: A Survey of Astronomy in English Literature.* Leicester, 1969: Leicester University Press.

Moskowitz, Sam. *Explorers of the Infinite.* Cleveland, 1963: World; rpt. Westport, Connecticut, 1974: Hyperion.

Moskowitz, Sam, ed. *Masterpieces of Science Fiction.* Cleveland, 1966: World; rpt. Westport, Connecticut, 1974: Hyperion.

Nicolson, Marjorie. *Voyages to the Moon.* New York, 1948: Macmillan.

Philmus, Robert M. *Into the Unknown: The Evolution of Science Fiction from Francis Godwin to H. G. Wells.* Berkeley and Los Angeles, 1970: University of California Press.

Pizor, Faith K., and T. Allan Comp, eds. *The Man in the Moone and Other Lunar Fantasies.* New York, 1971: Praeger.

Rosen, Edward, trans. and commentary. *Kepler's Somnium: The Dream, or Posthumous Work on Lunar Astronomy.* Madison, 1967: University of Wisconsin Press.

Russen, David. *Iter Lunare.* Introduction by Mary Elizabeth Bowen. Boston, 1976: Gregg Press.

Tucker, George (pseudonym Joseph Atterley). *A Voyage to the Moon.* Preface by David G. Hartwell. Boston, 1975: Gregg Press.

Versins, Pierre. *Encyclopédie de l'utopie des voyages extraordinaires et de la science fiction.* Lausanne, 1972: Editions L'Age d'Homme.

Von Braun, Wernher, Frederick I. Ordway III, and Dave Dooling. *Space Travel: A History* (4th ed. of the von Braun–Ordway *History of Rocketry and Space Travel*). New York, 1985: Harper & Row.

Wright, Hamilton, and Helen Wright, eds. *To the Moon!* New York, 1968: Meredith.

The Spaceship as Icon: Designs from Verne to the Early 1950s

RON MILLER

One of the most pervasive technological images of the twentieth century is the rocket—in fact, a very specific rocket, as we shall see. The automobile and airplane may outnumber the rocket in sheer quantity and variety of appearances, but the rocket has had the unique function of being used to enhance the image of its rivals. It has been used to give an impression of speed and modernity to the automobile and airplane, themselves once archetypal emblems of those very qualities. A typical example, and perhaps the best-known and most widely applied rocket symbol, was the Oldsmobile Rocket 88, whose swept-winged V-2-like hood ornament looked more like a prop from some 1950s science fiction movie than an emblem for an automobile.

For post–World War II society, the rocket was the symbol of the fabulous world of the future that Americans had been promised during four long, bleak wartime years. It appeared everywhere and in every possible—even if unlikely—context. And where a recognizable rocket did not appear, its stylized form was a ubiquitous decorative motif.

This motif was not just any rocketlike shape but a fairly specific silhouette that falls within very narrow parameters. In fact, I realize that I am able to write such a phrase as "rocketlike" knowing that readers will most likely understand exactly what I am describing *because* "rocketlike" has a very specific, limited meaning. I have discovered that children raised on the spacecraft of *Star Wars* and Japanese animation—which could not look less like the "classic" spaceship of the 1950s—will nevertheless respond to this primal outline, recognizing it as a rocket, just as baby chickens will respond to the silhouette of a hawk, even if they have never before actually seen such a bird. This primal, archetypal rocket shape is best demonstrated by the German ballistic missile of World War II, the A-4—better known to the world as the V-2.

It seems that virtually every spaceship depicted after the mid-1940s had more than a passing resemblance to the V-2. It was even used *as* a spaceship in numerous low-budget science fiction movies that replaced expensive special effects with cheap stock footage. The "classic" spaceship is generally spindle-shaped, with three or four fins at its rear; it may be winged as well. While it is a design that may be terribly dated (or maybe not, considering the trends of modern spaceplane design), it seems destined to be with us forever.

The history of spaceship design has thus had a dual nature: that of the spaceships of the imagination, and that of the spaceships of reality. Their evolution has not been mutually exclusive; there have been many parallels, overlaps, and cross-breedings. While the development of actual spacecraft has mirrored the state of the art of astronautic technology, the history of imaginary spacecraft has been an indicator of the *desire* to travel into space.

Several independent events or trends led to the modern concept of the spaceship: first, Galileo's discovery in 1610 that the Earth was indeed not alone in the universe, that there were other worlds than our own; second, the invention of the balloon, demonstrating that mankind was not necessarily earth-bound (and, peripherally, the notions elaborately developed in the eighteenth century that Galileo's new worlds harbored intelligent life); and, lastly, the development of the submarine boat.

■

History of the Spaceship *by Ron Miller, 1991, acrylic on canvas, 54 inches high by 100* *inches wide. Ordway Collection/Space & Rocket Center.*

Spaceships by Gaslight

It was the nineteenth century that finally conceived and gave birth to the machine we know as the *spaceship*. By the time Robert Goddard in the United States, Konstantin Tsiolkovsky in Russia, and the members of the Verein für Raumschiffahrt (literally, the "Society for Spaceship Travel" or, as it is more familiarly known, the VfR) in Germany, had designed or built their first liquid-propellant rockets, the *shape* of the spaceship had already been determined. It had evolved from the ungainly cubes and rubber bags of Tucker and Poe to Verne's stream-

lined projectile to, by the end of the century, the finned spindle shape that we are familiar with today.

The conditions that exist in the space between worlds were fairly well known by the 1800s. The shape the spaceship finally took was in great measure dictated by these conditions. Space is airless, so any vehicle meant to travel through it must be as hermetically sealable as a submarine. Unlike a submarine, which can surface at any time to renew its air supply, or send a snorkel to the surface to suck down some oxygen if it is too risky to expose the submersible boat, the spaceship's occupants are wholly dependent upon the air supply carried within it.

Prudent fictional spaceship designers went even further than allowing tanks of compressed or lique-fied air; they provided the means to *make* fresh air as the trip through space progressed. This was done either by chemical means or by the use of green plants. The supposed extreme cold of space had to be counteracted by thick layers of insulation (in actual fact, the vacuum surrounding a spaceship is itself an excellent insulator—so efficient that in the inner solar system getting *rid* of excess heat within the spaceship can be a problem). Also, some kind of armor protection would be required to shield the ship and its crew from meteorites.

Sufficient food provisions would have to be carried for the duration of the trip. Here the authors took a clue from the Arctic expeditions that were assaulting the Pole at this time: preserved, compressed, and canned foods took up little space and would keep indefinitely.

If it became necessary to leave the spaceship while on some airless world, such as the Earth's moon, some sort of personal protection would be required: something on the order of a diving suit, suitably insulated and provided with oxygen. An airlock, like that used in inventor Simon Lake's new submarines (in turn inspired by the airlock on Jules Verne's *Nautilus*), would allow the astronauts to safely leave and reenter the spaceship. Spaceship designers in the latter part of the century were to borrow heavily from the submarine inventors: more and more the illustrations of spaceships that accompanied the stories resembled nothing so much as flying submarines. And why not? Weren't the conditions faced by the two machines almost exactly analogous?[1]

Jules Verne wrote *De la Terre à la Lune* (*From the Earth to the Moon*) in 1865. His anonymous projectile (the cannon from which it was fired had a name, however: the *Columbiad*) was the first spacecraft to resemble the modern image. It was a squat bullet, 12 feet tall and 9 feet wide, cast entirely in solid aluminum. Its shape was dictated by its human passengers; this shape would be more stable than a sphere, which would tumble. Within was every amenity Verne could think of for his astronauts' safety and comfort: gas lighting, replenishment and purification of the atmosphere, condensed and preserved foods, an elaborate system to protect against the acceleration of takeoff (for which his passengers were to lie prone), and so on. There was even a test flight made

with a scaled-down model, with animals as subjects. (This latter item was included in the book for the subtle effect it would have on the reader. Verne was well aware that his method for launching his projectile would have fatal effects on its passengers. By having the animals survive a test shot, he laid the groundwork for having his readers believe in the success of the manned projectile.)

Even more remarkable, but less obvious, than the design of the projectile were the elaborate calculations Verne made for the Moon flight. Actually computed by his cousin, Henri Garcet, a mathematician at the Lycée Henri IV in Paris (the mathematics were considered so "graceful" that it was rumored that famed astronomer Sir John Herschel had collaborated), they represent apparently the first time in history that a trip to the Moon was placed on a mathematical basis. If so, then it would be no exaggeration to credit *From the Earth to the Moon* with the foundation of astronautics.

Five years later, in 1870, a sequel appeared entitled *Autour de la Lune* (*Round the Moon*). In it, Verne relates the adventures of the three astronauts as they hurtle through space toward their destination. After the takeoff all three had lost consciousness due to the terrific acceleration (over 20,000 G, it has been calculated). A powerful water cushion was expected to, and in the story did, sufficiently soften the shock—although in reality they would have been reduced to thin smears on the floor of the capsule. At first, they think something has gone wrong, since no one recalls hearing the noise of the explosion. Yet when they look out of a porthole for the first time they see, to their amazement, the retreating form of the Earth! It eventually occurs to them that they did not hear the explosion because they were traveling faster than its sound!

At a distance of over 4,500 miles from the Earth they cross the path of a large meteorite. They narrowly avoid a collision, but their course is sufficiently perturbed that a landing on the Moon is impossible. They calculate that the projectile will now circumnavigate the Moon, affording them an excellent view of both sides but no chance of actually wandering around on the surface.

The reasons Verne chose to keep his space travelers off the Moon remain obscure. But we can surmise what they might have been. First of all, by resorting to a cannon as the source of the velocity necessary to propel the spaceship from the Earth, it would have been hard for Verne to devise a scheme

Four illustrations from Jules Verne's From the Earth to the Moon *and* Round the Moon *(clockwise from top left): the cannon* Columbiad; *immediately after firing as the space capsule departs for the Moon; making a trajectory adjustment with rockets; ocean recovery. Ordway Collection/Space & Rocket Center.*

whereby the projectile could take off from the lunar surface and return to the Earth. Where would his astronauts have found a suitably powerful cannon? Perhaps he wanted to prevent his travelers from landing on the Moon because he *knew* there was almost no chance of lunar life and hence could not develop an interesting tale amid such barrenness and solitude.

While the frustrated voyagers gaze at the Moon, the projectile approaches so close that it seems that it might, after all, impact onto the surface. As a precaution, steps are immediately taken to reduce the spaceship's velocity, a feat to be accomplished by powerful fireworks placed inside 20 steel-lined tubes that protrude from the projectile's flat base. Their last calculations show that they are just barely going to miss the Moon. As the projectile begins to pull away, they fire the rockets in a final attempt to change direction and make a landing. Instead of landing, however, the spaceship heads back toward the Earth. Fortunately, it falls into the Pacific Ocean instead of crashing onto land, and is eventually picked up by an American corvette, the USS *Susquehanna*. The adventure is over.

Today we recognize the debt modern astronautics owes to the fictional works of Jules Verne. He was read with great respect by that minute fraction of humanity that urges the world forward. Towering above the vast majority of later writers—many of whom were little more than imitators, though they, too, have their place—his books remain popular to this day.

The illustrations—by A. de Neuville and E. Bayard—accompanying the second novel were the first to show a rocket operating in interplanetary space, and the first to make any attempt at a realistic representation of the Earth and Moon as seen from space.

Greg, Lasswitz, Wells, and Others

Only one type of spacecraft diverged from the trend toward the "classic" rocket shape: the anti-gravity ship—always a maverick. By its very nature, an anti-gravity spaceship can be any shape that its inventor finds convenient. Spherical shapes and geometric solids were the most popular. Anti-gravity was, and still is, the modern equivalent of flight by magic.

Innumerable authors have attempted to rationalize its use by dressing it up in elaborate pseudo-scientific explanations. But whether it is supposedly created by magetism, electricity, atomic energy, gyroscopic forces, or "apergy," it is magic nevertheless. Still, spaceships flown by anti-gravity have their place in this history. If the story is a good one, such as H. G. Wells's *First Men in the Moon* (1901), it can serve to excite the reader about the possibilities of spaceflight and exploring other worlds. And even anti-gravity spaceships have to deal with the realities of outer space and the conditions on other planets, so the design of the ship itself, and its appointments, can be interesting and important.

Between the time of Verne's two lunar novels and the flight of the first liquid-fueled rocket by Goddard in 1926, most of the theoretical groundwork for spaceflight had been laid and most of the possibilities had been imagined. To mention a very few: Edward Everett Hale described the first artificial manned satellite in his novelette *The Brick Moon* (serialized in *Atlantic Monthly* in 1869–1870), in which he listed nearly every function applied to modern satellites. In 1881 Hermann Ganswindt first described his interplanetary spaceship. While never quite grasping the principles of rocket propulsion, Ganswindt did take into consideration the possible need for artificial gravity. He created this by spinning his spacecraft; he anticipated Hermann Oberth by nearly 40 years in suggesting that two spacecraft could be joined by a cable and spun around their common center. Although he made errors in detail, he was one of the first to suggest the use of rockets in spaceflight, and the drawing he commissioned to illustrate his invention is one of the few nineteenth-century depictions of a rocket operating in space.

The year 1880 saw the appearance in *St. Nicholas* magazine of the charming short story "A Christmas Dinner with the Man in the Moon," by Washington Gladden. The giant space liner *Meteor* travels to the Moon on the "great electric currents" that pass between the Earth and its satellite. The iron hull of the spaceship is magnetized to take advantage of the currents. The *Meteor* is spindle-shaped (like one of "Winan's cigar-steamers"—incidentally one of the inspirations for Verne's *Nautilus*) and equipped with giant paddle wheels that raise it to the upper atmosphere. Because of the thinning atmosphere, Gladden equipped his passengers with respirators.

A sign of the changing times came with the publication, in 1880, of Percy Greg's two-volume novel *Across the Zodiac*. In the story, a mysterious force called "apergy" is used to negate gravity, providing the means for a voyage through space to Mars. The spaceship *Astronaut* is a monstrous affair with 3-foot-thick metal walls. The deck and keel are described as "absolutely flat, and each one hundred feet in length and fifty in breadth, the height of the vessel being about twenty feet." The apergy receptacle was placed above the generator, both located in the center of the ship, and from there "descended right through the floor a conducting bar in an antapergetic sheath, so divided that without separating it from the upper portion the lower might revolve in any direction through an angle of twenty minutes." This sheath is used to direct a "stream of repulsive force" against the Sun or any other body. Greg's "apergy" was apparently such an appealing element that it appeared in several other novels, notably John Jacob Astor's *A Journey in Other Worlds* (1894).

It is not particularly important what happens on Mars, which Greg's voyagers reach in a little over 40 days. What is important is that the red planet is beginning to receive the attention of writers of space fiction that it astronomically deserves. By the onset of World War I, more than 100 novels and stories had been published dealing with flights to Mars. All of this was a result of increasing observational knowledge of the planet itself and the development of some meticulously worked out concepts of the origin of the solar system, of which Mars was an especially interesting component. It was the period of the discovery of *canali* on Mars by Giovanni Virginio Schiaparelli (who interpreted them as naturally occurring channels or grooves) and their

popularization—or perhaps sensationalization—by Percival Lowell (to whom they were artificially constructed canals), the discovery in 1877 of Mars's two small moons by Asaph Hall (which Greg described), and of other phenomena that seemed to suggest that Mars might be much like the Earth, only older. For years, Lowell excited professionals and laymen alike with his proposition that Mars was inhabited by an advanced race of intelligent beings.

Kurd Lasswitz's *Auf zwei Planeten* carried the Mars theme several notches higher in the literary scale. Published in 1897 (but not translated into English until 1971 as *Two Planets*), it took a very logical look at the supposition that since Mars was the happy abode of a higher intelligence than Earth's, it would not be Earthmen who would first go to Mars but rather the opposite. Thus it is Martian space travelers who fly to the Earth and

■

The spaceship Callisto *flying through the tail of a comet in John Jacob Astor's novel* A Journey in Other Worlds. *Ordway Collection/Space & Rocket Center.*

H. G. Wells wrote his acclaimed *The War of the Worlds,* serialized in magazine form in 1897 and published as a book in 1898. This was a hair-raising tale of a Martian invasion of our planet. What appears initially to be a successful conquest of the Earth ends in failure, as Wells has the Martians die from terrestrial diseases against which their organisms have no defense. In a retaliatory vein, Garrett P. Serviss wrote *Edison's Conquest of Mars,* which began serialization even before the last installment of the Wells novel saw print. In this story, Serviss created the first-ever scenes of massed fleets of interplanetary spaceships. Serviss was an experienced astronomer

set up a base on the North Pole. Why they chose such a seemingly inconvenient location is explained in the dialogue: "You must realize . . . that the Martians can only land on Earth in the areas of the north or south poles. Their spaceships try, as soon as they have reached the outer border of the atmosphere, to approach in the direction of the axis of the Earth. But it is dangerous for them to enter the atmosphere. Therefore, everyone agreed with the suggestion my father had made to build a station outside the atmosphere but in the direction of the axis of the Earth, on which the ships would remain and from where they would descend to the Earth in a different manner." The method of crossing space relied on a gravity-nullifying material, although the actual propulsion is provided by rockets. Lasswitz's novel enormously influenced later interest in rocketry and spaceflight in Germany.

Capitalizing on the growing popularity of Mars,

and science writer and, while he was eventually to write far more polished fiction, this, his first novel, has a much sounder scientific basis than even the Wells original.

In 1889 appeared a three-volume set of novels, *Aventures extraordinaires d'un savant Russe* (*The Extraordinary Adventures of a Russian Scientist*), by G. Le Faure and H. de Graffigny. It is a veritable catalog of imaginative spacecraft, ranging from Vernian projectiles to rockets to solar sails. The three books deal with adventures on the Moon, the inner planets, comets, asteroids, and the giant outer planets. A fourth volume, *Les mondes stellaires*, was published but immediately withdrawn and destroyed, with the result that only a handful of copies are reported to have survived.

In 1903, Tsiolkovsky published the first of his spacecraft designs; it employed liquid fuel and gyroscopic stabilization. In outward appearance his spaceship laid the groundwork for the modern spaceship to come. In it he made a subtle but important conceptual innovation. There had already been torpedo-shaped spacecraft, but these still owed something to their nautical origins—especially the submarine—in the matter of orientation. In spacecraft before Tsiolkovsky's, an interior deck would run parallel with the long axis of the spaceship, so that a person standing on it would be perpendicular to that axis. One-half of the ship would be the "top" and the other the "bottom." So definitely distinct were these that some spacecraft, such as George Griffith's *Astronef* in *Honeymoon in Space* (1900), could have an exterior deck running the length of the ship, as well as a conning tower. In a Tsiolkovskian spaceship, the decks ran at right angles to the ship's long axis, so that a person standing upon one had his head pointing toward the nose and his feet toward the tail, and—unlike all previous spacecraft—his rockets were symmetrical around the central axis.

Between 1913 and 1916, André Mas, Drouet, and de Graffigny devised schemes for centrifugally launched spacecraft, thrown from the rims of rapidly spinning flywheels. Arthur Train and Robert Wood described a remarkable spaceship in their 1917 novel *The Moonmakers*. *The Flying Wheel* was a 66-foot-diameter torus propelled by an atomic motor suspended in gimbals from the apex of a tripod over the center of the doughnut-shaped ship. The fuel was uranium, producing a beam of alpha particles as it disintegrated.

Scenes from Le Faure and de Graffigny's Extraordinary Adventures of a Russian Scientist *(clockwise from bottom left):* from volume 1, Chuir, *one of the principal towns on the far side of the Moon; announcement of volume 2,* The Sun and the Small Planets; *a spaceship entering the shadow cone of Jupiter's moon Callisto in volume 3; announcement of the fourth volume,* Stellar Worlds, *which was published but immediately withdrawn from the market. Ordway Collection/Space & Rocket Center.*

The Space Artists

The late nineteenth century saw the visual arts finally catch up with the breadth of vision in fiction and scientific speculation. If the authors of scientific romances were creating more and more imaginative— and increasingly plausible—schemes for leaving the Earth, artists were beginning to illustrate the reasons we had for wanting to leave. The situation was analogous to the opening of the American West: while the designers and builders of Conestoga wagons and clipper ships provided the means to reach California, for example, word and visual images of a vast, fertile, rich land helped to create the desire to go there. Although writers and artists ultimately worked toward the same end—inspiring mankind to leave Earth and explore space—their roots could not have been more different.

Space art could not have existed before the romantic nineteenth century and its revolutionary discovery of the visionary landscape. Perhaps inspired most by the writing of Jean-Jacques Rousseau, the romantic artists did not merely observe nature, they rediscovered it in moments of intensely heightened vision. Landscape painting evolved from the merely decorative and pastoral to the highly charged emotional.

Almost diametrically opposed to the romantic landscapes were those of the pre-Raphaelites, yet these, too, were ancestors of space art. The pre-Raphaelites insisted upon a strictly accurate recreation of nature in the most minutely observed detail, with as little interpretation from the artist as possible. Although not a member of the pre-Raphaelite Brotherhood, John Constable expressed their inten-

tion well when he said that an artist must make it his primary job to create "a pure and unaffected representation" of what he saw. He would refuse to put a bird in the sky of a painting if there was none visible at the time he was working. He would rather wait, he explained, no matter how long it took, "till I see some living thing; because if any such appears, it is sure to be appropriate to the place. If no living thing shows itself, I put none in my picture."

The American version of the romantic landscape came from the Hudson River School, whose practitioners were enamored with the American wilderness. Like the European romantics, they looked for the grandiose and awe-inspiring, but like the pre-Raphaelites they were also fascinated by detail. Probably because they were Americans and inheritors of a tradition of Yankee practicality, they were akin to the geologists, botanists, and other scientists who were then exploring the unknown west of the Mississippi.

Artists accompanied these scientific expeditions as a matter of course. Thomas Moran, for example, was the official artist with the first official survey of the Yellowstone region. It is difficult to overestimate the effect of their paintings on the American people. Vast canvases, some measuring more than a dozen feet wide, were circulated throughout the East, drawing crowds as popular motion pictures do today. They revealed to an astonished public awesome wonders no one had thought could exist outside the mind of the most imaginative poet or novelist. In so doing, they changed the national view of the land from an adversary to a source of awe. The visions that artists such as Thomas Moran, Alfred Bierstadt, and Frederick Church brought back from places like Yellowstone, Yosemite, and Niagara Falls were directly responsible for the creation of the first national parks on this planet.

Space art as it existed by the 1920s was heir to this realistic romantic-naturalist tradition. Just as the painters of the Hudson River School changed our perception of the American wilderness, space art was destined to change our perception of the universe.

Many of the science fiction authors of the time were being well served by their illustrators, perhaps none better so than Jules Verne, whose fame could command the best artists for his books. Other books, such as *Honeymoon in Space, A Journey in Other Worlds,* or even *Edison's Conquest of Mars,* are as well known for their outstanding artwork as they are for the original stories.

By the first years of the new century, certain artists were beginning to specialize in astronomical renderings. One of the first was British illustrator Scriven Bolton. His work, appearing often in *The Illustrated London News,* was consistently dramatic, if not overly accurate. He originated a technique by which he first constructed model landscapes of plaster, then photographed and retouched them, and finally added starfields and planets. Bolton's work inspired a young American artist named Chesley Bonestell, who had been providing architectural renderings for *The Illustrated London News,* to "indulge in space painting." Bolton's contemporary, G. F. Morrell, not only created some splendidly expressionistic extraterrestrial landscapes, but made something of a specialty of showing how other worlds might look were they to replace the Earth's moon. For example, one painting shows what Saturn would look like seen from 238,000 miles away—the Moon's mean distance from the Earth. Morrell's masterpiece might be his strikingly surrealistic illustration of Saturn's rings as they would appear from London, if that city were to be transported to Saturn.

■

A typical lunar landscape, by Scriven Bolton. From The Illustrated London News, *1927. Miller Collection.*

The Abbé Théophile Moreux (1867–1954), whose work first appeared in the late nineteenth century, had his astronomical renderings published widely. One fine image he created was a scene of Saturn as seen from Titan, the planet reflected in a pool of liquid on that moon's surface. The Abbé was the first of the rare astronomer-artists; he was director of the Observatory of Bourges, France. In the 1920s Howard Russell Butler (1836–1934) contributed paintings to the American Museum of Natural History, one of which, a dramatic scene set near the central peak of a lunar crater, was later copied by artists working for a dozen different publications.

Publishers of popular books on astronomy began to realize the attractiveness of realistic astronomical art, and the work of artists such as Bolton, Morrell, and lesser-known and often uncredited painters appeared in great numbers. However, the pioneering specialist in astronomical art, and the one who first brought both scrupulous scientific accuracy and fine art together, was the French illustrator-astronomer Lucien Rudaux (1874–1947). He can rightly be regarded as the grandfather of astronomical art. Originally a commercial artist, he eventually became a highly regarded astronomer (the crater on Mars that is named for him was in honor of his work as an astronomer, rather than for his art). He created hundreds of illustrations to accompany his own articles and books as well as those written by others.

His masterpiece is the 1937 deluxe Larousse volume *Sur les autres mondes* (*On Other Worlds*). Its more than 400 illustrations, including 20 full-page color paintings, gave readers an unprecedented look at the solar system. These paintings achieved a level of accuracy and believability that was not to be challenged for nearly 20 years. As a careful astronomer and a superlative observer, Rudaux knew what the surfaces of the planets ought to look like. Many of his images look as though they could have been based on NASA photos. His portrayals of the lunar surface are especially remarkable. At a time when other artists were still producing the stereotyped craggy, saw-toothed mountain ranges that dated back to James Nasmyth and James Carpenter's 1874 work *The Moon,* Rudaux was showing us the rounded mountains and rolling landscapes found by the Apollo astronauts. He pictured Venus as an eroded, rocky dustbowl, Mars as flat and boulder-strewn, its sky sometimes reddened with pink dust clouds.

Beginning in the late 1930s, the science fiction magazine *Astounding Stories* displayed several astronomical paintings on its covers. Probably the finest was by Charles Schneeman, a view of Saturn as seen from Iapetus that remains one of the outstanding astronomical paintings published in the first half of this century. Others during this period were contributed by Gilmore, Hubert Rogers ("Einstein Eclipse"), and "A. von Munchausen."

The paintings provided by Charles Bittinger for the July 1939 issue of *National Geographic* show how far ahead of "respectable journals" the science fiction pulps were when it came to the accurate depiction of astronomical subjects. Although Bittinger's paintings were among the first space art to appear in a respected and nationally distributed journal (if we do not count Rudaux's appearances in the Sunday supplement *American Weekly*), and were described as "combining a fine sense of color values and artistic composition with a painstaking effort to achieve scientific accuracy," they are generally rather crude both artistically and scientifically and don't approach the standards set in both areas by Rudaux and many science fiction magazine illustrators.

Only two other prespaceflight artists had a major influence on the shaping of astronomical art as a genre in its own right—yet their contribution outweighs all of their predecessors' combined. The first was Chesley Bonestell (1888–1987), who can rightly be called the father of astronomical art (if we regard Rudaux as the grandfather). It is not easy to overestimate Bonestell's influence and inspiration: his was the right kind of art at the right time. The best of his work appeared between the end of World War II and 1960, when the American public was on a postwar technology high. Spaceflight symbolized everything that the postwar period promised, and it seemed as though it was just around the corner. Magazines, books, and motion pictures that featured anything about the coming age of space travel became best-sellers, and Bonestell was contributing something to them all.

His space art first appeared publicly in *Life* in 1944: a series of paintings showing Saturn as it might appear from its various moons. Nothing like them had ever been seen before. He combined a highly polished technical skill as a painter with his experience as a Hollywood special effects matte artist to create images that looked more like picture postcards than "artist's impressions." Bonestell's paintings possessed an intense believability that was far more important than their carefully researched un-

Astronomer-artist Lucien Rudaux's interpretation of the lunar surface with the full Earth hanging low on the horizon. From Lucien Rudaux, Sur les autres mondes. *Larousse, Paris, 1937. Ordway Collection/Space & Rocket Center.*

derpinnings. Rudaux's astronomical works, by contrast, accurate as they were—and they were more accurate than Bonestell's—nevertheless looked like paintings. There was always a nagging doubt in his viewers' minds that perhaps he might just have made the scenes up. Bonestell managed to remove himself from between the viewer and the scene being depicted. Never before had the planets taken on such a reality.

These paintings and many others were gathered into a best-selling book, *The Conquest of Space* (1949), with a text by Willy Ley. This was followed by countless magazine articles (including the classic *Collier's* series discussed in Liebermann's chapter), books, and space-movie special effects art (*Destination Moon, When Worlds Collide, War of the Worlds,* and *The Conquest of Space*). All of this contributed to making the 1950s a golden age of space enthusiasm.

The second artist was Ralph A. Smith (1905–1959) of Great Britain, whose work was almost exclusively connected with the British Interplanetary Society and, until recently, only collected in one book, *The Exploration of the Moon* (1954, with text by Arthur C. Clarke). Working from the founding of the BIS in the late 1930s continuously until his death in 1959, Smith used his engineering background to recreate meticulously the detailed space program developed by the society. Unlike Bonestell, who simply rendered the designs created by Wernher von Braun, Smith was an active contributor to the design of the spacecraft he illustrated. In particular, he was the codesigner of the "Smith-Ross" space station, an adaptation of the 1929 Hermann Noordung "Rotary House" and immediate predecessor of von Braun's giant wheel. Also unlike Bonestell, Smith was relatively uninterested in astronomy per se, and his lunar and Martian landscapes exist only as subtle backgrounds for his spacecraft and colonies. In fact, I am aware of no Smith artwork showing any planet beyond Mars, nor any not including some sort of hardware.

At its best, space art has served the same function as the paintings of the Hudson River School, in inspiring a sense of wonder about the universe. There is an educational side to this art form, but bald scientific facts are not the main point—any more than Moran or Bierstadt were trying to teach their audience geology. What space art ought to teach is not so much what the other planets are like, but that they are there at all, that they are *real*. Believability is at least as important as accuracy, for if no one believes that the scene represents some place in reality, all the scientific accuracy in the world is for naught.

During the 20 or 25 years separating Bonestell's first published work and the 1970s, space art was reserved, generally, to a few specialists. While numerous artists occasionally dabbled in astronomical illustration, or were forced to accept a space art assignment, fewer than half a dozen made any attempt to take the art form seriously.

Spaceships Enter the Real World

The year 1923 saw the publication of Hermann Oberth's seminal *Die Rakete zu den Planetenräumen* (*The Rocket into Planetary Space*), one of the theoretical cornerstones of modern spaceflight. In it he first proposed his Model E, an enormous manned rocket that finally settled the outward form of the classic spaceship. It was an artillery-shell-shaped hull 35 meters tall and 10 meters in diameter that stood erect on the tips of four big fins. Oberth later elaborated upon the design in the 1929 revised edition of his book, *Wege zur Raumschiffahrt* (*Ways to Spaceflight*). In it he described a fictional circumlunar flight by the Model E spaceship *Luna* (on 14 June 1932). It was a three-stage rocket launched from the Indian Ocean. The pilots were ensconced in a small cabin, an oblate spheroid in shape, contained in the nose of the third stage. This was equipped with a parachute for the final descent to the Earth. Oberth, with his typical meticulous care, considered every detail: how his crew were to eat in free-fall, waste disposal, heating and cooling, etc. Oberth's Model E formed the basis for the design of the spaceship *Friede,* which he provided for Fritz Lang's 1929 motion picture *Frau im Mond* (*The Girl in the Moon*), the first realistic spaceship in movie history.

At about this time Max Valier was actively publishing his own designs for spacecraft. Although he

Three real photo postcards published in 1929 by Ufa, the German film company, for Fritz Lang's classic Frau im Mond (The Girl in the Moon). Top: *Actors Mahmud Terja Bey* (left) *and Borwin Walth* (right) *studying a scale model of* Friede, *an Oberth-designed manned Moon rocket*. Middle: *Actress Gerda Maurus pointing out trans-lunar trajectory*. Bottom: *Actors Gustl Stark-Gstettenbauer* (left), *Willy Fritsch* (center), *and Gerda Maurus* (right), *on the Moon in front of* Friede's *capsule. Liebermann Collection.*

evolved his spaceships from existing aircraft (they even took off more or less horizontally from inclined ramps), the final design was aesthetically more pleasing than Oberth's rather ultrafunctional rocket. Valier's final design was a chunky streamlined spindle with curved fins at the rear and two outrigger nacelles containing the rocket motors near the front of the craft. A similar design, but with the rockets in the rear, would have been launched from the back of an enormous rocket-powered flying wing. This version was elaborated upon in Otto Willi Gail's novel *Hans Hardts Mondfahrt* (*Rocket to the Moon*, 1930).

Gail, combining the ideas of Valier and Oberth, described the spaceship *Geryon* in *Der Schuss ins All* (*A Shot into Infinity*, 1925)—a three-stage rocket with folding wings (a feature of which Oberth disapproved). It reappeared in *Der Stein vom Mond* (*The Stone from the Moon*, 1926), along with the space station *Astropol*. In this novel—which mixes space travel with the bizarre "Cosmic Ice Theory" of Horbiger then popular in Germany—the spaceship *Ikaros* makes a voyage to Venus (it remained in orbit while a small lander made the actual descent).

R. H. Romans's novel *The Moon Conquerors* (1930) described the 1945 flight of the spaceship *As-tronaut*. The rocket was the result of an international competition for the best scheme for reaching space (152 of the submitted plans "were for a Goddard rocket"). It was a slender torpedo with narrow fins running its length. Romans described the rocket in some detail. It was launched horizontally, its initial velocity provided by an electromagnetic cannon (a method proposed seriously by E. F. Northrup in *Zero to 80*, 1937). For propulsion between the Earth and the Moon, it used the pressure of sunlight on special black vanes.

Most of these concepts were illustrated by Frank R. Paul (1884–1963), who was almost solely responsible for the artwork in Hugo Gernsback's large stable of magazines. Trained as an architect and engineer, Paul produced spacecraft with an unprecedented aura of believability.

Many other fictional rockets contributed to the collective and cumulative design of the spaceship. The 1922 animated film *All Aboard for the Moon* featured a streamlined rocket launched from a rooftop, carrying tourists to the Moon. Miral-Viger's 1922 novel *L'Anneau de Feu* (*Ring of Fire*) based its atomic-powered spaceship on the theories of Robert Esnault-Pelterie, the French aviation and space pio-

■

Otto Willi Gail's vision of the Moon. Left, *explorers gazing at the lunar surface from their spaceship;* right, *solar power station predicted for the year* A.D. *3000. Ordway Collection/Space & Rocket Center.*

■

Left: *a spaceship designed by* "Mr Jex" for David Lasser's *1931 article* "By Rocket to the Planets" *appearing in* Nature. *These striking Art Deco* drawings are emblematic of *the times, as was the space- ship from the 1930 film* Just Imagine (right). *Miller Collection.*

neer. The 1930 Hollywood musical *Just Imagine* featured the ultimate Art Deco spaceship. It became the representative prewar spaceship since it was recycled in the immensely popular Flash Gordon serials.

By this time—in the real world—Tsiolkovsky had published extensively, and his plans included not only large manned rockets but lunar rovers and self-contained space colonies. Nicholai Tsander designed enormous biplane spaceships that fed upon their own structure for fuel, and Franz Ulinski published his schemes for electrically propelled spacecraft. In 1925, Walter Hohmann not only designed his "powder tower" spaceship, an enormous cone-shaped rocket with an egg-shaped manned capsule at its apex, but his work on interplanetary orbits became

■

Outside their spaceship, crew members gaze at the rings of Saturn in Miral-Viger's Ring of Fire *(1922).* Ordway Collection/Space & Rocket Center.

so fundamental that these energy-saving orbits have been named for him.

Franz von Hoefft proposed an evolutionary spaceship design, employing the lifting body concept. Using standardized units, spaceships could be customized for particular missions. He laid out a systematic and progressively more ambitious scenario for the exploration of outer space, employing a series of eight spacecraft, designated RH I–VIII. Von Hoefft's unique design resembled the blade of a shovel with a pair of slender pontoons beneath, since the larger ones were to be launched from water.

In the late 1920s Eugen Sänger began his researches into spaceflight, basing his hopes on the development of an "aerospace-plane." This eventually resulted, a decade later, in his famous "silver bird" antipodal bomber concept, the immediate precursor of today's space shuttle and modern aerospace planes.

By the time Goddard and the VfR had flown

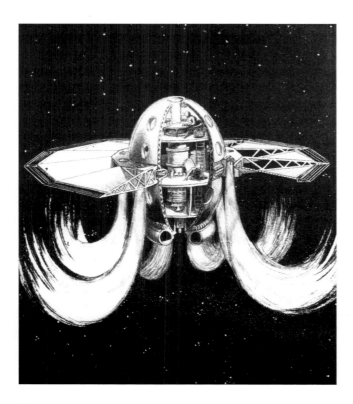

Austrian engineer Franz
Abdon Ulinski proposed this
electrically propelled spaceship
in 1927. Ordway Collection/
Space & Rocket Center.

their first liquid-fueled rockets, these dreamers and
theorists, and scores of others, had not only established that space travel would ultimately take place,
but had anticipated virtually every step on the road
to achieving it.

The Victory of the Imagination

By the outset of World War II, the outward shape
of the spaceship had been fairly well established.
From the speculations of scientists, science fiction,
and the countless images of science fiction illustrators came the familiar sleek, finned spindle shape.
There was no question in anyone's mind as to what
spaceships were eventually going to look like.

The science fiction spaceship—and the science fiction magazine was still virtually the sole source of
any speculative imagery concerning spacecraft, and
thereby the most influential—had evolved as much
as the technology and theory itself had. Where
Paul's vaguely art nouveau spaceships had once
dominated, there were now the flowing, organic
lines of Howard Browne's functional-looking designs. After the war, Browne's baton was handed to
Jack Coggins, who replaced the former's art mo-
derne designs with a series of highly functional, almost prosaic spacecraft that looked as though they
had come straight off some engineer's drawing
board. These and others of Coggins's work were
collected in a pair of books (*Rockets, Jets, Guided
Missiles and Space Ships,* 1951, and *By Spaceship to the
Moon,* 1952) that were probably as influential on a
generation of space enthusiasts as anything published in that decade.

However, while reality was still far from catching
up with the dream, progress was being made. Now
a mutually enhancing exchange of ideas and images
was taking place. High-altitude balloonists were taking their "spaceships" to the limits of the Earth's
atmosphere (by the mid-1930s altitudes of 12 miles or
more were being reached); rocket-powered gliders
and aircraft were being flown, great advances being
made in this area by the Germans and Russians; and
the Germans developed the V-2.

It is difficult to imagine and difficult to overestimate the influence of the V-2. It was larger by far
than any other rocket ever built and it flew faster,
higher, and farther. And, not the least of its important attributes, it looked great. It took hold of the
public imagination, becoming synonymous with
spaceship, because it *was* a spaceship.

The popular science writer and expatriate German
rocket experimenter Willy Ley said so himself. He
pointed out that the ton of explosives the V-2 carried could easily be replaced by a pilot and his life
support equipment. This was an idea that had also
occurred to the Nazis, who had drawn up tentative
plans to boost a manned version of the V-2 to New
York via a super-rocket called the A-10. After the
war the British Interplanetary Society took a scheme
similar to Ley's to the British Ministry of Supply.
They proposed using a modified V-2 to launch a
manned capsule into a ballistic, suborbital flight. After reaching a maximum altitude of about 190 miles,
the capsule would separate from the rocket and re-

turn to the Earth by parachute. Like the lunar
lander designed by the BIS in 1939, the "Megaroc"
bore a remarkable resemblance to things to come,
notably Alan Shepard's Mercury capsule that inaugurated America's manned entry into space.

The V-2 played a role in the first science fiction
movies to appear after the war. George Pal's *Destination Moon* (1950) begins with the launch of that
missile, and the vehicle used for the manned trip to
the Moon is clearly a linear descendant. The *Luna*
was designed by artist Chesley Bonestell and art di-

■
*Germany's wartime V-2
clearly inspired this 1948
Chesley Bonestell painting of
a winged spaceship on the
Moon. The wings were to*

*permit a glide reentry into
the Earth's atmosphere. Ordway Collection/Space &
Rocket Center.*

rector Ernst Fegte. *Destination Moon* was beaten to the theaters by the low-budget *Rocketship XM,* made to cash in on the bigger movie's publicity. Its low budget forced its producers to use stock footage of the launch of a V-2 for the launch of the movie rocket—even though it bore little resemblance to the model (itself lifted from a *Life* magazine article) used in the remainder of the film!

The 1951 space opera *Flight to Mars* also owed its spaceship to *Destination Moon,* but in a roundabout way. The *Mars 1* was originally designed by Bonestell as the *Luna,* but the design was rejected. The producers of *Flight to Mars,* one of whom had worked on *Destination Moon,* frugally adopted the unused spaceship for their own movie.

The *Mars 1* might be the quintessential 1950s spaceship, but the producer of *Destination Moon* had other, more realistic designs yet to come. The Bonestell-designed Space Ark from Pal's *When Worlds Collide,* with its spectacular if impractical launch ramp, was easily the most impressive rocket launch in film history. But the peak was reached with the spacecraft in *The Conquest of Space,* inspired by the series of articles in *Collier's.* Taking the flying-wing Mars glider from the book version of the 1954 Wernher von Braun article "Can We Get to Mars?," Bonestell and art director J. MacMillan Johnson adapted and even managed to improve the original design. In spite of silliness of plotting—of which there is a great deal—the film is like watching the *Collier's* articles and their illustrations by Bonestell, Fred Freeman, and Rolf Klep brought to life. The graceful toroidal space station, a delta-winged ferry rocket, space taxis, and the elegant Mars glider are all brought to the screen in color and extraordinary realism.

By the middle of the decade the golden age of space travel was in full swing, spurred primarily by the appearance of the *Collier's* serial, a series of programs on space travel produced by Walt Disney and aired on the "Tomorrowland" segment of the "Disneyland" television show, and the general postwar euphoria about the future that space travel represented. However, this was in a way self-defeating as well as self-fulfilling. The imaginative spaceships gradually gave way to the real-life ones that they helped to inspire. Backs were turned on the sleekly beautiful spacecraft of the 1930s, 1940s, and 1950s in order to embrace the less aesthetic if more functional Mercury and Gemini capsules, Vostoks, Apollo command modules, and space shuttles. Is it possible that some of the waning interest in space travel might be due to the disappointing appearance of our spacecraft? The space shuttle is a wonderful piece of hardware, but it looks like a brick with wings; and with its boosters and external tank it looks exactly like the compromise it is. It's no *Luna.*

For decades experts had told us that the needle-nosed, streamlined, winged spaceships of science fiction, which could fly into space in a single stage, were the products of fantasy. Flatly contradicting them, and vindicating hundreds of science fiction illustrators and movie makers, are the several proposed aerospace planes, more than one of which appear to have come straight off the cover of some 1950s pulp magazines. The American National Aero Space Plane is a businesslike dart with rakish wings and stabilizers, while the racy German Sänger II looks as much like a stylized hood ornament as a seriously proposed spacecraft. These are spaceships as God meant them to be! Perhaps the promises made by the 1950s are yet to be fulfilled.

Note

1. In 1858–1860, Narciso Monturiol performed experiments pertinent to the physiology of spaceflight by studying the effects of prolonged confinement on the crew of the Spanish submarine *Icteneo.* He studied the problems and solutions of oxygen use and regeneration, the condensation of water vapor, and temperature control, as well as the psychological effects of prolonged confinement in close quarters.

For further reading

Durant, Frederick C., III, and Ron Miller. *Worlds Beyond: The Art of Chesley Bonestell.* Norfolk, 1983: Donning.

Green, Roger Lancelyn. *Into Other Worlds.* London and New York, 1958: Abelard-Schuman.

Hardy, David A. *Visions of Space.* Foreword by Arthur C. Clarke. Limpsfield, 1989: Paper Tiger.

Hardy, Phil. *The Encyclopedia of Science Fiction Movies.* London, 1984: Woodbury Press.

Kyle, David. *Science Fiction Ideas and Dreams.* London, 1977: Hamlyn.

Leighton, Peter. *Moon Travellers.* London, 1960: Oldbourne.

Miller, Ron, ed. *Space Art.* New York, 1979: Starlog.

Miller, Walter James, ed. and trans. *From the Earth to the Moon.* New York, 1978: Thomas Y. Crowell.

Nicholls, Peter, gen. ed. *The Science in Science Fiction.* New York, 1983: Alfred A. Knopf.

Pizor, Faith K., and T. Allan Comp, eds. *The Man in the Moone and Other Lunar Fantasies.* New York, 1971: Praeger.

Rudaux, Lucien. *Sur les autres mondes.* Paris, 1937, reprinted 1990: Larousse.

Sadoul, Jacques. *2000 A.D.* Chicago, 1975: Henry Regnery.

Wright, Hamilton, Helen Wright, and Samuel Rapport, eds. *To the Moon!* New York, 1968: Meredith.

The Growth of Science Fiction from 1900 to the Early 1950s

SAM MOSKOWITZ

Beginnings

Though science fiction developed and became explosively popular in the twentieth century, materials had been accumulating previously. For much of the nineteenth century, Richard Adams Locke's 1835 newspaper hoax about the discovery of life on the Moon inspired a series of subsequent writers. Not the least of those was Edgar Allan Poe, who in turn inspired Jules Verne to begin writing his string of fantastic adventures beginning with *Five Weeks in a Balloon* (1863). Following that, works of what today we term science fiction were often identified as the "Jules Verne type," though "wonder stories" also became a common means of identifying such literature.

In the United States, the advent of science fiction in the nineteenth century was unpredictable and sporadic; when it did appear, it was usually in magazines or newspapers. San Franciscans had a fondness for the genre, particularly as found in the weekly magazine *The Argonaut* (which began publication in 1877) and in William Randolph Hearst's newspaper *The San Francisco Examiner* (taken over by him in 1887). Between them, these two outlets published hundreds of works of science fiction, the most popular of which were by Robert Duncan Milne. A Scottish expatriate, he wrote 60 such tales between 1880 and 1900, some of which were collected in his *Into the Sun and Other Stories*.

In England, penny papers with titles like *Pearson's Weekly* and *Short Stories* found science fiction—particularly that dealing with future wars—to be a great circulation booster; from 1894 on, they made its inclusion a matter of policy. This, in turn, virtu-

ally launched the careers of such popular authors as George Griffith, M. P. Shiel, and Louis Tracy, while at the same time enhancing those of H. Rider Haggard and H. G. Wells.

It was Wells who elevated science fiction to a literary art. His short science fiction tales had been appearing frequently since 1893 in a variety of British magazines and some had been reprinted in American magazines and newspapers as well. He gained a critical success in England with *The Time Machine* (1895) and international popularity and financial success with *The War of the Worlds* (1897). The latter novel was successfully serialized in *Pearson's Magazine* in England and in *The Cosmopolitan* in the United States.

This success gave rise in England to the decision of mass-circulation magazine editors to publish occasional works of science fiction. Among the magazines following this policy were *The Strand, Pall Mall Magazine, The Idler, Windsor Magazine, The English Illustrated Magazine,* and *The London Magazine.* In the United States, only *The Cosmopolitan* regularly ran science fiction, though the genre did appear from time to time in publications like *Ainslee's, Everybody's,* and *Hampton's.*

As a holdover from the nineteenth century, dime novels continued to reprint several hundred offerings about Frank Reade and Jack Wright labeled "invention stories." This term became popular because such stories usually involved an airplane, a submarine, a tank, or some associated marvel. They were reprinted in England and formed a basic constituent of the dozens of boys' weeklies that flourished there.

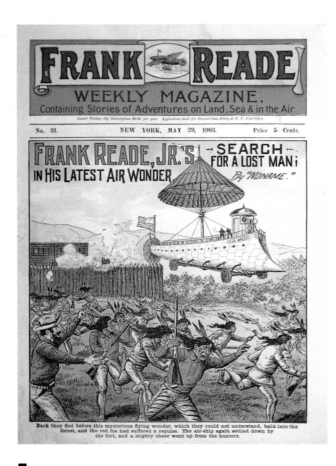

The Munsey Pulps

In October 1896, the American publisher Frank A. Munsey turned his smooth-papered, photograph-illustrated, popular-priced *The Argosy* into the first pulp-paper magazine in history. It regularly featured adventure fiction for men that dealt with the West, Africa, the sea, the desert, and sports, along with an increasing fare of science fiction novels and short stories. In 1897, Munsey published the eight-part novel *A Month in the Moon,* a reprint of *The Conquest of the Moon* (London, 1889) by French author André Laurie, in which the Moon is drawn by magnets down to the surface of the Earth. Two years later appeared the seven-part novel *A Queen of Atlantis* by Frank Aubrey, in which that fabled lost land and its flourishing civilization are discovered in the midst of the legendary Sargasso Sea.

With the advent of the twentieth century, we find H. G. Wells opening up the large-circulation family magazines to sporadic appearances of works of science fiction, and *The Argosy* providing a market for the genre in the newly created category of pulp magazines. Supplementing these were clever and sophisticated short science fiction tales that appeared in the group of publications best symbolized by *The Black Cat.* Established in 1895, this was a nationally distributed magazine that, until the turn of the century, ran one or more tales each month that could be labeled science fiction. This practice by *The Black Cat* inspired such imitators as *The Owl, The Grey Goose,* and *The White Elephant* to do the same.

In terms of output, *The Argosy* was certainly the leader. If one were to count each installment of a serial as a "unit," during 1901 alone 23 units of science fiction appeared in its 12 monthly issues. By maintaining this pace in ensuing years, it continued to attract readers with a predilection for the fantastic. *The Argosy* was one of the best-selling magazines in the world and by 1905 was charging advertisers on the basis of a circulation of 500,000 copies. Not surprisingly, its success led to the launching of a companion, *The All-Story Magazine.* Since this new entry also stressed adventures appealing to men, science fiction was included in almost every issue. A second companion, *The Cavalier,* was introduced in 1908 and also carried a generous quota of science fiction.

All the while, H. G. Wells was continuing to write science fiction, *The Cosmopolitan* favoring novels like *The First Men in the Moon* (1900–1901), *Food* of the Gods (1903–1904), and *In the Days of the Comet* (1906). The practice of serializing these novels in eight to ten installments, each lavishly illustrated, helped science fiction to become an important feature of this prestigious family magazine.

Despite Wells's broad appeal, two events would soon curtail *The Cosmopolitan*'s emphasis on fantasy and science fiction. First, its publisher John Brisben Walker needed money to develop and promote the steam automobile; he was convinced that it and not the internal combustion engine would be the transportation wave of the future. To raise money to pursue his automotive interests, in 1905 he sold the magazine to William Randolph Hearst for $400,000. Second, advertising agencies had discovered that women, not men, were making most of the purchasing decisions for the home; in the light of this, virtually all of the mass-circulation magazines soon began to slant their editorial policies to appeal to female readers. Because science fiction was not particularly popular with them, H. G. Wells felt obliged to cut down on this kind of writing and turn to love stories and socialist tracts.

Competitors to the Munsey pulps, typified by *The Popular Magazine* (1903) and *The Blue Book Magazine* (1905), began to offer some science fiction but never matched Munsey in quantity or quality. Their secondary position became all the more evident when *The All-Story* magazine discovered Edgar Rice Burroughs and serialized his first work, *Under the Moons of Mars,* from February to July 1912. The story told of a decadent planet of great canals, advanced science, monstrous creatures, and savage creeds; it was published in book form in 1917 as *The Princess of Mars.* One success in one year was not enough for the enthusiastic Burroughs, who promptly offered *All-Story* a quite different adventure tale: *Tarzan of the Apes* (October 1912). With John Carter (hero of the Martian adventure) and Tarzan on the literary market, H. G. Wells soon became last year's news when it came to imaginative fiction.

Burroughs brought into being and made immensely popular a form of science fiction frequently called the "scientific romance." It stressed imaginative, colorful, and romantic adventures set on other worlds, in other dimensions, and in otherwise remote locales. Stories following this formula were cultivated by a number of highly skilled imitators who were encouraged and published by *The Argosy* and *All-Story Weekly.* (The latter went weekly with the 7 March 1914 issue that incorporated *The Cava-*

A COMPANION STORY TO "SHE" BY H. RIDER HAGGARD IN THIS NUMBER

■

A sequel to H. Rider Haggard's fantastic classic She, *entitled* Ayesha: The Further History of She, *was a blockbuster that helped estab-* lish the widely circulated The Popular Magazine. *The story received cover attention on this January 1905 issue. Moskowitz Collection.*

lier.) These imitators included (independently and simultaneously) George Allan England with a trilogy of fine post-holocaust novels (1912–1913); Charles B. Stilson with a Tarzan-like antarctic superhero (1915); J. U. Giesy with a hero who journeys out of our solar system by spirit migration to a distant star (1918); A. Merritt, an unsurpassed literary stylist, who introduces a realm beneath the Earth (1918–1919); Ray Cummings, who dwindles people to worlds of the atom (1919); at a later period, Ralph Milne Farley, who makes the newly popular radio an integral part of his stories (1924); and still later Otis Adelbert Kline, who would slug it out planet-by-planet with Edgar Rice Burroughs (1929). And there were many others.

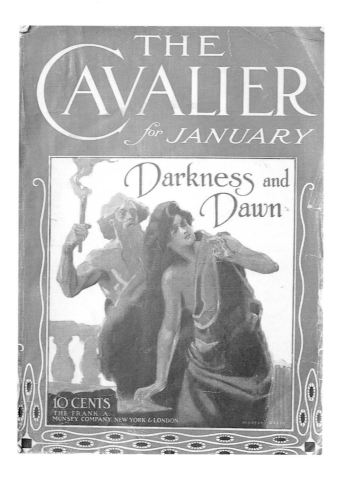

Bernarr Macfadden and Hugo Gernsback

Simultaneously, science fiction was taking hold in two other unlikely sectors. As early as 1904, Bernarr Macfadden's *Physical Culture Magazine* had begun publishing it. Now it so happened that Macfadden was an extremist strength-and-health advocate, promoting his ideas on nutrition (including vegetarianism), in addition to muscle building. He hired two full-time writers, John Coryell (one of the original authors of Nick Carter) and Milo Hastings, whose duties included writing utopian science fiction to order, usually—but not always—underscoring what supermen people of the future could become if they followed Macfadden's strength-and-health theories.

Macfadden even set up a utopian colony of his own in Spotswood, New Jersey, and opened a chain of health resorts and health restaurants. The extremes he resorted to in his advocacy of science fiction were displayed when he launched *True Story Magazine* in 1919. In it, each of his regulars, Coryell and Hastings, contributed a science fiction novel of the future "that might be true." The one by Hastings, *The City of Endless Night,* appeared in hardcovers by Dodd Mead in 1920 and bears favorable comparison with *We* by Eugene Zimiatin and *1984* by George Orwell.

The man who undoubtedly had the most impact on science fiction of anyone in the twentieth century was Hugo Gernsback. As an outgrowth of a radio catalog prepared for a mail-order business he had established, in 1908 he launched the monthly *Modern Electrics.* America's first radio magazine, it appeared at a time when there were no stations, no commercial receivers, and when ships at sea transmitted by Morse code. Finding his April 1911 issue with space to fill and no material on hand, Gernsback dashed off the first chapter of *Ralph 124C 41 +,* into which he crammed as many new inventions as he could conceive of. So popular was the first installment that he stretched his story out to 12 and featured it on the cover of the magazine.

To track a Martian spaceship carrying off his girlfriend, the hero Ralph relied on what we now call radar. In fact, he described and diagramed it so effectively that the United States Patent Office later refused to consider it a new invention when Britain's Sir Watson Watts applied for a patent. Other ideas revealed in *Ralph 124C 41 +* included fluorescent lighting, skywriting, plastics, a radio directional range finder, juke boxes, tape recorders, loudspeak-

The early pulp magazines, typified by the January 1912 issue of The Cavalier, *frequently featured science fiction. The cover of this issue announces "Darkness and Dawn," a popular post-holocaust novel by George Allan England that was to spawn two sequels and appear in book form in 1914. Moskowitz Collection.*

England, Merritt, Cummings, Farley, and Kline were all good enough to attain preservation in hardcovers, though none of them would approach the many millions of Burroughs's books sold. The latter's readership, incidentally, was by no means limited to the United States; Burroughs was also internationally published and, as early as 1922, had become extremely popular across the vast terrain of the Soviet Union.

ers, night baseball, solar energy, television, micro-film, nylon, aquacades, vending machines dispensing hot and cold foods, and scores of others.

Ralph 124C 41 + was such a circulation builder that as soon as Gernsback was able to obtain enough science fiction material from authors known to him, he included one or two stories in every issue of his electrical, radio, experimental science, and popular science magazines. His volume was such that by 1925 he was collectively publishing more units of science fiction than *Argosy All-Story Weekly* (these two periodicals had been combined under the new title with the 24 July 1920 issue). The only other possible competitor to confront Gernsback was *Weird Tales,* which had been introduced in 1923. A monthly publication specializing in supernatural and horror, it nevertheless offered in each number several "weird scientific" stories.

At a time when westerns were the rage due in large part to the best-selling popularity of Zane Grey, Gernsback went against the trend, and in April 1926 he introduced the first all–science fiction magazine, *Amazing Stories.* From the readers of his own scientific magazines plus those of *Argosy All-Story Weekly, Physical Culture,* and *Weird Tales,* he found a ready-made audience. Not unexpectedly, the magazine became an instant success and soon spawned *Amazing Stories Quarterly* after a single *Amazing Stories Annual.*

Gernsback was wise enough to feature authors like H. G. Wells and Edgar Rice Burroughs, who had created the previous waves of interest in science fiction, backed up by others who were regularly writing for *Argosy All-Story Weekly* and *Weird Tales.* In addition, he soon developed his own cadre of writers, among whom were Philip Francis Nowlan, with two novellas from which Buck Rogers was derived; Edward E. Smith, who opened up new vistas by journeying to other star systems; David H. Keller, M.D., who explored the psychological impact on humans of future technology; Jack Williamson, whose versatility made his a name to conjure with for the next 60 years; and a solid group of others whose achievements have been dissipated by time: Harl Vincent, Miles J. Breuer, M.D., Francis Flagg, R. F. Starzl, and Stanton A. Coblentz.

One of Gernsback's nonfiction publications, *Your Body,* may have inspired a conspiracy that would force him into involuntary bankruptcy. *Your Body* was a magazine of health, strength, and nutrition of undeniable quality, portions of it written by medical doctors. As such, it was in direct competition with Bernarr Macfadden's flagship publication *Physical Culture.* Add to that Macfadden's previously mentioned fascination with science fiction and the fact that he was concurrently publishing a monthly fantasy magazine *Ghost Stories* and it can be seen that he and Gernsback were on a collision course.

Now it so happened that both men relied on the same printer, Art Color. Located in Dunellen, New Jersey, it was a huge operation, and Macfadden Publications—with *True Story, True Romances, True Detective,* and as many as 15 other publications—was

When the first science fiction magazine, Amazing Stories, *soared to instant success, Hugo Gernsback launched a companion* Amazing Stories Quarterly. *It ran the complete* When the Sleeper Wakes *by H. G. Wells in the inaugural (Winter 1928) issue; the cover was by Frank R. Paul. Moskowitz Collection.*

Magazines were to be the dominant form of development of science fiction in the first half of the twentieth century. The first to compete with Gernsback's magazines was Astounding Stories of Super-Science, *whose cover on the May 1930 issue by H. W. Wesso illustrates a scene from "The Atom Smasher" by Victor Rousseau. It was a prescient look at future weapons. Moskowitz Collection.*

20¢

ASTOUNDING
STORIES
OF SUPER - SCIENCE

A CLAYTON MAGAZINE

**MURDER MADNESS
By MURRAY LEINSTER**
Charley Bell Fights to Stem the Swiftly Rising Tide of a Continent's Utter Enslavement

THE ATOM SMASHER
An Adventure into Time
By VICTOR ROUSSEAU

Art Color's largest customer, responsible at times for as many as 10 million copies a month. Gernsback, who rarely printed more than 500,000 copies, was a slow payer and often heavily in arrears.

Under Macfadden's prompting, Art Color pressured Gernsback to either sell out to Macfadden or have all his past notes called simultaneously. Just when Gernsback was about to capitulate, the printer, for reasons that can only be surmised, conspired successfully to throw him into involuntary bankruptcy (possible at that period if three creditors presented their claims simultaneously). This occurred in February 1929; and, after a kaleidoscope of "owners," in the Statement of Ownership Bernarr Macfadden was revealed to be the actual publisher of the various periodicals in the *Amazing Stories* issue of December 1931. *Your Body* was quickly killed as a competitor to Macfadden's *Physical Culture,* while *Amazing Stories* and its companion *Amazing Stories Quarterly* successfully continued publication.

Magazine Fiction in the 1930s and Early 1940s

Having lost control of his firm, Gernsback solicited subscriptions for a new corporation and in May 1929 launched two new magazines, *Science Wonder Stories* and *Air Wonder Stories,* followed a few months later by *Science Wonder Quarterly.* Then, in January 1930, a worthy competitor entered the field, *Astounding Stories of Super-Science* edited by Harry Bates. Noting that there was indeed a viable audience for the genre, general adventure magazine publishers began to include it ever more frequently. Understandably, this was particularly true of *Argosy Weekly* (separated from *All-Story* from 5 October 1929), which regularly featured Edgar Rice Burroughs, A. Merritt, Ray Cummings, Otis Adelbert Kline, and other proponents of the scientific romance; and *The Blue Book Magazine,* which in addition to Burroughs's Mars and Tarzan novels introduced two immensely popular interplanetary works by Edwin Balmer and Philip Wylie. The titles, *When Worlds Collide* (1932) and *After Worlds Collide* (1933), suggest the exciting themes developed by their authors.

Spearheaded by sales of millions of copies of Edgar Rice Burroughs's Mars books in their low-priced Grossett & Dunlap editions, for a few years in the late 1920s and early 1930s a sampling of hardcover science fiction appeared. The mathematician

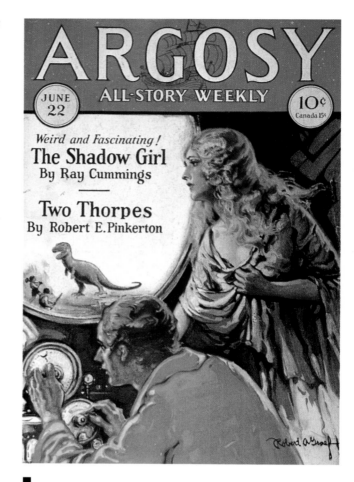

■

The non–science fiction/ fantasy adventure magazine that printed more of the genre than any other was Argosy. *It was a major outlet for science fiction before the advent of specialty magazines. The Robert A. Graef* cover on the 27 June 1929 issue depicts a scene from The Shadow Girl *by Ray Cummings, in which a televisor reveals a scene from Earth's distant past. Moskowitz Collection.*

Eric Temple Bell, writing under the pen name John Taine, produced a series of popular novels; the British author S. Fowler Wright had a best-seller in *Deluge,* which was made into a motion picture (1933); imitations of Burroughs were authored by Kline and Cummings; and the novels of M. P. Shiel were reissued. Then there were the incredible "histories" of the future by Olaf Stapledon. If it were not for the onset of the Depression, when $2.00 and $2.50 books became luxuries, this trend might have continued; but the economics of the times aborted it.

The Planet
of Peril

By
Otis Adelbert Kline

■

Riding on the popularity of Edgar Rice Burroughs, for a few years in the late 1920s science fiction began to appear in hardcovers. The Planet of Peril (1929) *by one of his more popular imitators, Otis Adelbert Kline, with a* Robert A. Graef *cover, was reprinted from* Argosy, *where the novel was first serialized. The onset of the Depression ended this experiment. Moskowitz Collection.*

In examining the establishment of the science fiction magazines, scrutiny is most often given to the quality of the contents, when realistically *distribution* was a more pivotal factor in their success. When *Astounding Stories* was purchased by Street and Smith in 1933, *Wonder Stories* by Standard/Beacon Magazines in 1936, and *Amazing Stories* by Ziff-Davis Publishing in 1938, all had something in common: new distribution by The American News Company, the most effective distributor of the period. It was no coincidence that all three became viable periodicals shortly after the change. Gernsback concentrated on his radio and popular science magazines, dropping science fiction.

Amazing Stories under Ziff-Davis ownership sparked a boom in science fiction magazines following the initial success of *Marvel Science Stories* (August 1938; issued by The Red Circle pulp chain). Robert O. Erisman, the head of this chain, had worked for Hugo Gernsback in the late 1920s and was therefore familiar with science fiction. The expansion of the field was given impetus by the Orson Welles radio presentation of H. G. Wells's *The War of the Worlds* on 30 October 1938. This newscast-style broadcast of Martians landing in New Jersey and devastating the horizon with heat rays sent many denizens of that state streaming into the streets with wet towels around their heads for protection. Orson Welles, in a letter to Nils Hardin, pulp magazine collector, dated 29 November 1976, revealed that for one year he had made his living as a pulp author (1932) and claimed to have written "a good deal of science fiction of the Lobster-Men type" published under the pen name of a friend. Unfortunately, Welles's science fiction stories have never been located or identified (he claimed to have been abroad at the time of publication and at no time to have actually seen them in print). Welles admitted only to having cashed the checks in payment for the stories.

A spate of new science fiction magazines appeared during the next two years, including *Startling Stories, Fantastic Adventures, Unknown, Science Fiction, Science Fiction Quarterly, Future Fiction, Dynamic Science Stories, Astonishing Stories, Super Science Stories, Captain Future,* and *Planet Stories,* until the newsstands set up special sections for them. So popular became science fiction that *Argosy* issued two titles, *Famous Fantastic Mysteries* and *Fantastic Novels,* that featured reprints from their old issues for those who had never read them. The new magazines proliferated until the entry of the United States into World War II. After the Japanese bombing of Pearl Harbor, the government curtailed publication by rationing the paper they required, and many fell by the wayside even though the market had by no means been saturated.

Astounding Stories had temporarily ceased to appear due to the difficulties of its publisher, Clayton Publications. When Street & Smith purchased the magazine in 1933, it offered the editorship to veteran F. Orlin Tremaine, who performed so brilliantly that the magazine soon became the leader in its field.

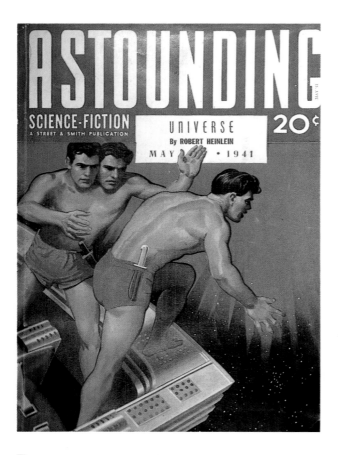

Astounding Science-Fiction, *edited by John W. Campbell, was the dominant influence on science fiction during the 1940s. Campbell developed a brilliant group of* new authors including Robert A. Heinlein, whose famed novelette of thousand-year space arks, "Universe," is featured on this cover by Hubert Rogers. Moskowitz Collection.

When Tremaine left in 1938, an assistant he had hired assumed control, John W. Campbell, Jr. By then, the new editor was one of the field's leading authors, writing under his own name and the pen name Don A. Stuart. He promoted constantly evolving ideas of what science fiction should be in concept and technique and was able to articulate these ideas to both new and veteran writers. With their cooperation, Campbell gradually popularized a more sophisticated brand of science fiction in which backgrounds were subtly woven into the narrative and where emphasis was placed on sociological, psychological, and even philosophical situations. He even developed certain rules for plots, such as that humans should usually win out over aliens.

As editor of what had become the leading science fiction magazine, with reliable monthly frequency and paying the best rates, Campbell was able to implement his ideas and quickly assembled a cadre of superior authors who were to become tops in the field. These included Robert A. Heinlein (1939), whose stories were the epitome of background blended with action; A. E. van Vogt (1939), who was hard to surpass when it came to original ideas approached from an unusual angle; Theodore Sturgeon (1939), stylistically the most innovative and adroit with his new discoveries; Isaac Asimov (1939), who featured robots and intergalactic politics; and Fritz Leiber (1939), who first appeared as an author of fantasies in *Unknown* and then employed witchcraft as a cover to expose corrupt religion. Campbell also witnessed the development and maturation of such already well-established talents as Clifford D. Simak, Eric Frank Russell, Lester del Rey, L. Sprague de Camp, Jack Williamson, Henry Kuttner, and C. L. Moore.

While Campbell and *Astounding Stories* were the unquestioned leader and innovator in the science fiction magazine field, several other major writers were developed by other markets. Prominent among them was Ray Bradbury, who was introduced by *Super Science Stories* in 1941 and reached his greatest peak of development in *Weird Tales, Planet Stories, Thrilling Wonder Stories,* and *Startling Stories* later in the decade. It was in the last three magazines that he placed the stories that were to compose *The Martian Chronicles* (1950), the book that made Bradbury's critical reputation. While *Astounding Science-Fiction* (the magazine's revised title) purchased Arthur C. Clarke's first two short stories for American publication (1946), this author's fictional development predominantly took place in such competing magazines as *Startling Stories, Famous Fantastic Mysteries,* and *Thrilling Wonder Stories.*

Further, there were occasional authors of science fiction who developed outside the traditional magazines and occasionally exercised great influence on them. The most important of these was Olaf Stapledon, an English socialist with a titanic imagination and, at his best, the possessor of a powerful, almost poetic style. Simply to describe the narrative line of his most influential books reveals his impressive scope. Stapledon's first published work, of verse, came out in 1914, followed in 1929 by his nonfiction treatise *A Modern Theory of Ethics. Last and First Men* (1930), his first attempt at fiction, was a future history of the human race for the next 200 million years. In it, Stapledon described not only the race's genetic evolution and physical adaptation to other planets, but each succeeding era's politics, art, music, sports, literature, and science. Even more impressive was *The Star Maker* (1937), which described the history of the *universe,* with even the stars imbued with thought processes and ambitions.

So fecund was Stapledon in ideas and concepts that he provided fuel for scores of prominent writers who contributed to the periodical literature. Among others who made a reputation in hardcovers and at the same time had an impact on magazine writers were S. Fowler Wright, whose recasting of Dante's *Inferno* into scientifically credible terms in *The World Below* (1929) was a landmark work, and Aldous Huxley, whose *Brave New World* (1932) conveyed political and social satire though highly inventive science fiction.

Specialty Presses, Anthologies, and Paperbacks

While the evolution of science fiction had been carried out predominantly in magazines and would continue so into the 1970s, as early as 1939 a new approach was taken that would carry the genre back into the respectability of hardcovers. August W. Derleth, a prolific contributor to *Weird Tales* and a regional novelist of some importance, together with science fiction author Donald Wandrei, had decided to honor the memory of their friend and correspondent, Howard Philips Lovecraft. Derleth and Wandrei published an omnibus Lovecraft collection entitled *The Outsider and Others,* whose stories included a substantial number that could be accurately characterized as science fiction. Though not the first to start a fantasy specialty press (theirs was called Arkham House), they were by all odds the most influential. They followed their initial offering with further volumes of Lovecraft stories as well as collections by Clark Ashton Smith and Donald Wandrei himself. Other authors attracted to Arkham House were Robert Bloch, Henry S. Whitehead, William Hope Hodgson, Frank Belknap Long, and S. Fowler Wright. A. E. van Vogt, whose novel *Slan* dealt with human mutants able to read minds and their persecution by normal society, was also published by Arkham.

Imitators quickly followed, with the Buffalo Book Company putting into print novels by Edward E. Smith, John Taine, John W. Campbell, and L. Ron Hubbard. A most important early specialty publisher was Fantasy Press, which was run by author Lloyd A. Eshbach. Borrowing the sales list developed by the Buffalo Book Company, he soon issued acknowledged classics by Edward E. Smith, Jack Williamson, John Taine, Stanley G. Weinbaum, Eric Frank Russell, Robert A. Heinlein, John W. Campbell, Jr., and A. E. van Vogt.

Fantasy Press was soon followed by Prime Press, which specialized in collections by Theodore Sturgeon and Lester del Rey and new works by David H. Keller, M.D.; the New Collector's Group, which offered two unfinished A. Merritt works completed by Hannes Bok from early chapters held by the Merritt estate; Gnome Press, which featured works by Robert A. Heinlein, L. Sprague de Camp, Robert E. Howard, Isaac Asimov, and Clifford D. Simak; Shasta Publishers, best known for its books by John W. Campbell, L. Sprague de Camp, L. Ron Hubbard, S. Fowler Wright, Murray Leinster, and Robert A. Heinlein; and an assortment of minor specialty houses.

A large portion of the sales of these houses was by direct mail, but they soon began to sell through distributors and bookstores, many of the latter installing for the first time science fiction shelves. The large trade book publishers looked on in amazement; but, despite earlier clues that there was a substantial market out there, they lacked knowledge of the field and were cautious to the extent that at first they did nothing.

Or rather almost nothing. As early as 1941, Wilfred Funk had produced *The Other Worlds,* a mixed anthology of science fiction and supernatural that enjoyed a fine continuing sale in a low-priced Garden City printing. And in 1945 under the editorship of Donald A. Wollheim, the Viking Portable Library had successfully issued *Novels of Science* with four works by H. G. Wells, John Taine, H. P. Lovecraft, and Olaf Stapledon in one volume. The real pay-off came a year later when Crown released *The Best of Science Fiction,* edited by Groff Conklin; it offered a spectrum of outstanding science fiction culled from the magazines. That same year, Random House produced *Adventures in Time and Space,* edited by Raymond J. Healy and J. Francis McComas. It was another omnibus composed mostly of the better tales from *Astounding Science-Fiction.* By the

standards of the 1940s, these collections were best-sellers, and they still remain in print.

There is no question that the compilation of both these anthologies was galvanized by the dropping of two atomic bombs on Japan the previous year. Science fiction was no longer comic book, pulp, or kid stuff; it had some thought and substance to it. Still, for the most part the big trade publishers were slow to respond until August W. Derleth got a small New York firm to issue a series of science fiction anthologies of very high literary quality: *Strange Ports of Call* (1948), *The Other Side of the Moon* (1949), and *Beyond Space and Time* (1950). At that point, main-line publishers got into the act. Among the early ones was Charles Scribner's Sons, which procured the juvenile *Rocket Ship Galileo* (1947) from Robert A. Heinlein, who had resumed writing after World War II. His output continued at the rate of one a year with *Space Cadet* (1948), *Red Planet* (1949), and *Farmer in the Sky* (1950). Each became increasingly more adult in style and enjoyed a wide and enthusiastic audience.

In the same period (1949), Frederick Fell, a small nonspecialist publisher, started *The Best Science Fiction Stories* on an annual basis. The series was edited by Everett Bleiler and Ted Dikty. The same publisher issued a quartet of novels in 1949 by Edmond Hamilton, Frank Belknap Long, Oscar J. Friend, and William F. Temple that were reviewed by the prestigious *New York Times*. Also, the low-priced reprint house Grossett and Dunlap published Henry

■

Specialty publishers returned science fiction to hardcovers in the 1940s, the leader being Fantasy Press headed by sci-

ence fiction author Lloyd A. Eshbach, among whose titles were these four. Moskowitz Collection.

Kuttner, A. E. van Vogt, Jack Williamson, and S. Fowler Wright in dollar hardcover editions. By the end of 1950, the influential and respected publisher Doubleday had Isaac Asimov, Ray Bradbury, Robert A. Heinlein, and Hal Clement in its stable. Simon & Schuster and Greenberg Publishers were also signing up top science fiction authors who heretofore had been the pride of the specialty houses. Science fiction had clearly advanced into the lists of mainstream book publishers, a circumstance that led to the virtual extinction of specialty houses during the 1950s. To an overwhelming extent, hardcover books were reprints of stories that had earlier appeared in magazines.

The boom in paperback publishing began in 1939 and would lead to hundreds of titles appearing on the same newsstand as magazines. The emphasis was on reprints simply because publishers recognized the sales value to offering a $3.00 book for 25 cents. The paperback houses were reluctant at first to publish science fiction and fantasy, preferring such other genres as western, detective, adventure, and love stories. Avon Books took a chance by republishing all of A. Merritt in paperback and was delighted by the sales that resulted. Bantam Books followed with an irregular program of publishing science fiction, leading off in 1950 with an anthology by Judith Merrill, *Shot in the Dark,* and continuing with Curt Siodmak, Frederic Brown, and Ray Bradbury. During the 1950s, Avon would become a leader in the field. Dell, which would also become a strong competitor, got started in science fiction in the 1940s with H. G. Wells, Alfred Hitchcock, and Orson Welles.

Bart House, under the former editor of *Astounding Stories,* F. Orlin Tremaine, entered the field back in 1944 by publishing the earliest H. P. Lovecraft paperbacks, Thomas Calvert McClary, and P. B. Maxon. However, Bart's efforts were severely hampered by paper shortages, more so than other houses because it had *started* during the war years and consequently been granted no paper quota by the government based on past usage. For a period it barely survived on quality book paper and short print orders. It was a period of 25-cent prices with distribution following the practice of magazines—through newsstands and candy stores. In general, paperbacks were a minor factor in science fiction publishing until the 1950s, when several houses began to specialize in the genre.

The Postwar Picture

After 1945, publishers at first still faced a severe paper shortage. Government allotment of paper left virtually no room for new expansion on the part of the chain publishers, since they did not wish to divert supplies from their non–science fiction magazines. Since they were already able to sell all copies of magazines for which paper had been approved, there was little incentive to take risks. In the case of book publishers, established authors understandably were accorded priority.

Despite war-generated difficulties, the potential of science fiction was not overlooked. As the paper shortage gradually began to ease, *The Avon Fantasy Reader* appeared in 1947, a magazine of reprints edited by Donald A. Wollheim. *Super Science Stories,* which had gone into mothballs for the duration of the war, resumed publication in 1948 along with a companion reprint magazine, *Fantastic Novels.* In 1949, Raymond A. Palmer, who had been editing *Amazing Stories,* left to form his own firm that would publish *Other Worlds Science Stories. A Merritt's Fantasy Magazine* also appeared, named after the immensely popular author of recent decades; and, most important, *The Magazine of Fantasy and Science Fiction* tentatively made its entry as a quarterly. Toward the end of 1950, no fewer than 28 science fiction and fantasy titles appeared on the newsstands, and that was not yet the highwater mark. Repressed demand had manifested itself; and, temporarily at least, the need for writers to fill it exceeded their ability to produce. This led 11 of the 28 magazines to rely on reprints to fill their pages.

From the vantage of hindsight, the most influential of the new titles were to be *The Magazine of Fantasy and Science Fiction* and *Galaxy Science Fiction.* The former, headed by the prominent detective fiction writer, editor, and authority Anthony Boucher, featured science fiction and fantasy—both new and reprints—and among its other accomplishments ran the early version of *A Canticle for Leibowitz* by Walter M. Miller, the novelette form of *Flowers for Algernon* by Daniel Keyes (later made into the motion picture *Charley*), and *Bring the Jubilee* by Ward Moore, the famed tale in which the South had won the Civil War. *Galaxy Science Fiction* was edited by H. L. Gold, formerly a writer, who steered his authors in the direction of Freudian psychology and helped build the reputations of Alfred Bester and Frederik Pohl. He lured away from *Astounding Science-Fiction* an enviable group of authors that included Isaac Asimov, Clifford D. Simak, Fritz Leiber, and Theodore Sturgeon. Gold also secured Ray Bradbury and developed Philip K. Dick.

As the 1950s ended, periodicals were the avant-garde of modern science fiction, even after pulp magazines had all but collapsed by 1955. Still decades ahead was the era when the field would be dominated by original paperbacks and when hardcovers would appear, often in multiples, on the best-seller list of the *New York Times*. Meanwhile the magazines—now converted to digest format—continued to be major avenues of development for the field.

For further reading

Ashley, Mike. *The History of the Science Fiction Magazine*. Volume 1, 1926–1935; Volume 2, 1936–1945; Volume 3, 1946–1955. New York, 1974, 1975, and 1976: New American Library.

Bleiler, E. F., ed. *Science Fiction Writers*. New York, 1982: Scribner's.

Goodstone, Tony, ed. *The Pulps*. New York, 1970: Bonanza.

Gunn, James. *Alternate Worlds: The Illustrated History of Science Fiction*. Englewood Cliffs, New Jersey, 1975: Prentice-Hall.

Haining, Peter. *The Fantastic Pulps*. London, 1975: Gollancz.

Moskowitz, Sam. *Explorers of the Infinite*. New York, 1963: World; rpt. Boston, 1974: Hyperion.

Moskowitz, Sam. *Science Fiction by Gaslight: A History and Anthology of Science Fiction in the Popular Magazine, 1891–1911*. New York, 1968: World; rpt. Boston, 1974: Hyperion.

Moskowitz, Sam. *Seekers of Tomorrow*. New York, 1966: World; rpt. Boston, 1974: Hyperion.

Moskowitz, Sam. *Strange Horizons: The Spectrum of Science Fiction*. New York, 1976: Scribner's.

Moskowitz, Sam. *Under the Moons of Mars: A History and Anthology of "The Scientific Romance" in the Munsey Magazines, 1912–1920*. New York, 1970: Holt, Rinehart & Winston.

Nichols, Peter. *The Science Fiction Encyclopedia*. New York, 1979: Doubleday.

Rogers, Alva. *A Requiem for Astounding*. Chicago, 1964: Advent.

Smith, Curtis C., ed. *Twentieth-Century Science-Fiction Writers*. New York, 1981: St. Martin's.

Tuck, Donald H. *The Encyclopedia of Science Fiction and Fantasy*. 3 vols. Chicago, 1974, 1978, and 1982: Advent.

Tymn, Marshall, and Mike Ashley. *Science Fiction, Fantasy and Weird Fiction Magazines*. Westport, Connecticut, 1985: Greenwood Press.

Part Two

Rocketry and Spaceflight

The Rocket from Earliest Times through World War I

FREDERICK I. ORDWAY III

The discovery that the reaction principle is the key to space travel is one of the great milestones in the history of human thought. Not only did it solve a problem that had intrigued man for ages, it opened the universe to his exploratory instincts. Though used sporadically for many hundreds of years, until the twentieth century the rocket remained a relatively minor artifact of civilization. Even writers of speculative fiction virtually ignored it as a means of transporting their heroes into the heavens. Prodigious efforts would be required, accelerated by two twentieth-century world wars, before the technology of rocketry could be translated into the reality of astronautics.

The reason for its earlier neglect lies in the fact that the reaction principle was not associated with the idea of traveling to neighboring worlds. It could have been figured out by cosmic adventure writers from the time of Isaac Newton onward, but it wasn't. A rocket operates much like a machine gun mounted on a rowboat. In reaction to the discharge of bullets, the gun, and hence the boat, move in the other direction with equal and opposite momentum, in accordance with Newton's Third Law of Motion (each action is accompanied by an equal and opposite reaction) described in *Philosophiae Naturalis Principia Mathematica* (1687). A rocket motor's "bullets" are minute particles resulting from the combustion of propellants in a suitable chamber. The reaction to the discharge of these particles causes the rocket to fly in the opposite direction.

We know that the reaction principle was demonstrated long before the advent of the rocket. In his *Noctes Atticae*, Aulus Gellius described the pigeon of Archytas, which dated back to about 360 B.C. Hanging from a string, it was made to move to and fro by steam blowing out through small exhaust ports. The reaction to the discharging steam provided the motive power to the bird.

Origins of the Rocket

The invention of the rocket is inextricably tied to black powder, credited by most historians of technology as a Chinese discovery. They base their belief on studies of Chinese writings and inquiries made by early Europeans who settled in or made prolonged visits to China, where they undertook detailed studies of its history and civilization. Despite some opinion to the contrary, it appears probable that, before the tenth century A.D., the explosive properties of the powder were unknown. Joseph Needham and his colleagues (*Science and Civilization in China*, volume V, part 7) state that around the middle of the eleventh century Tseng Kung-Liang and his assistant "were writing down the first gunpowder formulae to be printed and published in any civilization." They add that the essentials of the mixture had doubtless been known "at least a century previously." But this does not mean that gunpowder was immediately used to propel rockets.

By the thirteenth century, there is no longer much doubt that powder-propelled fire arrows had become rather common. The Sung Dynasty, under continuous pressure from the north, relied on such technological developments as incendiary projectiles, explosive grenades, and possibly cannons. They also made good use of rocket fire arrows at the battle of

K'ai-fung-fu (then called Piang-king) in 1232 when that town was besieged by the Mongols. According to Père Antoine Gaubil's *Histoire de Gentchiscan et de toute la dynastie de Mongous, ses successeurs, conquérants de la Chine* (1739) (*History of Genghiz Khan and of the Mongolian Dynasties, Their Successors, Conquerers of China*), the Chinese brought into play a new fire weapon that had a strong effect on the Mongols. "When it was lit," he explained, "it made a noise similar to thunder that extended to about a hundred *li* [approximately five leagues]. The place where it fell was burned and the fire extended more than two thousand feet." Another ecclesiastic, Père Joseph Anne-Marie Moriac de Mailla, in his *Histoire générale de la Chine*, volume 9 (1777–1784) (*General History of China*), wrote, "Moreover, the besieged had at their disposition flying fire arrows [*fei-ho-tsiang*]." When lit, they would take off rapidly, fly along a straight trajectory, and upon landing spread fire over a distance of 10 paces.

Needham and his colleagues believe that the rocket appeared some time after the mid-eleventh century, becoming present "in full force by +1340." They suggest that the origin can be traced to the "ground-rat" or "earth-rat" (*ti lao shu*), which was a firework device first used to scare troops and molest cavalry. Later, this same device was fitted with an arrow shaft and used to project firepower over long distances. "We shall suggest that the rocket originated, as it were, from the tube of the fire-lance filled with gunpowder, but detached from its handle, and therefore free to travel in whatever direction chance dictated."

The late-sixteenth-century *Wu Pei Chih* by Mao Yuan-i contains much historical information and many illustrations pertaining to these early rocket devices, including a launcher whose fire arrows "rush out on a solid front like 100 tigers." It

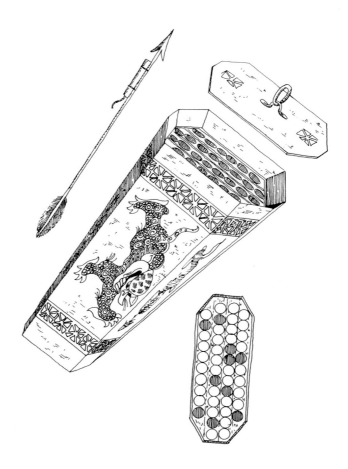

■ Left, *a Chinese rocket with its carrying case, from the* Wu Pei Chih (Treatise on Military Equipment) *by Mao Yuan-i;* above, *"Leopard-herd-rush-transversally" rocket, also* from the Wu Pei Chih. *The text explains that with this device "one can attack the enemy to both left and right." Ordway Collection/ Space & Rocket Center.*

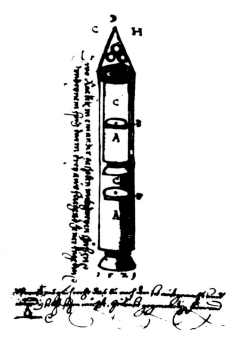
weighed 5 or 6 pounds, enabling a soldier to transport it and still maintain his mobility.

By the late thirteenth century the Mongols had introduced rockets to the western borders of their empire. The Arabs seem to have learned about them following the Mongol capture of Baghdad in 1258. The French sinologists Joseph Toussaint Reinaud and Idelphonse Favé, writing in the October 1849 issue of the *Journal Asiatique,* tell us something about rockets from information contained in MS 1128, fol. 103v and 105, Bibliothèque Nationale (ancien fonds) in Paris: "One attached the rocket near the iron base of the lance and the fuse was placed at the opposite end."

In western Europe, Marchus Graecus, who flourished in the second half of the thirteenth century, describes in his *Liber ignium ad comburendos hostes* (*Fire-Book*) devices that sound like rockets. He talks of *tunica ad volandum* or casing destined to fly and *ignis volatilis in aere* or flying fire. When lit, it would fly immediately toward the desired destination.

A number of relevant works appeared from the fifteenth through the eighteenth centuries, including Giovanni da Fontana's 1420–1430 manuscript *Belli-*

corum instrumentorum liber, in which military rockets are suggested. An anonymous French work on gunnery and fireworks, the *Livre de cannonerie et artifice de feu* (1561), tells how to make both 3½-foot and 4-foot rockets. Other works on pyrotechnics and fireworks, many profusely illustrated, include a sixteenth-century manuscript by Konrad Haas revealing that as early as 1529 he had conceived a multi-stage rocket; Battista de Valle di Venafro's *Vallo Libro . . .* of the same year; Vannoccio Biringuccio's *De la Pirotechnia* (1540); Jean Appier ("Hanzelet") of Lorraine's *La pyrotechnie militaire*

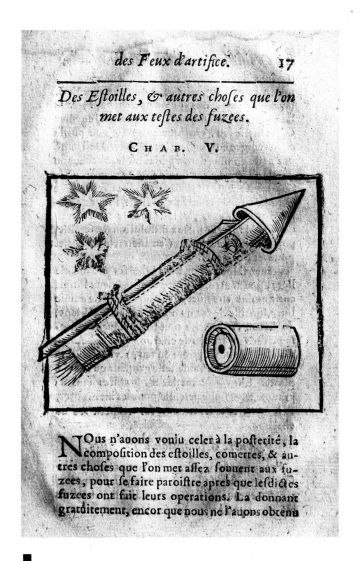

Johannis (John) Bate, author of the 1635 work The Mysteries of Nature and Art, *described—among many subjects—the preparation of rockets. Ordway Collection/ Space & Rocket Center.*

Two plates illustrating a variety of rocket types from Polish general Casimirus Siemienowicz's Artis magnae artilleriae . . . (The Great Art of Artillery), *1650. Ordway Collection/Space & Rocket Center.*

(1598) and *Recueil de plusiers machines militaires, et feux artificiels pour la Guerre, & Recréation* (1620); John Babington's *Pyrotechnia, or, A Discourse of Artificiall Fire-works* (1635); John Bate's *The Mysteries of Nature and Art* (1635); Polish general Casimirus Siemienowicz's *Artis magnae artilleriae* (1650; translated into English as *The Great Art of Artillery*, 1729); Robert Anderson's *The Making of Rockets* (1696); Amédée François Frézier's *Traité des feux d'artifice* (1747); and Perrinet d'Orval's *Traité des feux d'artifice pour le spectacle et pour la guerre* (1750).

The Italians were the first Europeans to advance seriously the art of fireworks making. In a 1572 work on artillery, Vannoccio gives credit to the Florentines and Sienese as being the first to place fireworks on wooden pedestals. Great fireworks displays were held regularly in many parts of Italy, which, until the end of the seventeenth century, reigned supreme in pyrotechnic displays. Then, under the influence

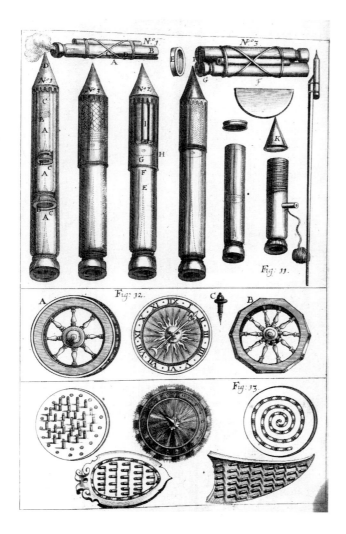

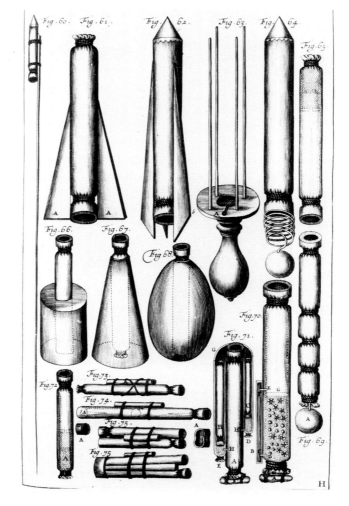

Fireworks display at Strasbourg, 23 February 1749. Ordway Collection/Space & Rocket Center.

■

A sketch of Indian war rockets appears on the title page of volume II of this work by Quintin Craufurd. Such rockets were about 8 inches long and 1½ inches in diameter and were fitted to 4-foot-long bamboo sticks. National Air and Space Museum.

first of Louis XIV and later of Louis XV, France began to take over the leadership, with such pyrotechnists as Morel Torre and the brothers Ruggieri making outstanding contributions. Rocket-based pyrotechnic displays became routine at major celebrations in France and throughout much of Europe.

Rockets as Weapons

Despite the outpouring of pyrotechnic manuscripts and books over the years, it was not until the late eighteenth century that Europeans became seriously interested in the possibilities of employing the rocket as a weapon of war. The incentive for this development came not from Europe itself but from faraway India. What happened there has been described by British and Indian historians. We learn that Hyder Ally of Mysore had built up a corps of rocketeers that, by 1788, numbered 1,200 men. Subsequently, his son Tippoo Sultan increased the corps to 5,000, using rockets successfully against the British during the battles of Seringapatam in 1792 and again in 1799.

In a 1793 work by Alexander Diron entitled *A Narrative of the Campaign in India, which Terminated the War with Tippoo Sultan,* Indian rockets are described as

SKETCHES

CHIEFLY RELATING TO THE

HISTORY, RELIGION, LEARNING, AND MANNERS,

OF THE

HINDOOS.

WITH

A concise Account of the PRESENT STATE of the NATIVE POWERS of HINDOSTAN.

THE SECOND EDITION, ENLARGED.

IN TWO VOLUMES.

VOL. II.

LONDON:

PRINTED FOR T. CADELL, IN THE STRAND.

MDCCXCII.

consisting of an iron tube about a foot long, and an inch in diameter, fixed to a bamboo rod of ten or twelve feet long. The tube being filled with combustible material, is set fire to, and, directed by the hand, flies like an arrow, to the distance of upwards of a thousand yards. Some of the rockets have a chamber, and burst like a shell; others, called the ground rockets, have a serpentine motion, and on striking the ground, rise again, and bound along till their force be spent. The rockets make a great noise, and exceedingly annoy the native cavalry in India, who move in great bodies; but are easily avoided, or seldom take the effect against our [British] troops, who are formed in lines of great extent, and no great depth.

After word of the Indian rockets quickly reached Europe, Colonel (later General and Sir) William Congreve began to experiment with incendiary barrage rockets at the Royal Laboratory of Britain's Woolwich Arsenal. He had heard of the use the Indians had made of rockets and set out to investigate the possibility of employing them in military operations on the Continent. In discussing Indian operations, Congreve cites as his authority a Colonel Gerrard, "the late adjutant general of the Indian army, who served in all the campaigns of Lord Cornwallis, in the Mysore, and in Lord Lake's campaigns." It seems that Gerrard "once saw three men killed and four desperately wounded by the same rocket." In the trenches in front of Seringapatam, the British "suffered more from them than from the shells or any other weapon used by the enemy."

Congreve, who carefully recorded his many activities and proposals for posterity, is represented in the literature by several important rare books. Among them are the *Memoir on the Possibility, the Means, and the Importance, of the Destruction of the Boulogne Flotilla, in the Present Crisis* (1806) and *A Concise Account on the Origin and Progress of the Rocket System* (1817). Of special interest is the *Concise Account,* in which we learn how the idea of using rockets against French military targets developed in Congreve's mind. "In the year 1804 it first occurred to me, that, as the projectile force of the Rocket is exerted without any re-action upon the point from which it is discharged, it might be successfully applied, both afloat and ashore, as a military engine. . . . I knew that rockets were used for military purposes in India; but that their magnitude was inconsiderable, and their range not exceeding 1000 yards." He then designed and built a 2,000-yard rocket, which he proposed be used in combat, as

■

Congreve rockets at the Rotunda Museum, Royal Artillery Establishment, Woolwich, England. Left to right: *300, 100, 42, 32, 24, and 18 pounders. Rotunda Museum.*

part of a "plan for the annoyance of Boulogne."

Congreve described his 32-pound rocket in clear, semitechnical terms. Its "carcass is the largest of the kind that has hitherto been constructed for use; it is completely cased in a stout iron cylinder, terminating in a conical head; it is 3 feet 6 inches in length, 4 inches in diameter, and weighs, when complete, 32 pounds. . . . The stick is 15 feet long, and 1½ inches in diameter, and is so constructed, that it may be firmly attached to the body of the rocket, by a simple and quick operation, at any required time." He spoke of 13,109 rockets having been manufactured up to August 1806.

The Age of Congreve

Congreve rockets were used extensively during the nineteenth century. First Britain and later Austria, Russia, France, Italy, Sweden, Denmark, and other nations introduced them into their weapons inventories. Colonial powers brought them to bear during military engagements in Asia, Africa, and the Americas. One of the most important advances made to the Congreve rocket was spin stabilization, invented by William Hale. Other improvements were introduced by such men as the Austrian Major Vincenz Augustin, the Russians Alexandr D. Zasyadko and

Major General Konstantin Ivanovitch Konstantinov, and the Dane Lieutenant Andreas Anton Frederick Schumacher.

The rocket in France never assumed the importance it did in Britain. Although there were exceptions among individual military officers, only moderate interest existed among most French artillery generals and ordnance planners. This was due in part to the fact that no great innovator appeared on the scene to "sell" rocketry to the military, in part because of the swiftly changing military and political climate, and in part because of the nature of the wars conducted by French troops. Nevertheless, France accomplished a considerable amount of research and development on rockets, propellants, warheads, and launchers especially between about 1810 and the early 1860s.

To a greater or lesser extent, other nations became interested in rocketry and established rocket-armed troop units during the nineteenth century. Thus, the Austrians established rocket forces as early as 1815 which persisted until 1867, while in Sweden Wilhelm Teodor Unge didn't begin his work in rocketry until

■

Shipboard use of Congreve rockets. During the War of 1812, the British rocket ship Erebus *was used effectively in* *Chesapeake Bay engagements. Ordway Collection/ Space & Rocket Center.*

the 1880s—the very period during which other countries were closing down their activities. The Russians maintained an active interest in the rocket and fired hundreds during the Crimean War (1853–1856). Konstantinov shared with Congreve the honor of being the most prolific writer on rocketry in the nineteenth century. In the United States, rockets saw action in the War of 1812, the Mexican War, and the Civil War.

Between 1809 and 1811, Andreas Schumacher, then a young second lieutenant in the Danish Corps of Engineers, worked in secrecy to improve on Congreve rockets at a special laboratory on the island of Hjelm in the Kattegat. Austria and France persuaded King Frederick to allow Major Augustin and Captain Bruselle de Brulard to visit Schumacher's secret laboratory, where they acquired much valu-

army. We establish the war rocket as a part of the artillery materiel and hope to improve them both in caliber, with and without the center-mounted stick."

Turn of the Century through World War I

Despite such interest, as the nineteenth century waned so did the importance of the rocket. This was primarily because rockets were eclipsed by improvements in artillery—rifled barrels, breech-loading, and so forth. Recognizing the rocket's shortcomings, beginning in the 1880s, Unge mounted a rescue effort in Sweden. He hoped to develop a rocket that could be boosted to high velocity by a cannon and then ignited so as to increase its range over that of a conventional shell. In 1890, he interested Alfred Nobel, the inventor of dynamite, in this idea, and two years later the Mars Company was formed to carry out work with Nobel financing.

Initial trials were unsuccessful, so Unge tried to develop an improved propellant, one that would permit the rocket on its own to compete in range with long-range artillery of the day. On 12 September 1896, Unge flight-tested a ballistite-propellant rocket (using a so-called double base composed of a nitrocellulose-nitroglycerine mixture) from a small hill near the Mars Company shops in Stockholm. Not content with improving the propellants employed in his rockets, he also sought to improve their accuracy by increasing the spin rate. To do this, he patented three modes of spinning the inner tube of the launching device so that upon launch his rockets would have an initial spin.

By 1905, Unge's rockets could reach up to 5 miles with accuracy comparable to that of existing artillery. Despite this, the Swedish government exhibited little enthusiasm for his work and in 1908 he was forced to sell his patents and rocket stockpile to Friedrich Krupp, the German arms magnate. Krupp ordered some tests to be made at his company's range at Meppen, but interest soon died out. The

able information. Though disappointed that some of his findings had passed into foreign hands, Schumacher persisted and soon had a commitment from the king for the manufacture of incendiary rockets as well as those with grenade heads. Two years later, a rocket company was established with 4 commissioned officers, 8 noncommissioned officers, and 73 privates. On 17 March 1816, the company became a Rocket Corps with Schumacher as its commander.

And so it went, all across Europe and down into Turkey. In Austria, for example, Major Augustin was ordered to establish a rocket laboratory at Raketendorf near Wiener-Neustadt beginning in 1815. Soon thereafter, a Rocket Battery was formed whose nattily dressed men stood out from the otherwise conservatively clothed Austrian army regulars. And in Italy, King Carlo Felice of Sardinia had become so interested in rocketry that on 25 November 1830 he could observe: "We have been told that war rockets, after experimenting with them for many years, are now good enough to be used in our army. The staff officers and the Major General of Artillery have proved that war rockets of 3 inches and 2½ inches of the English kind, with sticks in the middle, can be used to good advantage in the field, in the mountains, and in fortresses. For these reasons, we are ready to accept everything that is worthwhile to our rocket seemed destined for the technological grave-yard.

As it turned out, it merely went into dormancy and, indeed, made a comeback of sorts during the First World War. Between 1914 and 1918, rockets were employed for signaling, for illuminating enemy positions, and for laying smoke screens. They also found roles in ground-to-air and air-to-air combat. French naval lieutenant Y. A. G. Le Prieur developed models that could be fired from the ground or more commonly from Nieuport biplanes against German Zeppelins and observation balloons. Typically these French pursuit planes would carry eight rockets, four mounted on each side of the fuselage and fired electrically.

With the signing of the armistice and subsequent demobilization of the armed forces, the rocket was all but forgotten by the military. Then, during the 1920s and 1930s, amateur experimenters began to design and test rockets that one day, they hoped, would carry man into space. Their work, in turn, came to the attention of farsighted ordnance and artillery officers who saw in the rocket a potentially devastating weapon. With military funding, the rocket soon flowered as a major element of our technological civilization.

For further reading

Brock, Alan St. H. *A History of Fireworks*. London, 1949: Harrap.

Brock, Alan St. H. *Pyrotechnics: The History and Art of Firework Making*. London, 1922: O'Connor.

Canby, Courtlandt. *A History of Rockets and Space*. New York, 1963: Hawthorn.

Hogg, O. F. G. *The Royal Arsenal: Its Background, Origin and Subsequent History*. London, 1963: Oxford.

Lancaster, Ronald, et al. *Fireworks: Principles and Practice*. New York, 1972: Chemical Publishing.

Ley, Willy. *Rockets, Missiles and Men in Space*. New York, 1968: Viking (final edition of book that first appeared as *Rockets* in 1944).

Needham, Joseph, Ho Ping-Yu, Lu Gwei-Djen, and Wang Ling. *Science and Civilization in China*, volume 5, *Chemistry and Chemical Technology*, part 7: "Military Technology; the Gunpowder Epic." Cambridge, 1986: Cambridge University Press.

Ordway, Frederick I., III. "La fusée, de l'Orient a l'Occident." In *Le Grand Atlas de l'Espace*. Paris, 1987: Encyclopaedia Universalis. Translated as "The Rocket—from East to West," in *The Cambridge Encyclopedia of Space*. Cambridge, 1990: Cambridge University Press.

Partington, J. R. *A History of Greek Fire and Gunpowder*. Cambridge (England), 1960: Heffer.

Plimpton, George. *Fireworks*. Garden City, New York, 1984: Doubleday.

Von Braun, Wernher, and Frederick I. Ordway III. *The Rockets' Red Glare: An Illustrated History of Rocketry Through the Ages*. Garden City, New York, 1976: Doubleday.

■

Pilot E. V. Frot sits on a wheel of his Nieuport pursuit plane that is armed with eight Le Prieur rockets. Musée de l'Air, Paris.

■

Wilhelm Teodor Unge worked on rocket development during the late nineteenth and early twentieth centuries. Kungloheim Armeemuseum, Stockholm.

Von Braun, Wernher, and Frederick I. Ordway III. *History of Rocketry and Space Travel*. New York, 1966, 1969, and 1975: Thomas Y. Crowell. Fourth edition revised in collaboration with Dave Dooling and published as *Space Travel: A History*. New York, 1985: Harper & Row.

Winter, Frank H. *The First Golden Age of Rocketry*. Washington, D.C., 1990: Smithsonian Institution Press.

Note: A series of histories based on symposia conducted by the International Academy of Astronautics contain survey chapters on the history of rocketry. Published under the series editorship of R. Cargill Hall by Univelt in San Diego, California, the books form part of its ongoing history series. The first volume assigned to the IAA symposia is 6.

Durant, Frederick C., III, and George S. James, eds. *First Steps Towards Space*. 1986 (volume 6).

Hall, R. Cargill, ed. *History of Rocketry and Astronautics*. 1986 (volume 7; in two parts).

Lattu, Kristan, ed. *History of Rocketry and Astronautics*. 1989 (volume 8).

Ordway, Frederick I., III, ed. *History of Rocketry and Astronautics*. 1989 (volume 9).

Skoog, Å. Ingemar, ed. *History of Rocketry and Astronautics*. 1990 (volume 10).

Sloop, John L., ed. *History of Rocketry and Astronautics*. 1991 (volume 12).

Foundations of Modern Rocketry: 1920s and 1930s

FRANK H. WINTER

Despite the clarity of Sir Isaac Newton's classic Third Law of Motion—"for every action there is an equal and opposite reaction"—rocket experts had never been quite certain how this applied to their devices. Gradually, two schools of thought emerged. The first, as stated in 1717 by the French physicist Edme Mariotte, proposed that the rocket moves because its exhaust flame pushes against the surrounding air, thereby causing movement in the opposite direction. The second theory, advanced a year later by Mariotte's compatriot John Theophilus Desaguliers, held that the burning exhaust gases themselves cause the rocket to rise. Desaguliers thus came close to associating rocket motion and the Newtonian law of equal and opposite reaction, though he never explicitly made the connection.

Despite Desaguliers, for many years theories based on "air pushing" predominated in discussions of rocketry. For example, J. L. Comstock in his *A New System of Natural Philosophy*, first published in New York in 1833, presented a curiously distorted view of action and reaction in explaining rocket motion: "The stream of expanded air, or the fire which is emitted from the lower end of the rocket, not only pushes against the rocket itself, but against the atmospheric air, which, reacting against the air so expanded, sends the rocket along." Comstock's *Philosophy* was evidently quite popular, and he repeated his faulty reasoning through several editions until 1856. Another example of this misunderstanding appears in the pages of the respected and widely circulated *Scientific American* during a lively debate on the nature of rocket motion early in 1862. Engineer Charles Potts of Trenton, New Jersey, steadfastly

believed Mariotte's theory to be "the most tenable" and held that "it is doubted whether a rocket would ascend at all in a vacuum." The air-pushing school persisted into the early twentieth century. Since it was widely held that the rocket would not work in a vacuum, the device was not considered a viable means of penetrating space. Even had the reaction principle been recognized, the state of the art of rocketry at this time was primitive indeed.

Experiments of Robert H. Goddard

The rockets of World War I were still based on the centuries-old technology of gunpowder. Wilhelm Unge's experiments with ballistite rocket propellants from the mid-1890s until the early 1900s had certainly been on the right track, as double-base powders pack considerably more energy per pound than gunpowder and therefore enable the rocket to attain faster exhaust velocities, which translates to greater lifting power (thrust), speed, and range; but Unge's accomplishments were not translated into military practice.

In 1915 Robert H. Goddard, a New England physics professor who was enamored with the idea of spaceflight by rocket, began experimenting toward this end. The notion of spaceflight was then of course absurd, especially since the only rockets around were of the gunpowder type. However, Goddard was scientifically trained and a methodical worker, with infinite patience to see his great dream turn to reality. He began at the basics, by testing the efficiency of large Coston signal rockets, developed

in the last century by U.S. Navy officer Benjamin Franklin Coston. Goddard opened them up, weighed the propellant mass, noted the burning times of loaded rockets, and calculated their exhaust velocities with a ballistic pendulum. He performed similar experiments with Du Pont Infallible shotgun powder, a double-base mixture. Coston's pasteboard projectiles, he found, delivered a paltry efficiency of only 2.5 percent and exhaust velocities of about 1,000 feet per second. Apparently unaware of Unge's earlier priorities, Goddard built his own metal-cased rockets and incorporated double-base propellant. To the exhaust end of the rocket he added De Laval nozzles (funnel-shaped nozzles invented in the 1880s by Swedish engineer Carl Gustaf De Laval for producing steam at maximum pressure from turbines). By these means, he dramatically elevated the rocket's efficiency to 64.5 percent and exhaust velocities of 8,000 feet per second.

All the while, Goddard was well aware that, theoretically, liquid-propellant rockets were vastly more efficient than solid-propellant systems. He had first formulated this idea in 1909 but had limited funds to pursue experiments along these lines, and he also needed to gain a basic grounding. An eminently practical man although a visionary, Goddard likewise felt it best to develop first a modest solid-propellant sounding rocket to explore the upper reaches of the atmosphere before tackling so grandiose a project as a liquid-propellant spaceship. Goddard's designs constantly evolved, and he soon produced a curious cartridge-fed mechanism in which the fuel cartridges were mechanically fed into a combustion chamber where they would burn until the next cartridge automatically came into place for combustion. The results of Goddard's solid-propellant work were eventually published in 1919 by the Smithsonian Institution as *A Method of Reaching Extreme Altitudes*.

Goddard faced many frustrating technical difficulties with this mechanism, however, such as cartridge jamming and misfires; in 1920 he resolved to devote his time to liquid-based systems. Due to their easy availability and relative cheapness, he selected liquid oxygen as the oxidizer and gasoline as the fuel. (An *oxidizer* is required to furnish oxygen for the combustion of the *fuel;* in ordinary gunpowder, the potassium nitrate, also called saltpeter, contains necessary oxygen atoms while the charcoal and sulfur serve as the fuel.) Operating under a small grant from the Smithsonian, Goddard gradually developed tanks for holding the fuel and oxidizer (collectively called the *propellants*), combustion chambers, injectors for squirting the right doses of propellants into the combustion chamber, and pumps or other fuel-feed devices. Liquid-propellant rockets are far more complicated than solid-propellant types, and Goddard was perpetually faced with problems such as the best way to cool rocket motors for long-duration runs; finding the most effective and fastest means of feeding the propellants; storing super-cold liquid oxygen (usually kept at −297 degrees Fahrenheit) and overcoming its rapid evaporation; providing

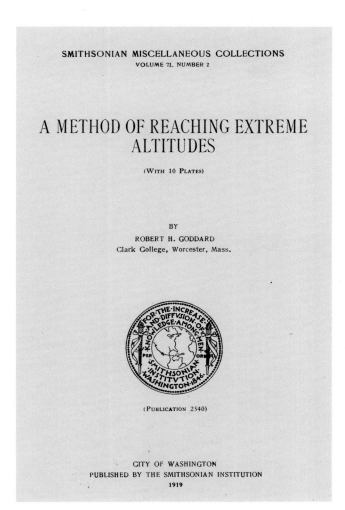

SMITHSONIAN MISCELLANEOUS COLLECTIONS
VOLUME 71, NUMBER 2

A METHOD OF REACHING EXTREME ALTITUDES

(WITH 10 PLATES)

BY
ROBERT H. GODDARD
Clark College, Worcester, Mass.

(PUBLICATION 2540)

CITY OF WASHINGTON
PUBLISHED BY THE SMITHSONIAN INSTITUTION
1919

Title page of Goddard's seminal work, A Method of Reaching Extreme Altitudes, *published in 1919. Ordway Collection/Space & Rocket Center.*

Goddard's launcher near Auburn, Massachusetts, after the successful 16 March 1926 firing of the first liquid-propellant rocket. The windshield is the larger object to the left of launcher, and in the background is the Ward Farm. Ordway Collection/ Space & Rocket Center.

precise ignition timing; stabilizing and recovering flight rockets; and many others.

Goddard's diligence and patience paid off. On 16 March 1926, he successfully launched the world's first liquid-propellant rocket. Puny by modern standards, it weighed about 10 pounds and soared 41 feet in 2.5 seconds, then landed 184 feet away in the snow on his Aunt Effie's farm at Auburn, Massachusetts. Outside of his wife and two assistants, plus Smithsonian officials, few knew about the flight at the time. Goddard requested that it not be publicized, mainly because he was waiting for a more spectacular flight. Goddard—and the Smithsonian—waited and waited. Goddard's main quirk was that he was secretive and almost fanatically guarded the details of his work. Continuing his experiments under grants from the Smithsonian as well as the Guggenheim Fund for the Promotion of Aeronautics, he made several other flights. (In 1930, to avoid too much publicity and to seek year-round good testing weather in a safe, unpopulated area, Goddard moved to Roswell, New Mexico, and pursued his experiments there until 1941.) But not until 1936, 10 years after his epochal first flight, did Goddard finally reveal in print, in his second Smithsonian publication, *Liquid-Propellant Rocket Development,* that he had made that first step.

Hermann Oberth and His Followers

Meanwhile, other great pioneering spaceflight theorists, notably Konstantin Tsiolkovsky and Hermann Oberth, played their roles in arousing widespread public interest in rocketry as applied to spaceflight; independently, they too had thought about liquid-fuel systems. Oberth's book *Die Rakete zu den Planetenräumen (The Rocket into Planetary Space)* of 1923 was especially crucial. Oberth laid out elaborate plans for liquid oxygen–alcohol Model A and Model B manned space rockets. He suggested the use of multiple stages (one rocket atop another) for achieving optimum velocity of the final rocket stage, also recommending super-light and strong aluminum alloys for construction materials, De Laval nozzles lined with asbestos to aid in their cooling, and so on.

Left, *Hermann Oberth in 1929;* right, *the cover of his* Die Rakete zu den Planetenräumen, *published in 1923. Ordway Collection/Space & Rocket Center.*

Oberth's ideas were so challenging to engineers and laymen alike that the Verein für Raumschiffahrt (Society for Spaceship Travel, or simply VfR) was founded in Breslau (now Wroclaw, Poland) in 1927. The most important of several spaceflight groups emerging from this period, the VfR at first gave lectures and published articles in their journal *Die Rakete.* Then, in 1930, they founded their Raketenflugplatz (Rocket Flying Field) in the Berlin suburb of Reinickendorf for conducting experiments. In essence, Reinickendorf, not Roswell, became the birthplace of modern rocketry.

From the start, the members of the VfR preferred liquid oxygen and alcohol, especially alcohol diluted with water, which helped cool the combustion. With meager funds (the Great Depression had hit Germany exceptionally hard) and plenty of enthusiasm, the amateur rocketeers worked relentlessly on the development of Europe's first liquid-fuel rockets. They were simple affairs and for this reason were called Miraks (contraction for "minimum rockets"). The propellants were ingeniously forced into the combustion chamber by pressure from an ordinary

carbon dioxide cartridge used to pressurize seltzer water bottles. In the first static (nonflight) ground experiment, a thrust of 14 ounces was attained. Later this was raised to about 4 pounds and after that to 7 pounds, then 9 pounds. The first large static test stand was completed early in 1931.

The years 1931–1932 were hence the most active for the VfR's idealistic and single-minded experimenters, though rocket explosions were common. The Miraks gave way to the improved Mirak II, Mirak III, the water-cooled Repulsor I, followed by Repulsors II to IV. The Repulsors were the first VfR rockets to fly and were designed to be recovered by parachutes, though there were often parachute failures. Repulsor I reached about 60 feet on 10 May 1931, while additional flights a few days later claimed altitudes of 150–200 feet. Johannes Winkler, the VfR's first president and editor of *Die Rakete,* had severed his connection with the Society in 1930 upon the cessation of *Die Rakete* and undertook his own private experimentation, successfully achieving a flight on 21 February 1931. Since Goddard's 1926 flight was virtually unknown at the time, the Ger-

for this type of rocket was 45 pounds and its thrust about 130 pounds.

By this time the VfR's high visibility had aroused the attention of a small group of German artillery officers headed by then-Colonel Karl Emil Becker, who saw great promise in the still crude "playthings" of the experimenters. Even earlier, from 1929, Becker had initiated a secret study of rockets, especially of the liquid-propellant type. Becker and his fellow officers of course had weapons in mind, though at that early stage they had no idea of the ranges that were possible nor the complexities in-

mans believed Winkler's was the first liquid-propellant flight anywhere.

To further complicate matters, it was claimed many years later that the German pyrotechnist Friedrich Sander flew his own liquid-propellant rocket in secrecy on 10 April 1929, though corroboration and details are wanting. In any case, the VfR group was the most visible and delighted in inviting the press and dignitaries to their tests, with the hope that the publicity would attract donations of both money and needed materials. Indeed, the amount of work accomplished was impressive. By May 1932, there had been 87 rocket flights (mostly with parachutes), more than 270 static tests, 23 demonstrations for clubs and societies, and 9 "for publicity." The highest altitude reached was by a Repulsor IV that went up to about 3,000 feet. The takeoff weight

volved in the perfection of these devices. (Smithsonian Verville Fellow Dr. Michael Neufeld has recently discovered a document in Germany that shows Becker actually financed and arranged for the establishment of the Raketenflugplatz, which had been a former army ammunition storage dump; undoubtedly Becker had clandestinely gotten the VfR experimenters started in order to exploit their findings and expertise in the near future.)

Indeed, by 1932 one of Becker's men, Captain Walter R. Dornberger, wearing civilian clothing so as not to arouse suspicions, paid several visits to the Raketenflugplatz. He cared little for calculations of spaceship trajectories to Mars and Venus, he afterward recalled, but was after useful data such as thrust-time curves, which fuel consumption and which fuel mixture were best, combustion temperatures encountered, and types of injectors. Yet despite their prodigious activities, the VfR lacked some of this essential data (particularly combustion temperatures) and even the requisite recording instruments. Dornberger was convinced that exacting rocket engineering development could more properly be undertaken by the army with a well-funded, well-staffed program.

What Dornberger and accompanying staff members did notice was the technical competence and intelligence of some of the VfR's leading experimenters, especially 20-year-old Wernher von Braun. Von Braun, then an engineering student intensely pursuing both rocketry and his degree, was soon approached by Dornberger who made the unbelievable offer of having the army give him both. Von Braun was only too happy to accept. Henceforward, from late 1932, he would become the civilian technical director of the German army's secret rocket development program and at the same time would acquire his degree from the University of Berlin—with the provision that his thesis on rocket combustion, which was to be conducted as a result of his work with the army, be classified secret. Soon, von Braun was joined by other former VfR members and the German army's rocket program began in earnest.

The VfR itself fell on hard times. Through some rather complicated in-fighting coupled to severe financial problems, the Society collapsed in the winter of 1933. The worsening Depression and political situation also made it more difficult for the private experimenters to continue and, gradually, several of

them followed in the wake of von Braun and joined the army rocket program.

American Rocket Society Experiments

Across the Atlantic, the American Interplanetary Society, formed in 1930 largely by science fiction fans rather than engineers, had been naturally much taken with the activities of the VfR. One of their members, G. Edward Pendray, in fact saw these activities firsthand when he and his wife visited the Raketenflugplatz in the spring of 1931. The American group (later renamed the American Rocket Society, or ARS, in order to attract bona fide engineers and scientists) thus began its own experimental phase that summer.

The ARS's record of experiments was not nearly as impressive as that of their German counterparts: only two successful flights were realized between 1933 and 1934, but by the latter year, the Americans realized that far more about rocket motor design and behavior could be learned from static tests than from flight rockets. Moreover, the flights ate up too

■

Assembling American Rocket Society rocket No. 2, at Marine Park, Staten Island, New York, in 1933. Attaching the tail fins is Bernard Smith, who built the rocket from parts scavenged from ARS rocket No. 1. At left is G. Edward Pendray, chairman of the ARS Experimental Committee. National Air and Space Museum.

much of the Society's paltry budget. Construction therefore began on the Society's first static test stand; by 1938 they had built their second. Their main problem was a technical one—seeking an optimum means of cooling rocket motors so that the liquid-propellant rocket would become a viable power plant instead of fizzling out or exploding due to overheating. Nichrome nozzles, water jackets, and heat-absorbing aluminum blocks around the combustion chamber were all tried but failed. Member James H. Wyld's solution, appearing at this time, was the regeneratively cooled rocket engine. The fuel was circulated in a cooling jacket around the chamber before being injected for combustion. Wyld's "regen" motor was successfully tested on ARS Test Stand No. 2 several times. Then, in December 1941, upon America's entry into World War II, Wyld with three fellow ARS members formed America's first commercial rocket company, Reaction Motors, Inc., which used the regen principle in a variety of later successful rocket projects including JATO (Jet-Assisted Take-Off) units for assisted take-offs of heavily laden planes, missiles, and rocket research airplanes, notably the Bell X-1 that was the first to fly faster than sound in 1947.

Pump-driven Goddard rocket being made ready for launching near Roswell, New Mexico, on 9 February 1940. Esther C. Goddard.

Goddard's rockets had become ever more sophisticated, and in 1937 one of his vehicles, featuring movable air vanes linked to a gyroscope for stabilization, climbed to between 8,000 and 9,000 feet. By 1940 his liquid oxygen–gasoline rockets were generating almost 900 pounds of thrust. Outside of a handful of assistants, Goddard was still working alone and no doubt could have accomplished far more if he had chosen to become part of a large, well-funded team. In 1940 he finally did agree to assist the U.S. Navy in developing liquid-propellant JATOs, continuing that association until his death in 1945.

Expanding Developments in Germany

The German army was under far fewer financial and manpower constraints in pursuing its own rocketry program. By 1934, under von Braun's able technical leadership, the first flying rocket, the A-2, was under development. Two models were built and humorously named Max and Moritz, after the characters in a German comic strip, known in America as the "Katzenjammer Kids." The 650-pound-thrust liquid oxygen–liquid alcohol regeneratively cooled motors enabled each of the rockets to reach altitudes of about 1.5 miles. (The regen and other basic rocket engineering techniques were arrived at by the Germans independently of the Americans.)

Soon, the army's rocket installation at Kummersdorf proved too cramped for further development of a greatly enlarged A-3 vehicle, which was 21 feet in length, weighed some 1,650 pounds at launch, and produced 3,300 pounds of thrust. But the technical success of the army's program had an unexpected consequence. At about that time (1935), air force Major Wolfram von Richthofen (cousin of the famous World War I fighter pilot Manfred von Richthofen) sought the use of rocketry in his own military branch and was much impressed with what he saw during a visit to Kummersdorf. He was primarily interested in adapting the rocket to aircraft.

■

The air force was thus induced to offer 5 million marks to build better and larger facilities elsewhere. Becker was incensed by the "impertinence of the junior service" and immediately appropriated 6 million marks to the army rocket group. With the 11 million now available, a much more expanded facility and operation could indeed be built. The result was the army's huge new secret rocket center of Peenemünde, on a remote island facing the Baltic, and the development of the much more ambitious A-4. Peenemünde officially opened in 1937.

Ultimately, the A-4 (whose combat designation was V-2), which stood at 45 feet long, weighed 12 tons at launch, and produced a thrust of 25 tons for 60 seconds, became one of the war's most awesome weapons and the direct ancestor of the spaceship.

■

A German experimental A-2 rocket in a test stand at Kummersdorf army proving ground near Berlin. Ordway Collection/Space & Rocket Center.

■

Preparing an A-3 test rocket for launch on 29 November 1937 from the island of Oie off the coast of Peenemünde in the Baltic Sea. Third from right is Wernher von Braun. Deutsches Museum.

For further reading

Bergaust, Erik. *Wernher von Braun*. Washington, D.C., 1976: National Space Institute.

Dornberger, Walter R. *V-2*. New York, 1954: The Viking Press; the German edition *V2. Der Schluss ins Weltall* was updated and published as *Peenemünde: Die Geschichte der V-Waffen*. Esslingen, 1981: Bechtle Verlag.

Durant, Frederick C., III, and George S. James, eds. *First Steps Towards Space,* Smithsonian Annals of Flight No. 10. Washington, D.C., 1974: Smithsonian Institution Press; rpt. San Diego, 1985: Univelt, as the sixth volume in the American Astronautical Society History Series and the first volume in the International Academy of Astronautics History series. (The book is a collection of 27 historical papers on rocket technology presented before International Astronautical Congresses. One paper is an analysis of the contributions of Wilhelm Teodor Unge and another treats the development of regeneratively cooled liquid rocket engines in Austria and Germany, 1926–1942.)

Goddard, Esther C. *The Papers of Robert H. Goddard*. 3 vols. New York, 1970: McGraw-Hill. (Selected correspondence, writings, and diary entries of Goddard throughout his life.)

Lehmann, Milton. *This High Man*. New York, 1963: Farrar, Straus & Giroux, Inc. (The authorized biography of Goddard.)

Ordway, Frederick I., III, and Mitchell R. Sharpe. *The Rocket Team*. New York, 1979: Thomas Y. Crowell; London, 1979: William Heinemann; rpt. Cambridge, Massachusetts, 1982: MIT Press. (Chronicles the history of the von Braun "rocket team" from their work at Peenemünde to their subsequent contribution to the postwar American missile and space program.)

Winter, Frank H. *Rockets into Space*. Cambridge, Massachusetts, and London, 1990: Harvard University Press. (Details the evolution of rocket technology as applied to the launch vehicle.)

Planning for Spaceflight: 1880s to 1930s

FRANK H. WINTER

From Lukian of Samosata's fierce whirlwinds drawing up a sailing ship into the heavens to Jules Verne's huge cannon shooting a manned projectile to the Moon, the first space vehicle concepts were literary fantasies with generally little regard for scientific possibilities. The dawning of modern (scientific) spaceflight theory did not come until the 1880s, when the provincial Russian schoolteacher Konstantin Eduardovich Tsiolkovsky began the seminal studies that, in his own country, have earned him the posthumous title of "the father of cosmonautics." The main focus of his work was space propulsion and all its various parameters. It is perhaps less recognized that he also attempted the first systems approach to the problems of flight beyond Earth's atmosphere. In sum, Tsiolkovsky was the first spaceflight planner.

To Tsiolkovsky must go the credit of being the first scientifically trained individual to recognize the reaction principle as the key to travel into space, and of initiating its supporting theory on a scientific basis. He began this process in 1883 in his manuscript "Izmenenie sily tyazhesti" ("Modification of the Force of Gravity"), though he initially derived his inspiration from Verne's space novels, especially an 1875 Russian translation of his second lunar tale *Round the Moon*. Verne's fictional spaceship was not technologically feasible but his story was believable. Indeed, the French writer had taken pains to work in mathematically computed projectile velocities and other measurements. As a challenge, Tsiolkovsky sought the real solutions to these problems.

■

Konstantin Eduardovich Tsiolkovsky (1857–1935) began pondering the scientific basis of space travel as early as 1883. This photo was taken in 1934. National Air and Space Museum.

At the beginning, the rocket as a means of space propulsion eluded Tsiolkovsky. He vaguely spoke of overcoming gravitation and the infinite possibilities of scientific and spiritual discovery once this was achieved. Even before solving the great problem of getting into space, Tsiolkovsky already contemplated lunar and planetary expeditions, space stations, space cities, and asteroid mining. These thoughts, often expressed in a philosophical vein, were confined to his notebooks. He also published the fantasy story *On the Moon* in 1893 and the pamphlets *Reflections on Earth and Heaven* (1895), *Effects of Universal Gravitation* (1895), *Will the Earth Someday Be Able to Inform the Inhabitants of Other Planets of the Existence on It of Intelligent Beings?* (1896), and *The Duration of Stellar Radiation* (1897).

104

"For a long time," Tsiolkovsky afterward wrote, "I regarded rockets, in the same way as others did, as diversions of limited practical use." Once he did "grasp" the significance of the reaction principle operating in space and began to formulate it in 1898, he devoted the rest of his life to expanding the space rocket idea and many other, nonpropulsive components of spaceflight. Tsiolkovsky's first mathematical exposition of these revolutionary concepts appeared as "The Exploration of Space with Reactive Devices," in the journal *Nauchnoe Obozrenie* (*Scientific Review*) for May 1903, seven months before the Wright brothers flew the first successful manned airplane.

Besides propulsion, Tsiolkovsky's seminal 1903 article also began to explore, in a rudimentary way, the need for "automatic instruments" to control the spaceship's movement, anticipating computerized guidance and controls of today; and a crew and equipment section for "respiration" in the nose of the ship.

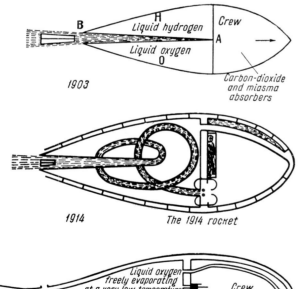

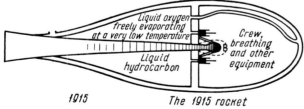

Whether Tsiolkovsky's early studies of the possibilities of flight into space reached the West at the time is unknown (besides his article, the May 1903 issue of *Nauchnoe Obozrenie* also contained a politically revolutionary piece that led to the confiscation of almost all issues by the authorities; Tsiolkovsky's subsequent astronautical writings were not widely circulated since he paid for their publication out of his own meager teacher's wages and few copies were printed). Among those inspired by his writings were Valentin Petrovich Glushko, Sergei Pavlovich Korolev, Igor Alexandrovich Merkulov, and Alexandr Ivanovich Polyarny. All pressed the development of rockets whose descendants would evolve into the modern Soviet stable of launch vehicles.

The spaceflight revolution also occurred in the West, pressed by researchers who apparently worked independently of Tsiolkovsky. It is often the nature of scientific discoveries that they appear in different places almost simultaneously and quite independently. Undoubtedly, one stimulus for widespread pondering of flight into space was the successful airplane flight by the Wright brothers. The French aeronautical and astronautical pioneer Robert Esnault-Pelterie began his career in aviation. He built a tailless biplane glider in 1904 and in 1906 constructed the first all-metal monoplane, which he successfully flew in 1907.

The following year he began to think of spaceflight; in February 1912, he delivered his first lecture on the subject in St. Petersburg, then the capital of Russia. But it is doubtful that he encountered Tsiolkovsky (who rarely left his home in Kaluga, about 400 miles to the southeast). In November of the same year, Esnault-Pelterie presented a similar

■

Tsiolkovsky's spaceship designs dated 1903, 1914, and 1915. Ordway Collection/Space & Rocket Center.

■

Sergei Pavlovich Korolev (1906–1966) was an early developer of rockets who helped organize the Moscow Group for the Study of Reactive Motion. After the war, he directed the development of launch vehicles that orbited the first Sputniks. K. E. Tsiolkovsky State Museum of Cosmonautics/National Air and Space Museum.

lecture in Paris in which he spoke not only about liquid-fuel rockets and optimum performance propellants, but also about the possibilities of flights to Mars and Venus. He worked out the flight times and speeds to these planets and believed that "the complete study of the question [of spaceflight] will lead to the study of the physiological conditions that must be fulfilled so that life will be possible under such conditions." The problem of human survival in the near-absolute cold of space especially troubled Esnault-Pelterie. Much could be learned of long-term regeneration of air in a spacecraft from experiences with submarines, he said. To achieve even temperature control, one-half of the spaceship could be "of a polished metal and the inside insulated." The other half had a black, copper oxide surface, so that the polished side facing the Sun would reflect its rays and the black side would absorb the heat. Esnault-Pelterie also concerned himself with the ef-

Robert Esnault-Pelterie of France began theorizing on spaceflight as early as 1907 and subsequently published several basic works on the subject. This picture was taken in 1929. Ordway Collection/Space & Rocket Center.

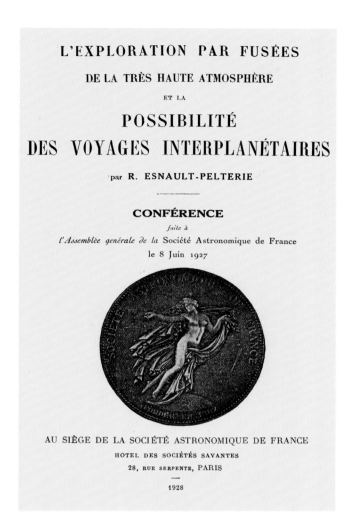

fects of extreme acceleration and weightlessness upon the human organism. His major works, *L'Exploration par fusées de la très haute atmosphère et la possibilité des voyages interplanétaires* (1928), *L'Astronautique* (1930), and *L'Astronautique-complément* (1935), laid the groundwork for later French achievements in rocketry and spaceflight.

Across the Atlantic, the American Robert H. Goddard became space-struck at age 16 when, in 1898, he read a newspaper serialization of H. G. Wells's terrifying Martian invasion story, *War of the Worlds.* Unaware of both Tsiolkovsky and Esnault-Pelterie, he methodically made notes on different possibilities of space propulsion and by 1909 realized that the rocket was the answer. In 1916 he proved, using an evacuated firing chamber, that rockets *do* work in a vacuum. Goddard calculated the minimum requirements of a multi-stage, *unmanned* solid-fuel rocket for the modest experiment of carrying and igniting a certain amount of flash powder on the

Moon. Unfortunately, the newspapers of the day misunderstood the real purpose of this exercise and ran sensationalized stories about the "Moon professor." Goddard was soon flooded with volunteers wishing to pilot the Moonship, and even spaceships bound for Mars!

Shy by nature, Goddard became increasingly secretive about his experiments and confided his more advanced spaceflight concepts solely to his notebooks. During his lifetime Goddard's more farsighted propulsive and nonpropulsive ideas on spaceflight were virtual secrets. As early as 1906–1910, for example, he postulated in some detail the use of a solar energy boiler aboard spacecraft as an internal power source; automatically photographing the Moon and planets in space and retrieving the pictures; instruments for detecting meteor hazards; steering space rockets by photosensitive cells; production of hydrogen and oxygen on the Moon; signaling from a planet; and a means of neutralizing zero gravity experienced by astronauts in space. Later (in 1918) he speculated on the "ultimate migration" of human beings to another solar system should the Sun die, but his private thoughts largely centered on unmanned interplanetary flight. From 1919, his *Method of Reaching Extreme Altitudes* and its wide press at least opened to the public the possibilities of *unmanned* travel to the Moon and planets.

Hermann Oberth's researches and speculations also extended well beyond rocketry itself, to orbital flight paths and trajectories, heat-resisting spacecraft materials, physiological and psychological effects of acceleration and weightlessness upon the astronauts, potential dangers in spaceflight (meteor hazards), space suits, types of experiments, artificial satellites, and space stations and their possible missions (weather observation and so on). His books detailing these ideas sparked a widespread spaceflight movement throughout the Western world. A flurry of books by other astronautical pioneers appeared. There were popularizations, like Max Valier's *Der Vorstoss in den Weltenraum* (*Advance into Space,*

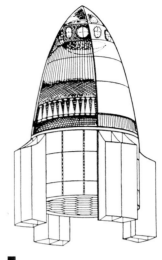

1924), which went through five additional printings to 1929 and an enlarged edition, *Raketenfahrt* (*Rocket Travel*) in 1930; Willy Ley's *Die Fahrt ins Weltall* (*Flight into Space*, 1926) and *Die Möglichkeit der Weltraumfahrt* (*The Possibilities of Spaceflight*, 1928); Felix Linke's *Das RaketenWeltraumschiff* (*The Rocket Spaceship*, 1928); and A. B. Scherschevsky's *Die Rakete für Fahrt und Flug* (*The Rocket for Travel and Flight*, 1929). David Lasser, founder of the American Interplanetary Society, wrote *The Conquest of Space* (1931), the first book on the topic in the English language, while Philip E. Cleator, founder of the British Interplanetary Society, produced *Rockets through Space* (1936). These works provided their general readerships with the fundamentals of spaceflight rather than detailed engineering "plans"; they were also optimistically speculative in nature. Another class of books made genuine contributions toward the development of the principles of astronautics and rocketry. These included *Die Erreichbarkeit der Himmelskörper* (*The Attainability of Heavenly Bodies*,

1925) by Walter Hohmann, and *Raketenflugtechnik* (*Rocket Flight Technology*, 1933) by Eugen Sänger. Hermann Noordung's *Das Problem der Befahrung des Weltraums* (*The Problem of Spaceflight*, 1929) presented the basics and also constitutes the first complete study of manned space stations. Werner Brügel's *Männer der Rakete* (*Men of the Rocket*, 1933) is an anthology of biographical sketches and technical summaries of the leading spaceflight pioneers of the day. In the Soviet Union there were counterpart works; probably the most famous (since translated into English as NASA technical translations TT-640 to TT-648) is *Mezhplanetnye Soobshchniya* (*Interplanetary Communications*, 9 volumes, 1928–1932), by Professor N. A. Rynin. Encyclopedic in scope, this is a collection of both technical and popular writings, including one volume devoted to Tsiolkovsky, a study of "astronavigation," a treatment of the spacecraft in science fiction, and a comprehensive bibliography.

Apart from the printed word, space clubs (also

Cover of Die Möglichkeit der Weltraumfahrt (The Possibilities of Spaceflight), *edited by Willy Ley and published in Leipzig in 1928. It* contained articles by many of Oberth's disciples as well as by Oberth himself. Ordway Collection/Space & Rocket Center.

David Lasser, president of the American Interplanetary Society and author of the book The Conquest of Space. *National Air and Space Museum and David Lasser.*

known as rocket societies) sprang up in Austria, Germany, the U.S., the USSR, and England during these years; similar groups were created a little later in France and elsewhere. With meager funds but great ambitions, these groups drew kindred souls together in seeking to promote the cause of spaceflight through public lectures, the publication of journals, and, in some cases, undertaking preliminary liquid-propellant rocketry experiments in order to advance the state of the art toward the eventual development of the spaceship. (In point of fact, long-range plans were rare, but these efforts were invaluable learning experiences nonetheless.) In retrospect, the early rocket societies performed several significant functions: they stimulated a wider audience to think about the possibilities of flight beyond Earth's atmosphere; they educated people on the correct theory of rocket motion; they provided training to future generations of rocketeers; and they laid some of the technological foundations for modern rocketry and spaceflight.

The concepts and plans as such were mainly conveyed in the rocket society journals. Many of the ideas were idealistic and impractical; for example, in 1930 Fletcher Pratt of the American Interplanetary Society, in his paper "The Universal Background of Interplanetary Travel," envisioned the development by the year 2050 of a 110-foot-diameter metal sphere to reach the Moon, propelled by ionized hydrogen and manned by a crew of 60 plus a dozen scientists. The Germans (and Austrians) tended to be more practical and scientific in their proposals, some of which were pioneering efforts in themselves. In a 1928 issue of the German Rocket Society's organ *Die Rakete (The Rocket)*, for instance, one can find "Medicine and Spaceflight" by member Max Valier; the series "The Conquest of Space" by Dr. Franz von Hoefft, projecting the gradual evolution toward spaceflight from a simple balloon-borne liquid oxygen–alcohol instrumented sounding rocket capable of a 62-mile altitude (the RHI, or Rakete-Hoefft I) to a Moon-, Mars-, or Venus-bound RHVII

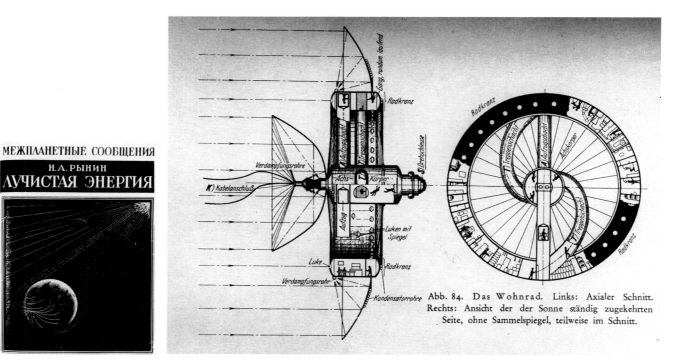

Abb. 84. Das Wohnrad. Links: Axialer Schnitt. Rechts: Ansicht der der Sonne ständig zugekehrten Seite, ohne Sammelspiegel, teilweise im Schnitt.

■

Cover of Nicolai Alexyvich Rynin's Radiation Energy, *the third volume of his nine-volume encyclopedia entitled* Interplanetary Communications. *Ordway Collection/ Space & Rocket Center.*

■

Hermann Potočnic (writing under the pseudonym Hermann Noordung) described his Wohnrad (living wheel) *space station in a 1929 book devoted entirely to the subject:* Das Problem der Befahrung des Weltraums *(The Problem of Spaceflight). The station was wheel-shaped, about a hundred feet in diameter, with the cable K to the left going to a separate observatory module. The S to the right is the airlock. A large mirror was relied upon to collect sunlight for power. In both drawings, stairs (Treppenschacht) and elevator shaft (Aufzugschacht) lead from the core to the rim. Ordway Collection/Space & Rocket Center.*

model; and the landmark 1928–1929 series "Travel Routes" by Guido von Pirquet, a mathematical study of trajectories to Mars and Venus that also set out to prove that the most efficient way of travel to the planets was using an Earth-orbiting space station as a takeoff point.

Finally, between 1937 and 1939 a bona fide concerted spaceflight plan was conducted by the Technical Committee of the British Interplanetary Society. This was the so-called BIS Moonship, which was carefully designed down to minute detail by specialists within the committee. A research chemist worked on the propellant section. A draftsman helped design the configuration. An electrical engineer was responsible for the wiring circuitry and an astronomer provided navigational data. Other con-

tributions were made by a mathematician, a biologist, an aircraft designer, and a turbine engineer. Considerations of cost-effectiveness led to a multicellular solid-fuel configuration. The cells or solid-propellant units could be ignited individually or in groups so that a certain amount of thrust control was possible. Ignition was electrically activated from the crew cabin. The ship consisted of six stages, 105 feet tall overall and 19.7 feet in diameter. The total weight was over 2 million pounds, the fuel comprising most of this. Hydrogen peroxide units provided fine velocity control and small liquid-propellant rockets adjusted the pressurized cabin for lunar landing. Great attention, of course, was given to the design of the three-man cabin with its custom couches and reinforced ceramic dome (to protect it from re-

No. 1.   JANUARY, 1934.   Vol. I.

Journal of the British Interplanetary Society.

34, OARSIDE DRIVE,
WALLASEY, CHESHIRE, ENGLAND.

Inaugural issue of the Journal of the British Interplanetary Society, *January 1934. Ordway Collection/Space & Rocket Center.*

BULLETIN

THE AMERICAN INTERPLANETARY SOCIETY

302 West 22nd Street, New York, N.Y.

David Lasser, President

No. 1.

C. W. Van Devander, Editor

New York   June, 1930

INTRODUCTORY

Among the principal aims of the American Interplanetary Society are the promotion of interest in interplanetary exploration and travel, and the mutual enlightenment of its members concerning the problems involved. To these purposes the monthly bulletins, of which this is the first, will be devoted.

The Society, despite its youth, has already begun to tackle seriously the peculiar problems in its field. Since the creation of public interest is of prime importance, the Society has sought to awaken interest in itself as well as the ideas for which it stands. Meanwhile, it has also begun the scientific consideration of the technical side of its program.

These varied activities will be reported here in full. In addition the bulletin will contain comprehensive summaries of developments relating to its subject everywhere in the world. The foreign news is expected to be of particular interest and value, and every effort will be made to make it a complete record of the research and experiments of foreign scientists in this field. All suggestions for improving the bulletin will be gratefully received.

NEWS OF THE SOCIETY

One of the earliest books on the subject of interplanetary travel, written by John Wilkins, Bishop of Chester, in 1640, has become the property of the Society through the generosity of one of its members, Hugo Gernsback. Captain Sir Hubert Wilkins, noted explorer and a descendant of the author, who is an honorary member of the Society, made the presentation in a ceremony at the American Museum of Natural History on April 30, David Lasser, president, receiving the small leather bound volume for the Society. The book, entitled, "The Discovery of a New World, or a Discourse Tending to Prove That There May Be Another Habitable World in the Moon, and Concerning the Possibility of a Passage Thither," becomes a valuable part of the Society's library.

- - - - - - - - - - -

A survey of the entire field of information relating to interplanetary travel has been begun by the Society, with C. P. Mason in charge of the investigation. It is the purpose of the survey to bring together all the comprehensive collection all the writings on that and related subjects, and to outline the problem with all its attendant difficulties, together with the proposals that have been made to solve them. The result should provide a complete reference library on the subject and a guide for scientists and others who may be interested.

First issue of the Bulletin of the American Interplanetary Society, *June 1930. The society later became the American Rocket Society and* *is now the American Institute of Aeronautics and Astronautics. Ordway Collection/Space & Rocket Center.*

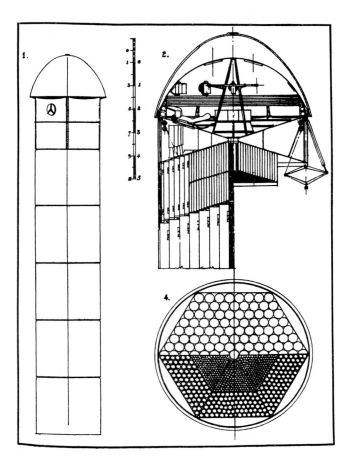

■

The design of a solid-propellant lunar spaceship undertaken by members of the British Interplanetary Society and published in the January 1939 issue of its Journal. National Air and Space Museum.

entry heating upon return to the Earth's atmosphere), instruments, parachutes, etc. Enough food, air, and water were planned for a 20-day round-trip lunar exploration mission, and a full program entailing space-suited astronauts conducting geological, photography, and gravity-probing activities was visualized. More details were promised in future issues of the *Journal of the British Interplanetary Society,* but World War II intervened.

For further reading

Durant, Frederick C., III, and George S. James, eds. *First Steps Towards Space*. Washington, D.C., 1974: Smithsonian Institution Annals of Flight no. 10. (See H. E. Ross's "The British Interplanetary Society's Astronautical Studies, 1937–1939," pp. 209–216.) Rpt. San Diego, 1986: Univelt (volume 6 in American Astronautical Society's History Series and first in series of histories organized by the International Academy of Astronautics).

Johnson, Leslie G. Readers' column, *Astounding Stories* 8 (October 1931), pp. 136–137. (The science fiction pulp magazines were also employed to educate their readers about the motion of rockets. This example is of particular interest in that Johnson later served as the first secretary of the British Interplanetary Society.)

Ley, Willy. *Rockets, Missiles and Men in Space*. New York, 1968: Viking.

Nicholson, Marjorie H. *Voyages to the Moon*. New York, 1948: Macmillan.

Pizor, Faith K., and T. Allan Comp, eds. *The Man in the Moone and Other Lunar Fantasies*. New York, 1971: Praeger.

Von Braun, Wernher, and Frederick I. Ordway III. *History of Rocketry and Space Travel*. New York, 1966, 1969, and 1975: Thomas Y. Crowell. 4th ed. as *Space Travel: A History,* with Dave Dooling. New York, 1985: Harper & Row.

Winter, Frank H. *Prelude to the Space Age: The Rocket Societies, 1924–1940*. Washington, D.C., 1983: Smithsonian Institution Press.

Winter, Frank H. *Rockets into Space*. Cambridge, Massachusetts, 1990: Harvard University Press. (Spaceflight concepts of Tsiolkovsky, Goddard, and Oberth are covered in detail.)

Gathering Momentum: Von Braun's Work in the 1940s and 1950s

ERNST STUHLINGER

Rocket Development at Peenemünde

At the German army's rocket center at Peenemünde, which had opened in 1937 with Wernher von Braun as technical director, rocket development and facility buildup proceeded quite smoothly until 1942. An island both geographically and in the security sense, the center's isolation permitted top secret work to be carried out far from the bustle and turmoil of the rest of the country. Moreover, as an army installation, Peenemünde was virtually off limits to Nazi Party functionaries who routinely sought to penetrate all nonmilitary segments of public and private life.

During the first two or three years after the beginning of World War II, Peenemünde remained relatively untouched by events swirling around the Third Reich. Hitler did not believe in rockets, and in any event he expected the war to be over before the A-4 could be developed into a weapon. It was only Army Ordnance's protective shroud that allowed Peenemünde to exist, albeit with low priorities for material and other needs.

As the months passed, it became clear that a gigantic effort would be needed to develop a large precision rocket, and that the full support of the armed services was indispensable. Von Braun, like most Germans at the time, did not envision a protracted war and was therefore confident that the A-4 would never be deployed in combat. Rather, he believed that military rockets would evolve primarily as defensive weapons and as deterrents to would-be aggressors. Eventually, reasoned von Braun, other

rockets would be developed to carry instruments for Earth observations, for communications, and to undertake scientific studies of the upper atmosphere and space. Still further in the future, rockets would be designed to transport crews and passengers to stations in orbit around the Earth and on to the Moon and planets. Although the pace of work at Peenemünde was always brisk, from time to time von Braun and his colleagues would gather privately to discuss such ambitious possibilities. (In February 1938, Peenemünde celebrated Mardi Gras under the motto "Mardi Gras on Mars"—there was a Martian goddess with her court who were visited by spacefarers from Earth. White-bearded "Professor emeritus" von Braun informed one and all that he was the Vagrant Viking of Space making a short stopover on the red planet.)

The scene changed when the Luftwaffe began to lose the Battle of Britain in 1941. Urged on by armaments and munitions minister Albert Speer, Hitler finally accorded Peenemünde top national priority. At the stroke of a pen, the center could now call on scarce manpower and materials needed to speed up development of the A-4. Technical work on its many components progressed to the point that by the spring of 1942 flight testing of complete missiles could begin. After two failures came success: on 3 October 1942 an A-4 soared into the skies, a perfect flight. Peenemünde's commanding officer, General Walter Dornberger, was overjoyed but nevertheless cautious. "Today," he told his col-

An unsuccessful launching of an A-4 at Peenemünde. The photograph shows the rocket in process of toppling to the ground, at which point it will violently explode. U.S. Army/ Ordway Collection/Space & Rocket Center.

An A-4 is successfully launched in field trials while another one, to the left, is being serviced. Ordway Collection/Space & Rocket Center.

leagues, "the spaceship has been born! But I warn you: our headaches are by no means over, they are just beginning!"

The truth of this prediction became evident almost immediately. Many of the rocket components were still unreliable and needed improvements; and, as a result of the October launch success, Hitler's representatives began to swarm all over Peenemünde demanding "immediate quantity production." A special A-4 committee was established in Speer's ministry and almost immediately began to draw up impossible-to-meet directives and production quotas.

Speer had been in close contact with the Peenemünde organization since 1939. In his book *Inside the Third Reich,* he tells how impressed he was by what was going on there and how he continued to support research and development even "after Hitler crossed the rocket project off his list of urgent undertakings." Speer judged von Braun quite correctly when he wrote: "For him and his team this was not the development of a weapon, but a step into the future of technology."[1]

In spite of his protective support of Peenemünde's programs and workers, Speer could not prevent Party officials from exerting influence over the expanding rocket research and development effort. In the summer of 1943, Reichsführer SS Heinrich Himmler visited the center to witness a test launching. For von Braun and Dornberger, the presence of the wily SS chief was a source of tension and concern, for they knew of his ambition to remove the A-4 from army control and place it under his own command. The launching proceeded well; but, after the rocket had reached an altitude of about 30 meters, it turned, tilted over, and hit the ground a few kilometers to the west. Himmler remarked drily: "I will go ahead now and order the production of ground weapons." Dornberger and von Braun were prepared for such a mishap. Less than an hour after the accident, another A-4 stood on the launch table, tanked, checked out, and ready for firing. The launch and subsequent flight were perfect, achieving an impact accuracy of one quarter of one percent.

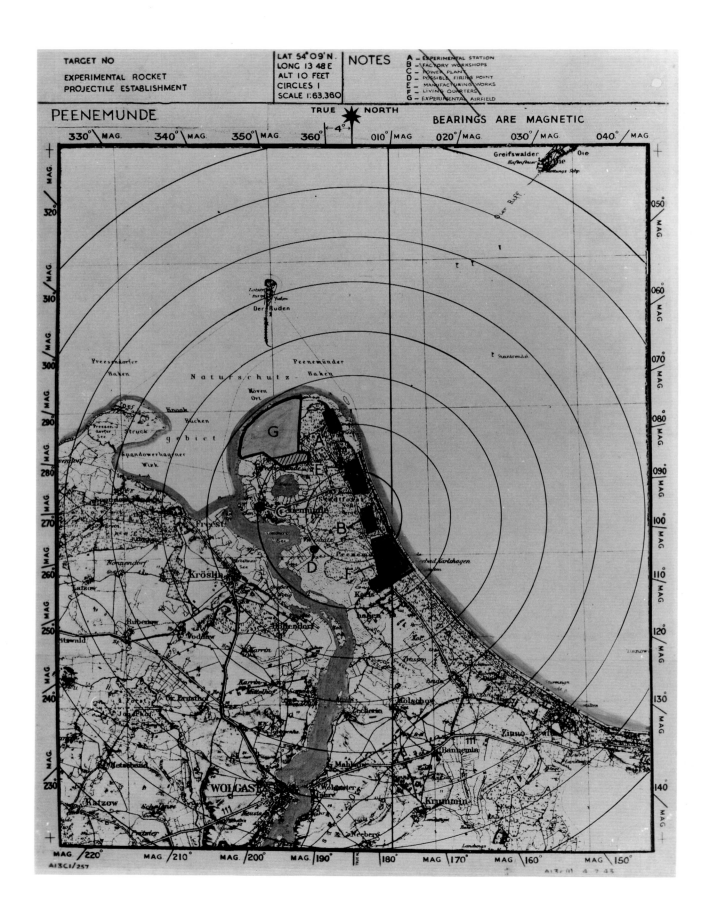

Aerial photograph of Test Stand 7 at Peenemünde, showing an A-4 rocket (A), *two mobile service towers* (B), *and an assembly hangar* (C). *Ordway Collection/ Space & Rocket Center.*

A photograph taken by the Royal Air Force on 20 May 1943 and issued in July of that year, showing installations at Peenemünde described as "Two large factory workshops. . . . It is believed that these buildings are intended for the manufacture and assembly of the rocket or firing apparatus." Ordway Collection/Space & Rocket Center.

Target map of what British air intelligence termed the Experimental Rocket Projectile Establishment, located at Peenemünde. Ordway Collection/Space & Rocket Center.

Von Braun remarked that the potential of the A-4 was demonstrated by the second launch, while the first launch underscored the fact that much additional work was necessary before it could be released for production and deployment. Himmler replied that he would discuss the matter with the führer.

A few weeks after Himmler's visit, some 600 Royal Air Force bombers from bases in England hit Peenemünde with 1500 tons of bombs. While damage to technical installations was not excessive, over 700 men, women, and children lost their lives. After the raid, Hitler ordered A-4 production transferred from aboveground facilities to underground installations and authorized Himmler to oversee the changeover. With this, the SS achieved full authority over the production and delivery to the field of A-4 missiles.

Production Commences

At Speer's direction, a large mine complex under the Harz Mountains near Niedersachswerfen was selected and quickly transformed into a facility for the assembly of various weapon systems. Not only were A-4s assigned to the plant, which was known as the Mittelwerk, but also pulse-jet-powered buzz bombs, airplane and submarine parts, jet engines, and a number of small rocket and other armament systems. Himmler, who commanded the infamous network of concentration camps that housed dissident Germans, resistance fighters from occupied countries, Jews, prisoners transferred from jails, and others whom the Nazi government simply wished to put away, assigned forced laborers to the Mittelwerk.

Horrified at this prospect, Dornberger and von Braun tried to persuade Nazi officialdom to postpone production until the A-4 had matured into a proven, combat-ready weapon. Their efforts were to no avail. A ruthless SS general, Hans Kammler, was put in charge of camp laborers, many of whom toiled to enlarge Harz Mountain caverns to accommodate A-4 missile assembly operations. A third to a half of the A-4 labor force (a total of 6,000 to 8,000 men), consisted of camp workers; the rest were civilian employees.

Peenemünde's history during the war years has been told in books by Walter Dornberger, Dieter Huzel, Frederick I. Ordway III and Mitchell R. Sharpe, and several others. Dornberger, who had reluctantly accepted production orders dictated by Himmler and Kammler, soon found himself transferred from Peenemünde to an administrative position in Berlin. As for Wernher von Braun, he was accused of thinking only of spaceflight at the expense of the country's war effort, arrested, and placed in a Gestapo jail in Stettin on Himmler's orders. Only Speer's personal intervention with Hitler permitted von Braun to leave jail two weeks later on probation.

The unsuccessful attempt to assassinate Hitler on 20 July 1944 resulted in an even tighter SS grip on the A-4 program. Military deployment of the still-immature missile was ordered late that summer. The first A-4s, henceforth called V-2 "vengeance" or retaliation weapons, began falling on Paris and London in early September 1944. "When I heard about this," von Braun commented later, "it was the darkest hour in my life."

As Allied forces drove into Germany in the closing weeks of the war, von Braun was ordered by Himmler to evacuate Peenemünde and transfer several hundred of his teammates and cratelords of documentation to southern Bavaria. The SS chief apparently planned to use the rocket team as ransom to gain his own freedom, or else to make sure that no member fell into Allied hands alive. Fortunately, Dornberger and von Braun succeeded in outwitting his schemes; on 2 May 1945, they surrendered with a number of companions to United States ground troops.

American intelligence officers, under the command of Colonel (later Major General) Holger N. Toftoy, interrogated von Braun and his associates and rounded up others who by war's end had become dispersed all over Germany. A limited number, 127 in all, were offered contracts to continue their rocket work in the United States.

A New Beginning in Texas and New Mexico

During the autumn and winter of 1945, these Peenemünders were brought to the United States under the code name "Project Paperclip" and sent to Fort Bliss, Texas, near El Paso. There, the army had established a Suboffice Rocket detachment that was located at first in a vacant barracks and later in an

unused annex of the army's Beaumont Hospital. In charge of the Paperclip specialists was Major James P. Hamill.

Together with members of the U.S. Army and employees of the General Electric Company, the von Braun team began to assemble V-2 rockets from parts and components that American troops had retrieved from the Mittelwerk and elsewhere in Germany. Some essential parts were missing while others were found to be damaged beyond repair; rough handling during collection, packaging, and transportation by rail, ship, and truck from war-torn Germany had taken its toll. So, when the V-2s reached their destination at the White Sands Proving Ground in New Mexico, they had to be fitted with American-made replacement components. Over a period of about seven years, 70 complete V-2 rockets were assembled and brought to the launch table. Of these, 67 more or less successfully achieved their missions.

Under the prodding of Ernst H. Krause and several colleagues, scientists were invited from all over the country to suggest experiments and develop instruments to be sent aloft in V-2s to altitudes of more than 100 kilometers. Such an opportunity had never before existed anywhere. Among the scientists who responded were Herbert Friedman, Richard Tousey, Homer Newell, John Naugle, James A. Van Allen, and Jesse Greenstain. Within a few years, instrumented V-2s had shed new light on the upper atmosphere and borders of space and had made possible the discovery of solar X rays, measurements of the Sun's far ultraviolet spectrum, clarification of the nature and origin of various layers of the ionosphere, and accurate measurements of atmospheric composition, temperature, density, and pressure.

Beyond preparing and firing V-2s for upper atmosphere experiments, the former Peenemünders had relatively little to do. To their surprise and disappointment, they were not asked to work on new rocket development projects, so—on their own initiative—they began to make plans for a kind of supersonic cruise missile. The idea was for it to be launched to cruising altitude by a V-2 and then continue under ramjet power to its destination. Design work, supplemented by ground and flight testing, proceeded at a rather slow pace, with little interest exhibited on the part of the army. With time still on their hands, von Braun and his teammates began to pursue a variety of other self-generated projects and studies.

Life in America meant a number of profound changes for the former Peenemünders. They were at last free to talk about their thoughts, and von Braun made immediate use of this freedom. On 16 January 1947, he gave a presentation to the El Paso Rotary Club entitled "The Future Development of the Rocket," describing first how a modern rocket

Wernher von Braun (right of center in front row, his left hand in his pocket) *with his teammates at the* *White Sands Proving Ground, New Mexico, 1946. Ordway Collection/Space & Rocket Center.*

works and then explaining Earth-orbiting satellites, manned stations in space, flights to the Moon, and expeditions to Mars. It was the first time in 10 years that von Braun could publicly express his spacefaring ideas, and his audience gave him a standing ovation.

Von Braun used much of his spare time in Fort Bliss to write, in collaboration with several colleagues, a book entitled *The Mars Project*. Based on the most advanced knowledge of rocketry available at that time, the book described an expedition to the red planet. It contained technical and scientific details concerning propulsion, guidance, communica-tions, life support and other systems, trajectories and celestial mechanics, the approach to and descent onto the target world, and the return to Earth.

Knowing what we do about Mars today, a basic correction to von Braun's scheme would be neces-sary. When he wrote his book, the atmospheric den-sity on Mars was believed to be just over 8 percent of the density of Earth's atmosphere at sea level. We now know that the Martian atmosphere is about ten times thinner than this. Therefore a landing craft on Mars could not, as he had suggested, rely on wings to land in glider fashion. Rather, retro- or counter-rockets would have to be employed to slow down the landing capsule as it approached the Martian surface.

Admittedly an expedition to Mars would be a gi-gantic undertaking. Von Braun did not advocate, much less himself believe, that the huge launch rocket, the wheel-shaped space station, the Mars

transfer vehicle, and the Mars landing and return craft he described could be built right away. His purpose was to show that a voyage to Mars from Earth would be possible based on reasonable extrapolations of late 1940s–early 1950s technologies. No mysterious new propulsion concepts nor still-unknown materials need be conceived and developed. "But," he would caution his coworkers, "we should begin to work on all these components to make them better and more efficient, first theoretically, and then with experiments, tests, and pilot models. Eventually, all of these components will reach a status that makes an expedition to Mars possible within reasonable limits of magnitude, complexity, and cost."[2]

Once *The Mars Project* had been published, first in Germany and then in the United States, von Braun stepped up the pace of his talks and lectures on rockets, satellites, and space travel. During the Fort Bliss and White Sands years, he came to the conclusion that developing rockets and making studies typified by his Mars project would not be sufficient if spaceflight were to be realized during his active life-

time. "Even if we continued our calculations until hell freezes over," he once remarked, "we will not touch or move anybody. . . . I will go public now, because this is where we have to sow our seeds for space exploration!" From then on, and for the next 25 years, von Braun grasped every opportunity, private and public, to talk and write about rockets and spaceflight. He addressed writers and publishers, educators and politicians, engineers and industrialists, scientists, economists, generals, and statesmen—the more prominent, the better!

■

In Washington on 17 March 1954, von Braun meets with military, government, industrial, and academic leaders to discuss Project Orbiter. Although this early American satellite proposal was not ulti- *mately accepted, it did pave the way for the later successful Redstone missile-launched Explorer series of artificial satellites. Frederick C. Durant III.*

The Move to Redstone

In the autumn of 1949, the Korean War began to cast its shadow upon Fort Bliss. The Beaumont Hospital now needed its annex that accommodated von Braun and his teammates. General Toftoy soon found new quarters for them at the sprawling Redstone Arsenal near Huntsville, Alabama; during the late spring and summer of 1950, they all moved east. At about the same time, Army Ordnance assigned them a development project—a 200-mile (320-kilometer) guided missile capable of carrying a heavy nuclear warhead. Work on the new project began in 1950; first flight tests were carried out in 1953; and, by 1958, the missile, named Redstone, was handed over to the U.S. Army for deployment at strategic sites in Europe.

As plans for the Redstone were being drawn up, von Braun quickly realized that the missile—if suitably modified—might be capable of orbiting a modest scientific satellite. By removing the hefty military payload, he reasoned, and substituting several upper

stages powered by clusters of small solid-propellant rockets, in theory at least the orbital objective should be attainable.

Von Braun talked about his satellite concept to his associates and in 1954 wrote a paper on the subject addressed to his superiors in Army Ordnance. Little happened despite continued and persistent proposing, planning, arguing, and persuading. Then in early October 1957 the Soviet Union triumphantly orbited its first Sputnik and the race was on. Nearly four years after von Braun had proposed using his Redstone to launch a satellite, he got the go-ahead, and on 31 January 1958 Explorer 1 was sent aloft. America, too, joined the Space Age.

Several years after that remarkable event, the Redstone had another opportunity to set a milestone in America's spaceflight program. On 5 May 1961, the missile lofted the first American astronaut, Alan B. Shepard, along a ballistic trajectory that briefly arced into space.

At about the time the Redstone missile was being readied for initial flight testing, Army Ordnance assigned another and more complex project to von Braun's rocket team in Huntsville—the development of the Jupiter intermediate range ballistic missile to be capable of reaching targets more than 1,500 miles away. In spite of this challenging new assignment and a multitude of other activities, von Braun continued resolutely to reach out to the public with plans for satellites, space stations, flights to the Moon, and expeditions to Mars. Fortunately, he found enthusiastic and influential brothers-in-arms who helped carry the torch: Willy Ley, Heinz and Fritz Haber, Fred Whipple, Chesley Bonestell, Cornelius Ryan from *Collier's* magazine, and the entertainment giant Walt Disney. During the early 1950s, the idea of spaceflight and space exploration began to expand dramatically.

Notes

1. Speer, Albert, *Inside the Third Reich: Memoirs* (New York, 1970: Macmillan), p. 367.
2. Recollections of author from frequent discussions with von Braun in the late 1940s and early 1950s.

For further reading

Collier, Basil. *The Battle of the V-Weapons 1944–1945*. Morey, Yorkshire, 1976: Elmfiel.

Collier, Basil. *The Defence of the United Kingdom*. London, 1957: Her Majesty's Stationery Office.

Dornberger, Walter. *V-2*. New York, 1954: Viking. Expanded German edition published as *Peenemünde: Die Geschichte der V-Waffen*. Esslinger, 1981: Bechtle.

Huzel, Dieter K. *Peenemünde to Canaveral*. Englewood Cliffs, New Jersey, 1962: Prentice-Hall.

Irving, David. *The Mare's Nest*. London, 1964: William Kimber.

Klee, Ernst, and Otto Merk. *The Birth of the Missile*. New York, 1964: Dutton.

Kooy, J. M. J., and J. W. H. Uytenbogaart. *Ballistics of the Future*. Haarlem, Netherlands, 1946: N.V. de Technische Vitgeverij H. Stam; New York and London, 1946: McGraw-Hill.

Lasby, Clarence G. *Project Paperclip*. New York, 1971: Atheneum.

McGovern, James. *Crossbow and Overcast*. New York, 1964: Morrow.

Medaris, Major General J. B., with Arthur Gordon. *Countdown for Decision*. New York, 1960: G. P. Putnam's Sons.

Middlebrook, Martin. *The Peenemünde Raid: The Night of 17–18 August 1943*. London, 1982: Allen Lane.

Newell, Homer E. *Beyond the Atmosphere: Early Years of Space Science*. Washington, D.C., 1980: National Aeronautics and Space Administration.

Ordway, Frederick I., III, and Mitchell R. Sharpe. *The Rocket Team*. New York, 1979: Thomas Y. Crowell; London, 1979: Heinemann; rpt. Cambridge, Massachusetts, 1982: MIT Press.

Speer, Albert. *Inside the Third Reich: Memoirs*. New York, 1970: Macmillan; and *Infiltration*. New York, 1981: Macmillan.

Stuhlinger, Ernst, and Frederick I. Ordway III. *Wernher von Braun: Crusader for Space*. Esslingen: Bechtle Verlag (in press).

Von Braun, Wernher. *The Mars Project*. Urbana, 1952: University of Illinois; rpt. 1991.

Von Braun, Wernher, and Frederick I. Ordway III. *History of Rocketry and Space Travel*. New York, 1966, 1969, and 1975: Thomas Y. Crowell. 4th ed. as *Space Travel: A History*, with Dave Dooling. New York, 1985: Harper & Row.

Part Three

The Golden Age of Space Travel

Recollections of Pre-Sputnik Days

FRED L. WHIPPLE

The Space Age began for me personally in the late winter of 1943–1944. After nearly three decades of reading, talking, and dreaming science fiction, I was still uncertain as to when we would break the gravity barrier. That winter, I was in the United Kingdom as "Chief of Chaff" (unofficial title) for the U.S. Army Air Corps. My war job involved the development, production, and tactical use of aluminum foil strips (code word Chaff) to be dropped out of aircraft to confuse enemy radars. The top secret V-2 rocket firings that were being conducted by the German army at Peenemünde on the Baltic coast did not impress me as a serious immediate war threat. But the information about the success of their program overwhelmed me when I viewed it as the morning twilight of the Space Age. It meant a high probability that I could actually see artificial satellites and, I hoped, manned space travel in my lifetime.

In 1946, I helped organize and joined the V-2 Panel that would guide the scientific project utilizing the "liberated" V-2 rockets.[1] That summer saw my first direct contribution to space travel at a secret meeting of the Rand Corporation, then managed by the Douglas Aircraft Company near Santa Monica, California. There I made preliminary (in retrospect rather poor) calculations of the hazards to spacecraft from tiny rocks orbiting among the planets. This space debris becomes meteors on striking the Earth's atmosphere at speeds up to 72 kilometers per second. Surprisingly tiny dust grains can puncture the skin of a spacecraft, because a typical encounter speed is some 40 kilometers per second.

My solution to the meteor problem was the "meteor bumper," now called the meteor deflection screen or the Whipple shield. The bumper was based on the principle that meteoric bodies explode when striking a solid surface. If an outer skin about a tenth of the thickness of the ship's skin is built around it, an impinging body will explode upon impact with the skin (bumper) and fan out as hot gas, which does not puncture the spacecraft. This reduces the meteor hazard by about a factor of ten with little cost in weight. The scheme has been successfully used on most long-lived satellites or deep space vehicles and, with improvements, is planned for the space station Freedom. When the meteor deflection screen caused considerable trouble on a Skylab flight, however, I was relieved that it was no longer called the Whipple shield.

Knowing that the military was working on intercontinental ballistic missiles (ICBMs) during this early postwar period, I realized that the day of artificial Earth satellites and space travel could not be too far in the future. So I tried to exert all the influence I could to encourage developments toward this end. From 1946 to 1952 I served on the U.S. National Advisory Panel on Aeronautics and from 1947 to 1952 on the U.S. Research and Development Board Panel. I also consulted with General Dynamics on problems relating to the upper atmosphere. Because of my specialized studies of meteors, I was welcomed into these high-altitude circles.

Before the advent of the V-2 and other powerful rockets, our knowledge of air temperature and densities in the upper atmosphere above 50 kilometers was very limited. Researching this area, I developed a system of photographing meteors that required two separate stations. Each station's camera had a synchronous motor to actuate shutters in order to photographically chop the trail of the incoming meteorite. By studying these time-sequenced photographs, I could measure air drag up to an altitude of about 100 kilometers. Although this method was crude, it gave quantitative information where other methods only yielded qualitative. Later, when rockets gave more accurate data, I was delighted because then I could reverse the logic and learn more about the physical processes and the nature of meteors.

In the late 1940s, a surprising number of people in the military establishment and airframe industry were excited about the more or less imminent possibility of Earth satellites and space travel. Many clandestine discussions of the subject occurred among scientists, engineers, and administrators. By 1951, knowledge of the possibilities was so widespread, even though it was not publicized, that Robert R. Coles, the chairman of the Hayden Planetarium in New York, was able to convince the director of the parent American Museum of Natural History to host the First Annual Symposium on Space Travel, on Columbus Day (12 October). Willy Ley, popular science author and manned space travel promoter, became the coordinator of the symposium and presented the first paper. Naturally, I was delighted at this public discussion of satellites and space travel, even though it was presented only as an abstract possibility.

The next public recognition of the increasing probability of space travel followed the New York symposium by less than a month. The Lovelace Foundation for Medical Education and Research of Albuquerque, New Mexico, in collaboration with the United States Air Force School of Aviation Medicine staged a four-day symposium in San Antonio, Texas, on the physics and medicine of the upper atmosphere. The presentations at this symposium were consolidated into a 611-page volume under the editorship of two physicians, Clayton S. White, M.D., of the Lovelace Foundation, and Brigadier General Otis O. Benson, Jr., M.D., Commandant of the U.S. Air Force School of Medicine, with an introduction by the Surgeon General of the U.S. Air Force, Major General Harry G. Armstrong, M.D.

Most participants at the San Antonio symposium hedged on the likelihood of ICBMs and satellites, although Wernher von Braun, who was not asked to speak, discussed the reentry problems of a "Winged Rocket Vehicle in a Satellite Orbit" in a piece that appeared in the published proceedings. Contributors to the symposium included most of the members of the V-2 Panel, among them Dr. James Van Allen, later to become immortalized as the discoverer of the radiation belts around the Earth, which subsequently were named for him. Another participant was Marcel Nicolet of Belgium, recently elevated to Baron for his studies of the upper atmosphere. I discussed the meteor hazard at high altitudes.

My most vivid memories of the symposium are of

■

Invitation and program from the First Annual Symposium on Space Travel. Liebermann Collection.

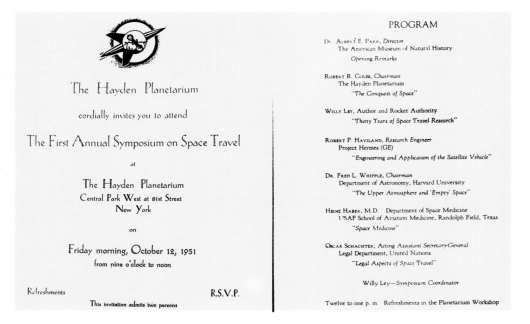

The Hayden Planetarium

cordially invites you to attend

The First Annual Symposium on Space Travel

at

The Hayden Planetarium
Central Park West at 81st Street
New York

on

Friday morning, October 12, 1951
from nine o'clock to noon

Refreshments   R.S.V.P.

This invitation admits two persons

PROGRAM

Dr. Albert E. Parr, Director
The American Museum of Natural History
Opening Remarks

Robert R. Coles, Chairman
The Hayden Planetarium
"The Conquest of Space"

Willy Ley, Author and Rocket Authority
"Thirty Years of Space Travel Research"

Robert P. Haviland, Research Engineer
Project Hermes (GE)
"Engineering and Application of the Satellite Vehicle"

Dr. Fred L. Whipple, Chairman
Department of Astronomy, Harvard University
"The Upper Atmosphere and 'Empty' Space"

Heinz Haber, M.D. Department of Space Medicine
USAF School of Aviation Medicine, Randolph Field, Texas
"Space Medicine"

Oscar Schachter, Acting Assistant Secretary-General
Legal Department, United Nations
"Legal Aspects of Space Travel"

Willy Ley—Symposium Coordinator

Twelve to one p.m. Refreshments in the Planetarium Workshop

an evening of cocktails, dinner, and an impassioned long-into-the-night discussion with von Braun, Joseph Kaplan (an upper atmosphere spectroscopist), and Cornelius "Connie" Ryan. Then a popular writer for *Collier's* magazine, Ryan is probably best known for his World War II book, *The Longest Day*. That evening he appeared to be highly skeptical about any possibility of artificial satellites or space travel, dashing our hopes for wide publicity in the pages of *Collier's*. Whether or not he was truly skeptical, we persevered. Von Braun, not only a prophetic engineer and top-notch administrator, was also certainly one of the best salesmen of the twentieth century. Additionally, Kaplan carried the aura of wisdom and the expertise of the archetypal learned professor, while I had learned by then to sound very convincing. The three of us worked hard at proselytizing Ryan and finally by midnight he was sold on the space program.

Ryan returned to his New York office at *Collier's* and convinced his editor to publish a feature article about artificial satellites and manned space travel. The article's success led to further articles about expeditions to the Moon and to Mars, training for spaceflight, and so on. Together, these were later the basis of books edited by Ryan: *Across the Space Frontier* and *Conquest of the Moon,* published by the Viking Press in 1952 and 1953. Perhaps most interesting is the fact that in 1951 von Braun and I both overestimated the actual time schedules—both for satellites (10 years instead of 6) and men on the Moon (a quarter century instead of 18 years).

In writing these articles we were all handicapped, not assisted, by knowing quite a bit about military plans for large ballistic missiles. For his part, von Braun was the technical director of the Army Ordnance Guided Missiles Development Group in Huntsville, Alabama. We were under top security wraps in discussing satellites or space travel. As a consequence, we had to write our articles without disclosing or suggesting any secret information. We could not outline the actual steps that probably would occur but had to jump over the realistic near future that we expected. Thus, the picture we painted carried much of the imaginative character of science fiction. We knew that only in the distant future could we expect the huge and complex vehicles we described. Any description of the likely series of events and instruments might prejudice our security status. On the other hand, the expected reality was much less exciting than the story we told. Only the

Apollo program nearly matched our imagination.

During more than a decade from February 1946, the V-2 Panel continued as the guiding angel of upper atmosphere research via rocket studies. The panel completely lacked any official status as sponsor, yet acted as the actual governing board for the scientific use of high-altitude rockets in atmospheric and other research. The story of its formation and activities is too complex for elaboration here. Suffice it to say that its founding members were affiliates of the National Advisory Committee for Aeronautics, the Army Signal Corps, the Army Air Corps' Wright Field, the universities of Michigan, Princeton, and Harvard, the Naval Research Laboratory (NRL), and the General Electric Company. Later, the panel included representatives of Army Ordnance, the Navy's Bureau of Ordnance, the Aberdeen Ballistics Laboratory, and the White Sands Proving Ground. Other interested observers attended unclassified meetings. The air force, of course, became interested after it was structured as a separate department of the U.S. armed services in 1947.

The upper atmosphere and related phenomena were not the only study objectives. Solar radiations, cosmic rays, and Earth's surface were of great interest. Members of the panel, supported by their various agencies, answered a host of questions about the upper atmosphere and varied phenomena, both about their military impact and their purely scientific interest.

Ernst Krause of the NRL was certainly the major force in establishing the panel and was the obvious choice for chairman. He was a unique leader with unbounded enthusiasm and orderliness. I had the privilege of visiting his basement laboratory at his home. Whereas my basement is a mess with odds and ends lying every which way, his was neater and cleaner than a hospital operating room. Practically nothing was to be seen except benches, tables, and large equipment. Everything was in drawers, and properly labeled. Even though Krause resigned the chairmanship in December 1957 to participate in nuclear bomb tests, he left his mark on the panel. Van Allen was a highly competent successor. One of the important panel members, Homer E. Newell, tells some of the story of the panel in his book *Beyond the Atmosphere: Early Years of Space Science.* David H. De Voorkin published more details of panel politics and vicissitudes in his article "Organizing for Space Research: The V-2 Rocket Panel."

In spite of the generally wider interest in space research that followed publication of the scientific results of the V-2 Panel scientists and the 1951 symposia, along with several magazine articles and two books on possible space travel, the subject remained just "in the air" until late in the planning for the International Geophysical Year (IGY), scheduled to begin 1 July 1957 (an idea spearheaded in 1950 by the world-renowned geophysicist Lloyd V. Berkner). Various international unions backed the idea of world-wide study of planet Earth, of its atmosphere, oceans, dimensions, magnetism, aurorae or polar lights, and simultaneous measurements of anything that could be measured. By 1952, an international committee, headed by Sydney Chapman of England along with Berkner, set the IGY idea into motion. In the United States, the National Academy of Sciences selected Joseph Kaplan as chairman of the U.S. National Committee for the IGY. Eventually, 67 countries joined the IGY, which held its largest meeting in Moscow in August 1958.

One American group in the IGY was the Technical Panel of Rocketry, of which I was the chairman. We made it known that the U.S. would use rockets in its IGY program. At the same time all of the pan-

el's members, as well as many others, were aware that satellites were in the offing, but we were scientifically handicapped by our ties to classified military information. At this time another highly active and enthusiastic man, much like Krause, *almost* changed the course of events. He was Lieutenant Commander George W. Hoover of the Office of Naval Research. At his initiative, a few satellite enthusiasts created an informal and clandestine group called project Orbiter. Von Braun was certainly another of the organizers as he was then technical director of the Guided Missile Development Group at the Redstone Arsenal and was in charge of planning the Redstone missile testing program. His idea was to peel off one of the test missiles, No. 28 as I recall, and fire it eastward from an equatorial base with a small payload to become the world's first artificial satellite. I was to set up four or more simple optical observing stations around the world near the equator to observe it. Had the program been realized, other types of stations would have received various scientific signals from it.

But around this time, S. Fred Singer of the Johns Hopkins Applied Physics Laboratory publicly announced his 45-kilogram instrumented satellite MOUSE, derived from Minimum Orbital Unmanned Satellite of Earth. In September 1953, the International Radio Union approved Singer's proposal at its 11th General Assembly in The Hague. Singer irked many of those who were better informed than he about satellite potentialities because the manner of his presentation implied that he was the sole originator of the idea. Nevertheless, he probably did space enthusiasts a good turn by publicizing the real potentials of satellites for research.

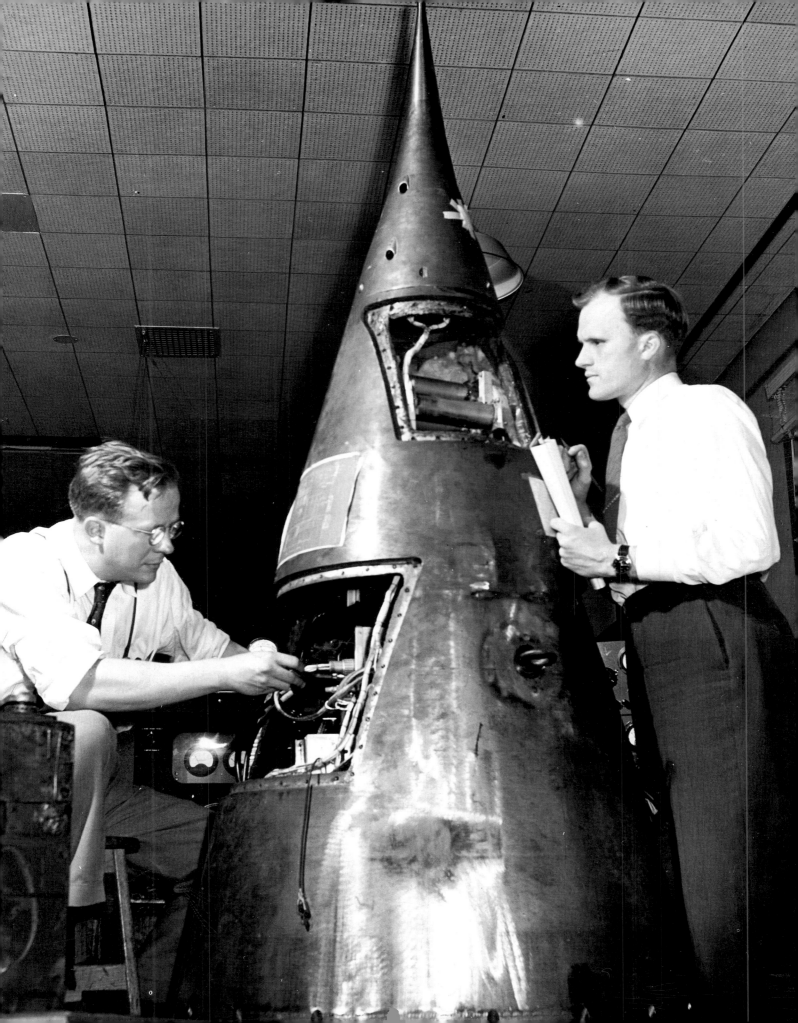

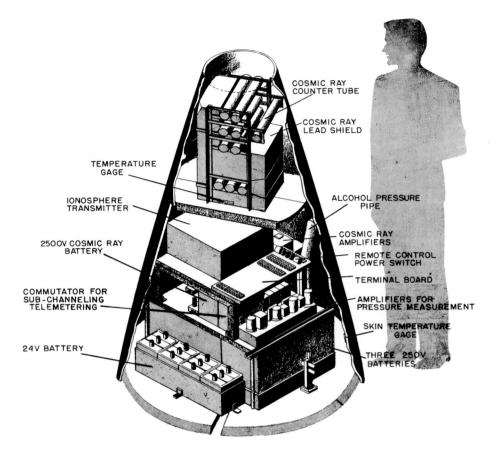

Diagram of the upper atmosphere instrument package sent aloft in the V-2. Liebermann Collection/U.S. Navy.

COSMIC RAY COUNTER TUBE

COSMIC RAY LEAD SHIELD

TEMPERATURE GAGE

IONOSPHERE TRANSMITTER

ALCOHOL PRESSURE PIPE

COSMIC RAY AMPLIFIERS

2500V COSMIC RAY BATTERY

REMOTE CONTROL POWER SWITCH

TERMINAL BOARD

COMMUTATOR FOR SUB-CHANNELING TELEMETERING

AMPLIFIERS FOR PRESSURE MEASUREMENT

SKIN TEMPERATURE GAGE

24V BATTERY

THREE 250V BATTERIES

Diagram of the V-2 equipped for upper atmosphere study, spring 1946. Navy Department/Ordway Collection/Space & Rocket Center.

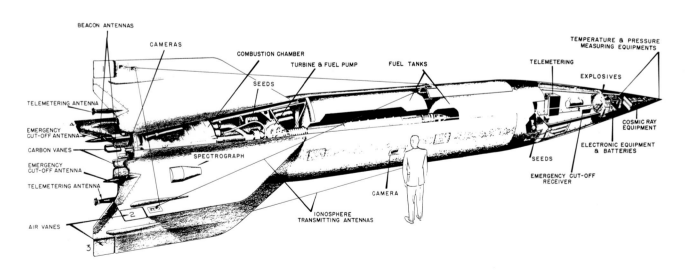

BEACON ANTENNAS

CAMERAS

COMBUSTION CHAMBER

TURBINE & FUEL PUMP

FUEL TANKS

TEMPERATURE & PRESSURE MEASURING EQUIPMENTS

TELEMETERING

SEEDS

EXPLOSIVES

TELEMETERING ANTENNA

EMERGENCY CUT-OFF ANTENNA

CARBON VANES

EMERGENCY CUT-OFF ANTENNA

TELEMETERING ANTENNA

SPECTROGRAPH

COSMIC RAY EQUIPMENT

ELECTRONIC EQUIPMENT & BATTERIES

SEEDS

EMERGENCY CUT-OFF RECEIVER

AIR VANES

CAMERA

IONOSPHERE TRANSMITTING ANTENNAS

Wernher von Braun (standing, left) *and Fred L. Whipple* (standing, right) *view a model of Lockheed's vertical takeoff aircraft design with Ralph S. Damon,* left, *President of Trans World Airlines, and Hall Hibbard,* right, *Vice-President of Engineering at Lockheed* *Aircraft Corporation. All had just participated in a symposium forecasting the progress of aviation 30 years hence (from the early 1950s) at the Hayden Planetarium in New York City. TWA/ George Jervas Studio, Ordway Collection/Space & Rocket Center.*

By 29 July 1955, official decisions had been made, and President Eisenhower announced from the White House that an artificial satellite would be a part of the U.S. program in the IGY. That very day, I set sail for astronomical meetings in Italy and heard the announcement aboard ship. Having testified before official committees along with von Braun and many others in favor of Orbiter, I daily expected a radiogram instructing me to return home and start organizing an optical observing program.

None ever came.

The Vanguard program had been approved and not von Braun's. The reason I heard for the rejection of the Redstone missile as a satellite launcher was that such a diversion of Redstone Arsenal's activities would reduce the efficiency of the organization and delay the production of ballistic missiles being developed there. I was certain that this was a rationalization, because the goal of producing an artificial satellite would have been a strong incentive for increased activity and efficiency by the staff. The reason I have heard and believe to be true is that to have based our first satellite on the efforts of a German-led team was unacceptable. Whatever the real reason for what I still consider to be a bad decision, it meant that I had to start over from scratch with a new satellite observing program after I returned to the United States in September 1955. I had just become director of the Smithsonian Astrophysical Observatory and moved its Washington-based headquarters to Cambridge alongside the Harvard College Observatory.

At that time the accuracy of international geodesy was about 100 meters uncertainty for positions on large land masses and up to a kilometer for islands. I claimed that I could reduce this uncertainty to 10 meters by photographing artificial satellites that would serve as markers for positions. I also claimed that amateur astronomers would be able to observe satellites visually for atmospheric drag measurements as the satellites made their final and rather unpredictable falls to the ground. My plan involved 12 photographic tracking stations located in regions that were relatively free of clouds. The National Academy of Sciences accepted the proposal for the IGY; after a number of vicissitudes, the project finally succeeded in attaining its objectives. A major contributor to the success of the satellite tracking project was J. Allen Hynek, an astrophysicist from Ohio State University who headed up the project operationally.

In Washington, D.C., the idea of a U.S. artificial satellite aroused quite divergent reactions. Among the old guard it was considered unlikely, mostly a lot of hot air intended only to arouse public interest. Many individuals were indifferent. Many others, however, were truly excited, seeing the satellite as a great step forward both in technology and in exploration, not to mention its cultural significance. To my surprise, some at high levels saw the satellite primarily as a public relations gimmick to show the world our scientific and technological superiority in the cold war. This attitude became evident as we at the Smithsonian Astrophysical Observatory began to organize amateur astronomers as visual satellite observers in the IGY's Moonwatch tracking program.

Fortunately, Armand Spitz was willing to accept the leadership of the organization and recruitment for Moonwatch. He was world famous both for his work at the Hayden Planetarium in New York and for his invention of a small inexpensive planetarium for general use. He aroused the interest of amateur astronomers by traveling widely and giving many popular lectures. On several occasions after Spitz had given a lecture in some far-flung area of the United States, I would get a phone call the next morning from a member of the administrative staff of the IGY. The message was always the same in content and concept. "Spitz has told the public that the USSR is also planning to launch an artificial satellite as a part of the IGY. *Shut the man up!*" In fact Spitz had read translations of internal publications from the USSR in which they described their plans. I gathered that in the unclassified IGY effort we were supposed never even to whisper about the possibility that the USSR might be able to launch an artificial Earth satellite. In any case, I never told Spitz about any of those phone calls.

During the buildup phase of the IGY, I gave a number of lectures to promote the satellite program. One of the analogies that I found amusing went as follows: The great pyramid of Khufu, it is said, required some 20 percent of Egypt's gross national product (GNP) for 20 years in its building. I averred that if the United States devoted 20 percent of its GNP for 20 years to satellites, it could place Khufu's pyramid into Earth orbit. Be that as it may, one of the worries concerned the satellite's eventual fall back to Earth and the hazard of something being hurt by it. I believe it was Dr. Karl Henize (recently an astronaut) who jokingly offered insurance, $10,000 for 1 cent per year, against such personal damage. So far as I know, no one has yet been hurt by a falling satellite, so Lloyd's of London would have done well with such an offering.

Another incident illustrates the absurdities to which government officials carried the cold war not long after the red-baiting campaigns of Senator Joseph R. McCarthy. For the Moonwatch program, the Edmonds Salvage Company had constructed, from surplus World War II materials, a small optical telescope with a 45-degree mirror so that an observer could look horizontally at a satellite crossing his meridian overhead. It was inexpensive, in the $20 range,

easily affordable by any amateur. In the spring of 1956, Dr. Alla Masevitch, a Soviet astronomer who was setting up in the USSR the equivalent of our Moonwatch program, visited us in Cambridge. Naturally we gave her one of the Moonwatch telescopes. Soon Washington let us know that they had heard that we were giving away government property to the Soviets and possibly optical information as well. They even suggested that we were committing subversive acts. Quickly four of us put $5 each in the pot and bought a replacement Moonwatch telescope, at least covering the accusation of having given away government property. We heard no more about subversive information transfer.

This was not the end of the incident, however. When the Soviet IGY scientists met in Washington, D.C., in October 1959, they gave the American IGY Committee the Soviet version of the Moonwatch telescope. Beautifully constructed, it probably cost the equivalent of $200 to $300 to manufacture, even in quantity. Our IGY administrators, however, would not let our Moonwatch people or the IGY people of the Smithsonian Astrophysical Observatory touch, let alone test, the telescope optically. It was 4 October 1957, the day Sputnik went up, totally surprising an unsuspecting world. The Soviets had barely missed *our* target date of 1 October 1957.

Note

1. The V-2 Panel was later called the V-2 Upper Atmosphere Panel and the Upper Atmosphere Rocket Research Panel. Herein the term V-2 Panel is used throughout to avoid confusion.

For further reading

De Voorkin, David H. "Organizing for Space Research: The V-2 Rocket Panel." *Historical Studies in the Physical and Biological Sciences* 18, no. 1 (1987), pp. 1–24.

Fraser, L. W., and E. H. Siegler. *High Altitude Research Using the V-2 Rocket*. Johns Hopkins University, 1948: Applied Physics Laboratory.

Krause, Ernst H. "High Altitude Research with V-2 Rockets." *Proceedings of the American Philosophical Society* 91, no. 5 (December 1947).

Newell, Homer E., Jr. *Beyond the Atmosphere: Early Years of Space Science*. Washington, D.C., 1980: National Aeronautics and Space Administration.

Newell, Homer E., Jr. *High Altitude Rocket Research*. New York, 1953: Academic Press.

White, Clayton S., M.D., and Otis O. Benson, Jr., eds. *Physics and Medicine of the Upper Atmosphere: A Study of the Aeropause*. Albuquerque, 1952: The University of New Mexico Press.

The Collier's *and* Disney Series

RANDY LIEBERMANN

*The reasonable man adapts himself to the world;
the unreasonable man persists in trying to adapt
the world to himself. Therefore, all progress
depends on the unreasonable man.*

—George Bernard Shaw,
Man and Superman: "Maxims for
Revolutionists"

For the majority of those born after Yuri Gagarin's orbital odyssey on 12 April 1961, manned space travel has become commonplace. Back in the early 1950s, manned space travel had largely been relegated to the preserve of science fiction. How—and when—did the general public first become aware of the real possibilities for space travel? How was the transition made from science fiction to science fact?

From the beginning, the visionaries of space science realized the importance of sales promotion to the success of major research and development projects. During the war, well-coordinated audio-visual presentations, complete with carefully detailed scale models, had aided Wernher von Braun and his colleagues in convincing German higher authority to finance the expensive development of the V-2. During the late 1940s and early 1950s, now in America, von Braun made a few public speeches to small groups on rocket development and the possibility of space travel. He realized that for the United States to make the expensive commitment to explore space, popular public support was essential, particularly during peacetime.

When Willy Ley began to organize the 1951 Space Travel Symposium held at the Hayden Planetarium, he saw publicity and education as essential goals: "the time is now ripe to make the public realize that the problem of space travel is to be regarded as a serious branch of science and technology."[1] Papers were to be presented by experts as diverse as Fred Whipple (on the physics of the upper atmosphere), Heinz Haber (on space medicine), and Oscar Schacter (on space law). Invitations to attend the symposium were "sent to institutions of learning, to professional societies and research groups, and also to the science editors of metropolitan newspapers and magazines (plus those out-of-town and foreign publications which have offices in New York)."[2] When the symposium took place on Columbus Day of that year, over 200 people attended, among them two journalists from *Collier's* magazine, then one of America's most widely read publications.

The *Collier's* journalists informed Gordon Manning, their managing editor, about what they had learned at the Hayden symposium. A short time later, Manning spotted a brief article in the *New York Journal-American* about a space medicine conference scheduled to take place in San Antonio, Texas, that 6–9 November. Manning gave Cornelius Ryan, one of his most capable associate editors, the assignment of traveling to San Antonio to see if he could find out anything that might be newsworthy. Ryan, who knew nothing about rockets or space travel, was skeptical about the trip's value but respected Manning's prescient nose for news. As Fred Whipple described in his chapter, Ryan was converted from space travel skeptic to believer by von Braun, Whipple, and Joseph Kaplan. Returning to his office in New York, Ryan enthusiastically sold Manning on the idea of having *Collier's* organize their own internal space travel symposium calling on the experts from the Hayden and San Antonio meetings.

Ryan could not then have known that the *Collier's* symposium would develop into a series of eight feature articles appearing in the magazine over a two-year period. Their authors included James A. Van Allen, Hubertus Strughold, Whipple, Kaplan, Heinz and Fritz Haber, and the preeminent authority von Braun himself. After dedicating 25 years of his life to the advancement of astronautics, von Braun finally had the opportunity to emerge out of his sequestered army environment and lay out a grand blueprint for manned travel to orbit, to the Moon, and eventually to Mars.

Due to the complex technical nature of the articles, *Collier's* art director William Chessman hired three of America's finest freelance artists to work with the writers: Chesley Bonestell, Fred Freeman, and Rolf Klep. To ensure technical accuracy, each artist established a close working relationship with the authors, particularly von Braun. The procedure for most of the paintings went as follows: from his base in Huntsville, von Braun sent his original engineering design drawings to Ryan at *Collier's* in New York. Ryan would make photostatic copies of each drawing and send them to Bonestell, who was living in California, or hand them to Freeman and Klep, who were both living in the New York area. Each artist created working drawings from von Braun's original designs. They sent these drawings to von Braun, who would then return them to the artists with corrections and comments. This cycle was followed throughout the entire process of creating the finished illustrations.

During the nearly two and a half years of the project, Fred Freeman developed a particularly close working relationship with von Braun. On at least two occasions, at *Collier's* behest, Freeman flew to Huntsville to discuss his renderings of von Braun's space "hardware." Freeman had developed a nationwide reputation as an artist specializing in technical subjects (he illustrated two now-classic volumes on U.S. submarine and destroyer operations in World War II for the U.S. Naval Institute).[3] This skill enabled him to properly position, in his compositions, all the necessary equipment von Braun called for. In

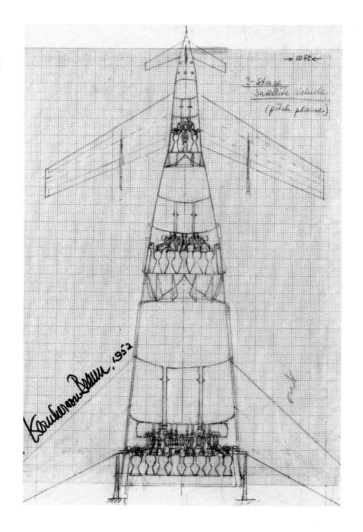

■

Three-stage reusable launch vehicle designed by von Braun for Collier's, *executed in December 1951 and signed* *1952. Pencil on Keuffel and Esser engineering paper.* Omni *Magazine Collection.*

a few of his preliminary drawings, Freeman corrected von Braun's original designs by adding doorways in spaceships or developing a feeding system for monkeys orbiting Earth. During the late 1950s and early 1960s Freeman would again illustrate the writings of von Braun, this time for the readers of *This Week* magazine and a related book, *First Men on the Moon*.

The first *Collier's* space issue hit the newsstands about a week before its 22 March 1952 cover date.

Bonestell's photorealistic cover depicted von Braun's huge three-stage launch vehicle undergoing staging en route to Earth orbit. The headline, "Man Will Conquer Space *Soon,*" challenged the reader to pick up the magazine and learn about man's imminent adventure in space. The opening article ("What Are We Waiting For?") begins: "On the following pages *Collier's* presents what may be one of the most important scientific symposiums ever published by a national magazine. It is the story of the inevitability of man's conquest of space. What you will read here is not science fiction. It is serious fact."[4] At the time, *Collier's* had a circulation of over 3 million copies; and, it was estimated, 4 or 5 people read each issue before it was discarded. This meant that more than 12–15 million people had the opportunity to judge for themselves *Collier's* bold claim. Space travel in the public consciousness was about to begin its transition from science fiction to science fact.

The first component in von Braun's blueprint was

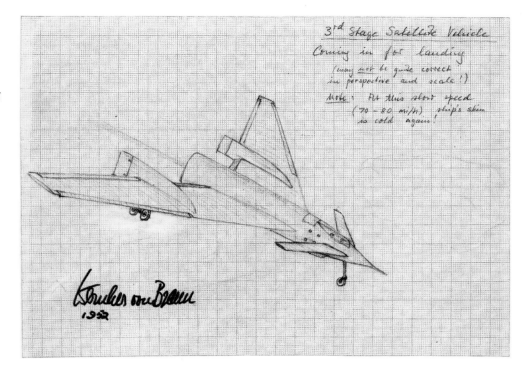

3rd Stage Satellite Vehicle
Coming in for landing
(may not be quite correct
in perspective and scale!)
Note: At this slow speed
(70 – 80 m/h) ship's skin
is cold again!

Staging en route to Earth orbit. Collier's *magazine cover illustration, 22 March 1952, by Chesley Bonestell. Oil on illustration board. Ordway Collection/Space & Rocket Center.*

Landing of third stage of reusable shuttle vehicle executed by von Braun in December 1951 and signed in 1952. Pencil on Keuffel and Esser engineering paper. Omni *Magazine Collection.*

the construction of a small fleet of three-stage launch vehicles with reusable upper stages (today we would call them shuttles). The 265-foot-high rocket's 51-engine first stage would produce a total thrust of 14,000 tons (in comparison, the first stage of the Saturn V Moon rocket as built had five engines and produced a total thrust of 3,750 tons). After launch, the first two stages would be retrieved from the ocean by ship to be readied for another flight. In the third stage, the crew of ten astronauts would continue their mission goal by attaining Earth orbit at an altitude of 1,075 miles. Its test mission completed, this stage would return to Earth and land like a conventional aircraft. Von Braun proposed this reusable design nearly three decades before NASA flew its first space shuttle.

The initial mission of the von Braun fleet was to ferry up into Earth orbit the necessary components for the construction of a permanently manned space station. Each shuttle flight would deliver $36\frac{1}{2}$ tons of payload into the same area, 1,075 miles above Earth. Astronauts working in space had the job of assembling prefabricated and inflatable nylon and plastic components into a wheel-shaped structure 250 feet in diameter. Once assembled, the station would house 80 men within its three levels. A concave condensing mirror, attached to the side of the station

and permanently facing the Sun, would provide the station's power by focusing solar rays onto a mercury-filled tube that ran through the center of the mirror. The heated vapor would power a turbo-generator producing electricity.

Space medicine experts of the early 1950s believed that man would be incapable of withstanding prolonged periods of weightlessness. For this reason, the station was designed to produce centrifugal force by rotating on its axis. The station level farthest away from the hub had the strongest artificial gravity.

Small rocket-powered "taxis" would be used to ferry personnel and supplies brought into orbit. They would dock in one of the station's two landing berths located at the hub of the wheel. The space station crew was to include scientists, engineers, technicians, and military observers. Meteorological and astronomical observations of the Earth and the cosmos would be conducted using a large free-flying telescope, not unlike today's Hubble space telescope.

The telescope was scheduled to perform another function. When the article was published, the U.S. was engaged in a hot war on the Korean peninsula and a cold war with the Soviet Union and its satellite Eastern Bloc nations. Von Braun emphasized that U.S. national security was the major reason for constructing the space station. A large percentage of

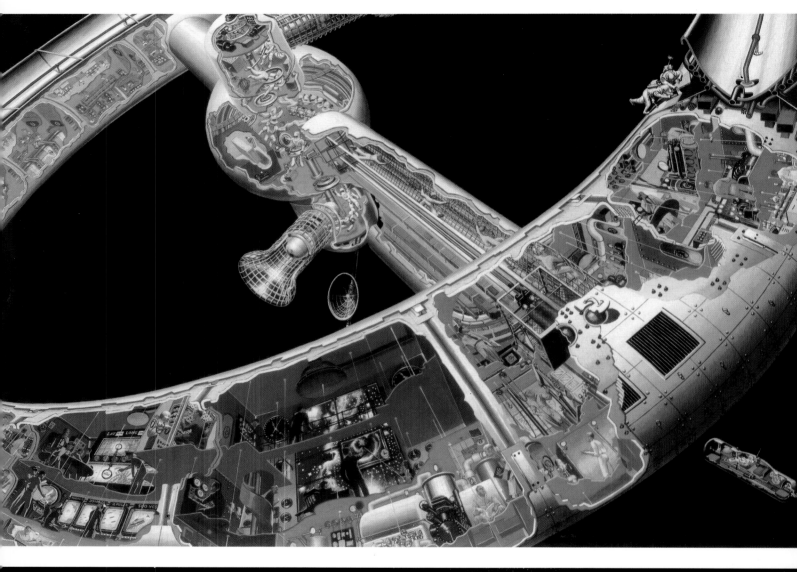

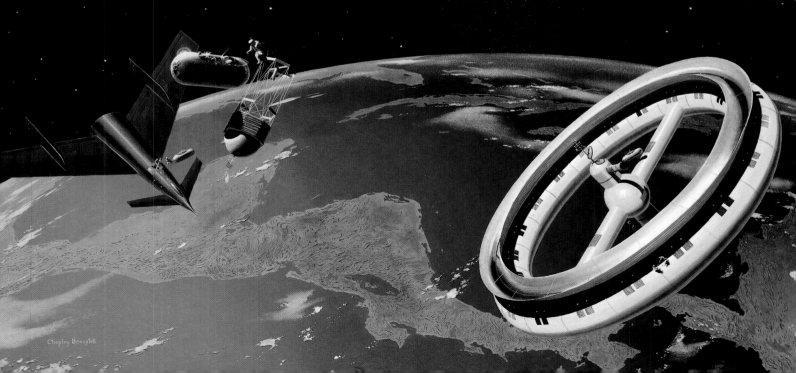

the station's men and equipment were to be devoted to military surveillance of potential U.S. enemies, and the telescope would be a handy tool for this kind of work.

Another advantage of the station was that it could act as a platform where interplanetary travel could begin and end. Thus a manned lunar surveying mission was planned. A nonstreamlined vehicle, assembled from components ferried up into orbit, was to leave for the Moon from the general proximity of the station. Upon reaching lunar orbit, the crew would begin to photograph the surface for possible future landing sites. Von Braun did not anticipate the advent of unmanned reconnaissance spacecraft such as Ranger, Surveyor, and Lunar Orbiter that NASA later developed to pave the way for the Apollo expeditions to the Moon. He projected that the entire program through manned reconnaissance of the Moon would cost $4 billion and take 10 to 15 years to accomplish.

Prior to the newsstand release of the magazine, Seth H. Moseley II, *Collier's* publicity director, organized a full-scale media campaign to promote the upcoming first space issue. The campaign, called "Operation Underground," included television appearances by von Braun; window displays of the *Collier's* artwork in the American Express offices in Manhattan and downtown Philadelphia; press publicity, which included sending out specially prepared major press releases to U.S. and foreign press associations and 12,000 daily newspapers; 2,800 press and radio kits for local radio and newspaper staffs and high school and college groups; and photo releases to all major photo syndicates. Live speaking engage-

ments by von Braun and Ryan also took place in New York and Washington, D.C.

Among von Braun's more important television appearances was his National Broadcasting Company (NBC) interview with John Cameron Swayze for the *Camel News Caravan.* An audience of five and a half million watched von Braun discuss manned space travel as a near-term event that could occur in the lifetimes of those who were listening. Other television appearances of note were interviews by Dave Garroway for NBC's *Today* with a viewership of two and a half million and Columbia Broadcasting System's *Gary Moore* with one million viewers. Scale models of the space station and launch vehicle were constructed under the direction of Gerd de Beek, a colleague of von Braun at Redstone Arsenal and formerly at Pennemünde. These models were convincing visual aides reinforcing von Braun's words for the television viewer.

Encouraged by the positive feedback received for its space issue, *Collier's* staff continued the series in the 18 and 25 October 1952 issues with von Braun's plan for sending a manned expedition to the Moon. Three nonstreamlined lunar landing ships, each 160 feet high, were to be assembled in Earth orbit out of prefabricated components lofted into space by giant launch vehicles. Two passenger ships would each accommodate a crew of 20 men, while the third would carry 10. This third craft would loft the necessary cargo for living on and exploring the lunar surface for six weeks. While traveling to the Moon, the crew would live in a "personnel sphere" located at the top of each ship.

Upon reaching the gravitational pull of the Moon, an automated system would control the ship's descent onto the surface. After landing, the crew would unload the cargo ship containing the mission's equipment. Three track-equipped lunar tractors would allow the explorers to travel a considerable distance from their base. The base itself was to be constructed out of the two halves of the cargo ship's hold. Each half would be lowered by crane into position within a lunar chasm. Setting up quarters below the lunar surface would provide protection against meteorite and cosmic radiation hazards. One-half of the hold would become a lunar laboratory, while the other would serve as living quarters. Each would contain its own life support system and draw power from a solar-powered turbogenerator placed on the lunar surface. Six weeks after landing on the Moon, the crews would split up

Wernher von Braun with a model of his reusable launch vehicle in Collier's New York office in March 1952. Ordway Collection/Space & Rocket Center.

and return to Earth orbit in the two passenger ships.

Von Braun projected that the cost for this advanced lunar expedition would be $500 million and that it could occur 15 years after the establishment of the space station and the undertaking of manned orbital reconnaissance.

Once again Moseley organized a coordinated media program in conjunction with the newsstand release of these two issues. Von Braun appeared on television and radio and gave interviews.

Collier's visible success led many other mainstream magazine and book publishers to begin to take space travel seriously. *Time* and *Look*, for example, featured articles on space travel during the period of the *Collier's* series. Viking Press, whose 1949 classic *Conquest of Space* had been written by Ley and illustrated by Bonestell,[5] contracted for two books based on the *Collier's* articles. *Across the Space Frontier*, published in September 1952, was an expansion of the *Collier's* 22 March 1952 issue; *Conquest of the Moon*, appearing a year later, expanded *Collier's* 18 and 25 October 1952 issues.

Responding to the flood of inquiries about how to become an astronaut, in the 28 February and 7 and 14 March 1953 issues, *Collier's* ran stories about the human aspects of space travel and the training of the men who would go into space. Various physical and psychological tests were described and illustrated. Extended training within high-pressure tanks, isolation chambers, and centrifuges reduced the number of candidates to a qualified few who would then continue the training in sophisticated astronavigation equipment and the use of emergency escape systems. The astronaut training program, laid out in these issues, could very well have formed the basis for training Mercury astronauts.

Publicity for the newsstand release of these issues was once again successfully handled by *Collier's* Moseley. The magazine received a great amount of positive feedback from elementary through high school–age boys who had been closely following the series. Many men who eventually went on to work in the U.S. space program attribute their initial spark of interest to the pages of *Collier's*.

The lunar cargo ship. This drawing was executed by von Braun in June 1952. Pencil on Keuffel and Esser engineering paper. Ordway Collection/Space & Rocket Center.

The seventh in the space series, appearing in the 27 June 1953 issue, focused attention on placing a "baby space station" containing specially trained Rhesus monkeys into a 200-mile-high Earth orbit. Researchers on Earth would have the opportunity to study the animals' reactions to prolonged weightlessness and possible cosmic radiation contamination via remote television cameras and telemetric sensors attached to the monkeys. Medical information would be vital to the success of any future manned mission. Twenty field stations, strategically placed around the globe, would receive data and transmit necessary course corrections to the station, which would remain in orbit for 60 days. Prior to the station's reentry and burning up in Earth's atmosphere, quick-acting lethal gas would kill the monkeys.

Von Braun claimed that the "cost of this project would be absorbed into the $4 billion ten year program to establish the [manned space] station. The baby station could be ready within five to seven years and five years later the manned station would be ready."[6]

Al Dann, who had taken over Moseley's position at *Collier's*, did not generate significant publicity for this issue. He did have von Braun travel to New York about a week before its newsstand release to record some radio and television interviews, which were aired about a week later. For its part, *Collier's* chose not to go to the expense of having de Beek create miniature scale models of von Braun's hardware.

During mid-summer 1953, *Collier's* decided to conclude its space series with a story of a manned expedition to Mars. The article, originally scheduled to follow the lunar expedition issues, was delayed due to the large number of readers requesting information about the training of astronauts. Later planned for release in the fall of 1953, the Mars article was again delayed due to political infighting. It transpired that Ryan, who had been editor of the first two *Collier's*-derived books, also wanted to edit the Mars book (which later appeared as *The Exploration of Mars*). When he learned that Chesley Bonestell and Willy Ley had already signed a contract with Viking to produce the book, Ryan became indignant and threw a monkey wrench into the *Collier's* Mars issue machinery, which delayed publication for six months. He did not easily accept the argument that back in 1950 Ley and Bonestell, knowing that Mars would be at perigee in relation to the Earth in

■

The baby space station in 200-mile-high Earth orbit. Long Island, New Jersey's shore, and Cape Cod are seen below. Bonestell painted this *for* Collier's *27 June 1953 cover. Oil on illustration board. Ordway Collection/ Space & Rocket Center.*

1956, had agreed to write a book for Viking that was to be published that very year.

When it finally came out, *Collier's* 30 April 1954 issue elaborated on von Braun's plan for a manned mission to the planet Mars. A flotilla of ten spacecraft were to be assembled in Earth orbit and launched toward the red planet on an eight-month journey. Once in Mars orbit, a manned landing "boat" would be assembled and glided to a soft landing. (At the time, it was believed that Mars had an atmosphere thick enough to make such a glide maneuver feasible.) The initial team was scheduled to land on the Martian north pole, from where it would travel to the equator in a combination tractor/living quarters vehicle. Arriving at an unobstructed area, the team was to prepare a safe landing strip for the additional landing boats that were still

orbiting the planet. Ultimately, a base was to be set up to house 70 explorers throughout the 15-month stay.

The eight-month journey to Mars and eight-month return to Earth would be the most stressful part of the mission. Living in proximity to other people and having little to do would severely test the psychological stability of each astronaut. Von Braun believed that such a Mars mission could take place within 100 years. He speculated that key technologies would emerge leading to a considerable reduction in travel time to and from the planet.

Collier's did not go to the trouble of generating concurrent newsstand release publicity for the Mars issue as they had on previous occasions; probably the long release delay had dampened management enthusiasm.

Many of von Braun's colleagues in the engineering and scientific community looked upon the *Collier's* space articles as speculative hoopla that served only the purposes of those who participated. But

history has clearly shown that the series was a seminal event in the space travel movement. They also formed the basis for three subsequent Walt Disney television films that brought space travel to an even higher level of public consciousness.

In the spring of 1954, Disney started to organize programing for his "Disneyland" television show, which was to be inaugurated on the American Broadcasting Company's network during the fall of that year. Each show was to follow one of the four themes of his Disneyland theme park then under construction: "Adventureland," "Frontierland," "Fantasyland," and "Tomorrowland." All but the last were covered by existing Disney films. Disney asked Ward Kimball, a key animator who had worked for the company since 1934 and been involved with such Disney classics as *Snow White and the Seven Dwarfs*, *Pinocchio*, and *Fantasia*, to come up with ideas for a television film segment to cover "Tomorrowland." Kimball told Disney about the *Collier's* space series that he had been following for the last two years;

The Challenge of Space: Linking Aspirations and Political Will

JOHN M. LOGSDON

Visions of space travel would have remained just visions, had they not become linked to individuals and organizations that controlled the resources necessary to turn vision into reality. In practice, this meant national governments and their leaders. In the years following World War II, the scope and expense of space travel were well beyond the means of private companies or wealthy individuals. Thus the story of the space era is not only a study of creative minds and human aspirations but also a story of the partnership between politics and dreams.

That partnership first came to fruition in the Soviet Union.[1] Like much in the history of space travel, it was linked to national security interests. The capability to launch an object of substantial weight into orbit or beyond is, in its basics, the same as the capability to launch weapons on ballistic trajectories over long distances. As the cold war rivalry between the United States and the Soviet Union emerged from the ruins of World War II, Soviet Premier Joseph Stalin gave top priority to two projects: the development of nuclear weapons and the development of rockets to carry those weapons across intercontinental distances. The Soviet Union, like the United States, profited from the experience of the German Peenemünde rocket team, but it was also able to build on the work of Soviet rocket pioneers Valentin Glushko and particularly Sergei Korolev.

By 1949, an all-Soviet upgrade of von Braun's V-2 rocket was tested. By 1952, an intermediate-range ballistic missile capable of carrying a warhead to targets in western Europe was in production. And by 1954, Korolev's design for a large intercontinental

missile to reach U.S. territory won Politburo approval. The first requirement for space travel, a booster with substantial lift capability, was under development.

In mid-1955, the Soviet Union announced its intention to launch an Earth satellite during the International Geophysical Year, which was to begin on 1 July 1957. But such a satellite launch only gained final approval after the first successful test of Korolev's booster, which occurred on 3 August 1957. In just over two months, the R-7 rocket launched Sputnik I, and the world would never be the same again.

The satellite launch was a propaganda bonanza for the Soviet Union. Within weeks, with the ebullient Nikita Khrushchev leading the way, the Soviet Union claimed that Sputnik not only validated Soviet claims to possessing a nuclear-tipped missile, but also demonstrated the overall scientific, economic, and political superiority of the Soviet society. Khrushchev may have been surprised by the worldwide acclaim that followed the satellite launch, but he was quick to recognize the profound propaganda victory. There was little doubt that the Soviet Union would continue to press for spectacular space achievements as long as Khrushchev was its leader. In doing so, it laid down a challenge to which the United States felt it had to respond.

The United States had also in 1955 announced its intent to launch a satellite during the International Geophysical Year. In contrast to the USSR, however, the Eisenhower administration separated the satellite project from rockets being developed for military purposes. When Wernher von Braun and his team claimed that they could launch a satellite in

1956 using the four-stage Redstone missile–based configuration known as Jupiter C (or Juno I) that they were then developing, Washington explicitly blocked such aspirations. The White House also seems to have dramatically underestimated the political significance of space achievement.

When the Sputnik launch forced a U.S. response, then, there had been little debate over the purposes that should guide U.S. space activities.[2] In the aftermath of Sputnik, President Eisenhower turned to his newly established Science Advisory Committee for counsel on the appropriate U.S. reaction, and that panel included scientists who saw space as an exciting new arena for discovery. They recommended a program focused on scientific return; the science advisers were also concerned that space science not divert money away from other fields of science, but rather be planned as a separate part of the overall national scientific effort.

The national security community was quick to sense the potential of space as an important arena for military and intelligence activities, not primarily in terms of active military operations but rather using space technology to perform necessary military support functions (such as communications, navigation, and weather forecasting) and surveillance functions central to strategic intelligence. From the start, there was little question that when space offered a more efficient or unique way of achieving a military objective, the Department of Defense would be authorized to carry out military-oriented space projects.

The capability to operate in space was also recognized early on as having the potential to lead to applications with both social and economic benefits, and this potential was seen as a legitimate justification for exploratory programs to investigate various applications. In particular, the potential of space technology for meteorological observation and for relaying communications was recognized as areas of early pay-off, and was rapidly pursued.

The most vigorous area of debate in the early years of the U.S. space program was over whether strategic political objectives such as national prestige ought to be pursued through space activity. The Eisenhower government explicitly rejected the idea of using large space technology projects to compete in symbolic, prestige-oriented accomplishments with the USSR; Eisenhower insisted on a policy of "calm conservatism" with respect to the political uses of space technology. This policy was diametrically reversed by President John F. Kennedy in May 1961, with his commitment to a man landing on the Moon "before this decade is out." Kennedy was straightforward in his rationale for Apollo; as he said in the speech announcing his decision, "no single space project in this period will be more exciting or more impressive to mankind."

In the annals of space travel, the initial tentative steps away from humanity's home planet that were taken during the Apollo program will clearly be milestones. Although travel to other celestial bodies had been a key element in the visions of the first half of the twentieth century, it was once again the linkage with political purposes and will that made these steps feasible. But when Kennedy took office on 20 January 1961, no one could have predicted that within four months he would create that link; thus, understanding how that decision was made is a key to understanding the early years of space travel.

The first months of 1961 were sobering for the new administration. Kennedy and his associates came to Washington pledged to get the country moving after eight years of Eisenhower presidency, but they seemed unable to make any substantial changes in government structures or activities. Late in March, after a month of intense deliberations, President Kennedy had almost decided to send American troops to fight the Communists in Laos; he rejected intervention only after learning that 60,000 troops would be needed. In Congress the ambitious New Frontier legislative program seemed bogged down.

Early on the morning of 12 April, even more galling news reached the White House. Before dawn in Washington, the Soviets announced that cosmonaut Yuri Gagarin had successfully orbited the Earth in his Vostok spaceship. The Soviet Union, first to launch a satellite in 1957, had now become the first country to achieve manned spaceflight. The Soviets were quick to capitalize on the propaganda significance of Gagarin's flight. Khrushchev, talking to Gagarin while he was still in orbit, boasted, "Let the capitalist countries catch up with our country." The Communist Central Committee claimed that the flight embodied "the genius of the Soviet people and the powerful force of socialism." Self-congratulation was not particularly necessary. The world was almost unanimous in admiration. Even the Vatican newspaper called the flight "a universal good."

Within a few hours, questioning and criticism began. Representative Victor Anfuso called for a full-scale Congressional investigation and suggested that the U.S. be "mobilized to a wartime basis" in order to beat the Soviets to the Moon. A Washington newspaper called the Gagarin flight "a psychological victory of the first magnitude for the Soviet Union." Kennedy told a late afternoon press conference on 12 April that "no one is more tired than I am" of being second to the Soviets in space, but that he hoped to find "other areas where we can be first and which will bring more long-range benefits to mankind."

However much Kennedy might have wanted to find some other arena of competition, within a few days he became convinced that the United States had to enter the space race in earnest. His science adviser, Jerome Weisner, remembers that "we talked a lot about whether we had to do this. He said to me, 'If you had a scientific spectacular on this earth that would be more useful or something that is just as dramatic and convincing as space, then we would do it.' " But, says Weisner, Kennedy "became convinced that space was the symbol of the twentieth century. It was a decision he made cold-bloodedly. He thought it was right for the country."

On the late afternoon of 14 April, Kennedy called a meeting to learn how to win the space race. Assembled in the cabinet room were Weisner; Kennedy's closest aide, Theodore Sorenson; Budget Director David Bell; NASA Administrator James E. Webb; and his deputy, Hugh Dryden. Kennedy wanted to know, "Is there any place we can catch them?" He got no clear answer. Dryden suggested an all-out lunar landing program, but Webb and Weisner were cautious, and Bell warned that the cost of such an undertaking could exceed $40 billion. At the end of the meeting Kennedy thought aloud: "When we know more, I can decide if it is worth it or not. If somebody can just tell me how to catch up." Then he turned to the others, adding, "There is nothing more important."

Kennedy's willingness to respond to the Soviet challenge was predictable, given the new president's views on the nature of his job and of the international and domestic political setting in which the challenge was placed. He believed in an activist pres-

■

President John F. Kennedy (left) *and NASA Administrator James E. Webb* (right). *NASA.*

idency and thought that he could couple his own forceful personality to the inherent power of the office in order to move the nation in the direction he chose. Kennedy, of course, came from a fiercely competitive family, and he was not accustomed to avoiding challenges. He held to the prevailing anti-Communist view of American foreign policy, one that saw the Soviet Union as a real threat to American security and to a democratic way of life. And Kennedy was an expert politician. He could sense public sentiment on an issue, and Sorenson says that "the Gagarin flight and the reaction to it around the world and in this country and in Congress demonstrated to the President the importance of going ahead with an all-out space effort and the willingness of the country and the Congress to back such an effort."

Sorenson also suggests that Kennedy had both "affirmative and negative" reasons for choosing to accelerate the space race. They were "affirmative in the sense that the United States intended to maintain its position of world leadership, its position of eminence in commerce, in science, in foreign policy and in whatever else might develop from space exploration. The negative side was that we did not want to have the Soviets dominating space to a point where, at some future time, it could be a military threat to our security." Weisner says Kennedy was concerned that "the rest of the world has been led to believe by Soviet space accomplishments, and particularly by the U.S. reaction to them, that the scientifically and technologically most competent nation now was the Soviet Union, not the United States. We were paying a price all kinds of ways—internationally, politically—and that was the issue the President was dealing with. Not was it time to go to the moon, but how could you get yourself out of this?"

Then came the Bay of Pigs. On 17 April United States–trained Cuban refugees attempted to invade Cuba and overthrow the Castro government. By the 19th Castro had crushed the invasion as the United States stood by, unwilling to intervene on behalf of its protégés. Pierre Salinger, Kennedy's press secretary, described these three days as the "grimmest" of Kennedy's time in the White House. How much Kennedy's state of mind resulting from the Cuban fiasco influenced or reinforced his resolve to proceed rapidly in space is not completely clear. The Bay of Pigs was never explicitly linked to changes in the space program during any of the meetings on space held at this time. But Weisner says of the Bay of Pigs, "I don't think anyone can measure it, but I am sure that it had an impact. I think the President felt some pressure to get something else in the foreground. It wasn't his primary motivation, but I think the Bay of Pigs put him into a mood to run harder than he might have." Sorenson says Kennedy's attitude was influenced by the fact the "the Soviets had gained tremendous worldwide prestige from the Gagarin flight at the same time we had suffered a loss of prestige from the Bay of Pigs. It pointed up the fact that prestige was a real, and not simply public relations, factor in world affairs."

Even though Kennedy seems to have decided as early as 14 April that he would approve an accelerated space program aimed at winning some firsts in the space race, he knew very little of the details of the space program. He needed more information before he could make a definitive decision. The day after the Bay of Pigs invasion collapsed, he acted to get that information. Kennedy's vice-president, Lyndon B. Johnson, did know a great deal about the space program. On the night that Sputnik I went into orbit in 1957, Johnson had set the wheels moving to begin a Congressional inves-

tigation of America's missile and space program by a Senate Subcommittee on Preparedness that he chaired. He was the chief Congressional architect of the bill establishing NASA in 1958. Then he became the Chairman of the Senate Aeronautical and Space Sciences Committee. After the 1960 election, Kennedy named Johnson to head the National Aeronautics and Space Council, the president's advisory body for space policy.

On 20 April Kennedy asked Johnson, as chairman of the Space Council, to make "an overall survey of where we stand in space" and especially to get information the president needed: "Do we have a chance of beating the Soviets by putting a laboratory in space, or by a trip around the moon, or by a rocket to land on the moon, or by a rocket to go to the moon and back with a man? Is there any other space program which promises dramatic results in which we could win?"

For the three years since Sputnik, Johnson had been an advocate of a more aggressive, politically oriented space program. He knew those in and out of government who shared his views. While Dwight Eisenhower was president, they had been unable to gain approval for space projects as ambitious as they thought were needed. After Sputnik the Eisenhower administration adopted a conservative space policy and stuck to that policy through the rest of Ike's second term. The policy ruled out a space race between the United States and the USSR. Now Kennedy had decided to reverse the Eisenhower policy, to enter the space race, and to approve space projects justified in political terms. Johnson called on his fellow space enthusiasts to help him prepare a new space program.

Given the presidential directive, Johnson quickly organized a series of meetings. It did not take long to find that there was a consensus on the project that gave the best chance of a U.S. first. Johnson's top staff assistant for space was Edward Welsh, who remembers that "running through the discussions was the theme, could we go to the moon, should we if we could, how much would it cost, what else did we need to do if we decided to go?" Answers to these questions were available, for much thought had already been given to the feasibility of a manned lunar landing program.

Both the air force and the army had developed plans for an ambitious military space program in the post-Sputnik rivalry for control of the nation's space

■

Left to right: *Senator Mer-* *and NASA Administrator*
rit Preston, Vice-President *James E. Webb at*
Johnson, President Kennedy, *Cape Canaveral. NASA.*

efforts. Each of these programs had featured a manned lunar landing as a goal; the services had thus developed preliminary analyses of what such an undertaking would require. One army plan, prepared by Wernher von Braun's team of German and American rocket experts (who worked at the Army Ballistic Missile Agency until it became part of NASA in July 1960) called for the establishment of a 12-man lunar outpost by the end of 1966.

In 1959, NASA planners also had chosen a lunar landing as the most valid goal of an advanced manned spaceflight program. Throughout 1959 and 1960, they studied ways of accomplishing this feat.

By 1960, their planning was advanced enough for NASA's leaders to ask for White House permission to begin building a spacecraft—called Apollo—for the initial steps toward a lunar landing: long-duration flight in Earth orbit and flights around the Moon. President Eisenhower refused to approve this request. His science advisers told him that the cost of a lunar landing would run from $34 to $46 billion and that this much money for space would not produce enough scientific knowledge to justify the investment. In December, just before leaving office, Eisenhower told NASA that he would not approve any project aimed at a lunar landing.

NASA did not abandon its plans; a new president would soon be in office. Meanwhile, a task force chaired by George Low made a quick but thorough assessment of all available material related to the lunar landing project. By the end of February 1961,

Low's group concluded that a lunar landing by 1967 was feasible. In late March, NASA asked President Kennedy to approve Project Apollo plans, but he deferred his decision. NASA had yet to launch a man into space, and the president preferred to wait for a few successful flights in Project Mercury before committing himself to a second-generation manned flight program.

The events of April altered the political climate, and Kennedy was no longer willing to wait. The planning that NASA had already done, which had convinced the agency's officials that a manned lunar landing was a technologically feasible goal, now was to be the basis for a decision to use the space program as an instrument of American political strategy. On 22 April, Webb told Johnson that "there is a chance for the U.S. to be the first to land a man on the moon and return him to earth if a determined national effort is made. A possible target date for a manned lunar landing is 1967."

Two days later the vice-president consulted space experts from the air force and navy and others whose judgment he trusted. Among those Johnson consulted, there was unanimous agreement that the lunar landing objective made sense. Wernher von Braun told the vice-president that the U.S. had "an excellent chance of beating the Soviets to the first landing of a crew on the moon." He believed that "a performance jump by a factor of 10 over their present rockets is necessary to accomplish this feat" and "therefore, we would not have to enter the race toward this obvious next goal in space exploration against hopeless odds favoring the Soviets." Von Braun thought that "with an all-out crash program" the U.S. could achieve a lunar landing by 1967 or 1968.

The next week was spent gaining assurances that the accelerated program would receive Congressional support. Finally, on Friday, 5 May, Johnson asked NASA and the Department of Defense to meet over the weekend to prepare a detailed set of recommendations incorporating the results of his consultations. Johnson wanted to present these to the president the following Monday before leaving on a two-week tour of Asia. That same Friday, Alan Shepard completed a 15-minute suborbital flight, thus becoming the first American in space. A wave of national relief and pride over this American success swept the country, removing whatever obstacles may have remained in the path of Kennedy's space decision.

Webb, Secretary of Defense Robert S. McNamara, and their staffs met at the Pentagon on 6 May. After an all-day session, they concluded that the manned lunar landing project did indeed provide the best chance of beating the Soviets to a spectacular space first. They thought that this project should be made a national goal in order to have both the international and domestic impact desired. A memorandum incorporating this recommendation and others concerned with every aspect of the space program was prepared the following day and given to the vice-president at noon Monday. Johnson approved the memorandum and gave it to Kennedy later that afternoon. Kennedy ratified the new space program without changing anything.

On 25 May, Kennedy announced his decision in a speech to a joint session of Congress:

Now is the time to take longer strides—time for a great new American enterprise—time for this nation to take a clearly leading role in space achievement, which in many ways may hold the key to our future on earth.

I believe that this nation should commit itself to achieving the goal, before this decade is out, of landing a man on the moon and returning him safely to the earth. I believe we should go to the moon.

Thus, less than four years after the launch of an initial primitive space probe, the United States committed itself to sending humans to another celestial body. The sheer bravado of that commitment is remarkable from the perspective of three decades later; there is little in history since to match it. And the commitment was made in the most public fashion.

We know that the Soviet Union, in secret, accepted Kennedy's challenge and entered a race to the Moon during the decade of the 1960s.[3] Europe, still struggling to recover from the devastation of World War II, chose to stand aside as the two superpowers competed in space. Only a modest cooperative European space science effort was begun in the early years of the Space Age, and Europe was dependent on U.S. launches for its access to space. By the mid-1960s, Europe attempted to create a cooperative launch vehicle development program, but without success. Although other countries began to launch satellites by the end of the 1960s, during the initial years of the Space Age only the United States and the Soviet Union regularly undertook space missions.

The U.S. response, then, was the dominant fea-

ture of the first decade of space travel. While the Soviet Union continued to pioneer in Earth orbit, sending aloft the first woman and the first multiperson crew and conducting the first space walk, its accomplishments paled in comparison to the grand sweep of human voyages to the Moon. The Apollo program was a worthy response to the ideas, images, and aspirations of the early space pioneers.

■

Left to right: Senator George Smathers, NASA Deputy Associate Administrator George Low, President Kennedy, astronauts Gordon Cooper and Virgil "Gus" Grissom, and Marshall Space Flight Center's Merritt Preston. A Gemini capsule is in the background. Courtesy NASA.

Notes

1. Much of the following information on early Soviet space activities is drawn from Walter J. McDougall, . . . *the Heavens and the Earth: A Political History of the Space Age* (New York, 1985: Basic Books).

2. The following account of the Apollo decision, including all quotations, is drawn from my *The Decision to Go to the Moon: Project Apollo and the National Interest* (Cambridge, 1970: MIT Press).

3. For a Soviet account of the Soviet lunar landing program, see the English translation of an article by Sergei Leskov, "How We Didn't Get to the Moon," which appeared in *Izvestiya*, 18 August 1969. The translation appears as Appendix A in Nicholas Johnson, *The Soviet Year in Space 1989* (Colorado Springs, 1990: Teledyne Brown).

For further reading

Clarke, Arthur C. *Profiles of the Future: An Inquiry into the Limits of the Possible*. New York, 1963: Harper & Row.

Logsdon, John. *The Decision to Go to the Moon: Project Apollo and the National Interest*. Cambridge, 1970: MIT Press.

McDougall, Walter J. . . . *the Heavens and the Earth: A Political History of the Space Age*. New York, 1985: Basic Books.

Wilford, John Nobel. *We Reach the Moon: The New York Times Story of Man's Greatest Adventure*. New York, 1969: Bantam Books.

Project Apollo in Retrospect

R. CARGILL HALL

Project Apollo, the astronautical venture that carried men to the Moon and returned them to Earth in the late 1960s and early 1970s, concluded twenty years ago. It has been viewed as a turning point in world history, a watershed in America's nascent space program, a marvel of technical and managerial ingenuity, and, occurring as it did at a time of stirring domestic social change, as an enormously expensive public diversion that wastefully shot billions of dollars into space. Whatever it may have been, as a public enterprise, Apollo—on virtually any scale of human endeavor save organized warfare—clearly was an undertaking of historic proportions.

Project Apollo cost $25.4 billion, about $95 billion in 1990 dollars. It launched astronauts to the Moon atop immense rockets that towered 36 stories high and produced 7½ million pounds of thrust at liftoff. For an entire decade this project consumed 51 percent of the budget of the National Aeronautics and Space Administration, the federal agency that directed and managed it. NASA committed to Apollo some 12,000 employees, about 30 percent of its personnel, while 17,000 American firms employing 300,000 engineers and scientists labored to produce its hardware and software. Moreover, the government created for Apollo and related NASA projects a vast array of space facilities around the United States, including what is today the Johnson Space Center at Houston, Texas, the Kennedy Space Center at Cape Canaveral, Florida, and a greatly expanded Marshall Space Flight Center at Huntsville, Alabama. During this period Apollo dominated the attention of NASA's leaders just as surely as it claimed, at least until the first lunar landing, the rapt attention of many Americans and their representatives in Congress.

■

Nearly full Moon, looking westward toward the large, circular Sea of Crises on the horizon. NASA.

Origins and First Years

President Dwight D. Eisenhower, who created NASA in the National Aeronautics and Space Act of July 1958, was not enamored of manned spaceflight. He had divided the nation's space effort between NASA-controlled civilian space science and application missions, and military spaceflight directed by the defense department. Eisenhower's interest and that of his scientific counselors focused on the instrumented satellites and space probes that contributed to increased scientific knowledge, on improved communications and weather reporting, and, increasingly toward the end of his second term in office, on military spaceflight efforts that, in an era of thermonuclear weapons and intercontinental rockets, promised advance warning of surprise attack. Although the president reluctantly accepted NASA's Mercury project, an attempt to orbit a man around the Earth, he opposed anything more than studies of future manned space missions including a NASA plan, called Apollo, that proposed eventually to fly a man to the Moon and return him to Earth. Indeed, in his last budget message, Eisenhower advised Congress that much more study would be needed simply to determine "whether there are any valid scientific reasons for extending manned space flight beyond the Mercury Program."

President John F. Kennedy received similar counsel from his science advisers when he assumed office in 1961. The American public, they told Kennedy, needed to better understand the importance of the instrumented military and scientific spacecraft that directly contributed to the nation's welfare, adding, "we should stop advertising Mercury as our major objective in space activities." While the new president considered their advice and the future of the nation's civil space program, he was soon overtaken and profoundly affected by international events (see preceding chapter). When he issued his bold challenge to land a man on the Moon before the end of the decade, few misunderstood the importance thus attached to Project Apollo: the outcome of the international political competition between the Soviet Union and the United States would turn in part on this quest for astronautical preeminence. The decision of the president and Congress, the author of NASA's apollo history observed, "owed nothing to any scientific interest in the moon. The primary dividend was to be national prestige."[1] Perhaps less obvious to those involved, the decision would focus America's civil space program almost entirely on the exacting and costly demands of manned space travel.

Whatever the understanding of Apollo's likely ramifications for the nation or the space agency, James E. Webb, whom President Kennedy selected as NASA administrator, knew well that he faced a staggering task. A former director of the Bureau of the Budget, Webb had encouraged the lunar landing decision. Now he was charged to design and build the system that would accelerate men into space at 25,000 miles per hour to escape the Earth's gravitational attraction, transport them to a celestial body 240,000 miles distant—itself traveling at 2,000 miles per hour relative to our planet—land them on its surface, and return them through the searing heat of atmospheric reentry *safely* to a landing on Earth *before* the end of 1969.

In the months and years that followed, Webb melded America's industries, universities, and crucial elements of the federal government into "a team of teams." To meet the overriding demands of Apollo within NASA, during 1961 he reorganized the space agency, dividing it between the Office of Manned Space Flight and what eventually became the Office of Space Science and Applications, the latter responsible for automatic satellites and space probes. Finally, he took the Space Task Group at the Langley Research Center in Virginia, charged with the Mercury project and now with all manned projects including Apollo, relocated that organization near Houston, Texas, and redesignated it the Manned Spacecraft Center.

At NASA headquarters in Washington, D.C., Webb worked closely with Robert C. Seamans, Jr., NASA's associate administrator, later deputy administrator, and he selected D. Brainerd Holmes, a hard-driving industrial executive, as director of the Office of Manned Space Flight. At Houston, Joseph F. Shea, the director responsible for Apollo spacecraft systems, reported to Holmes through the center director, Robert Gilruth. Altogether, NASA officials identified some 10,000 tasks that had to be accomplished to land man on the Moon and return him to Earth—each with its own particular objectives, manpower and funding requirements, and interrelated schedules. This complex of tasks was subdivided among NASA's centers, principally the Marshall Space Flight Center in Alabama, which would design and contract for the launch vehicles; a new center at Cape Canaveral, Florida, which would launch the manned lunar missions; the California

Institute of Technology's Jet Propulsion Laboratory in California, responsible for the large radio antennas needed to communicate with and receive data from spacecraft at lunar distances; and the Manned Spacecraft Center in Houston, which would contract for the spacecraft and integrate the efforts of the other centers.

Wernher von Braun, director of the Marshall Space Flight Center, lived and breathed manned space travel. When the German expatriate rocket team at Redstone Arsenal transferred from the army to NASA, becoming the George C. Marshall Space Flight Center in 1960, von Braun had already contracted for components of several enormous liquid-propellant rockets that if built, he assured NASA officials, could propel men to the Moon. The largest of these, called Saturn V, was a three-stage vehicle that clustered five Rocketdyne F-1 rocket engines in its first stage. Burning liquid oxygen and kerosene, each engine produced one and one-half million pounds of thrust. The second and third stages, NASA officials and von Braun agreed, would be driven by the more powerful combination of liquid oxygen and liquid hydrogen. In 1961, the Huntsville center also had plans on the drawing board for an even larger rocket called Nova that would cluster eight F-1 engines in its first stage for a combined thrust at liftoff of twelve million pounds. Whether a Saturn or a Nova would launch Apollo astronauts moonward, however, awaited a decision on just how the journey would be accomplished.

Late in 1961, NASA leaders considered three approaches for flying men to the Moon: direct ascent, Earth orbit rendezvous, and lunar orbit rendezvous. The first called for the entire spacecraft to be flown to the Moon and soft-landed, with enough propellant to lift off and return to Earth. Weight requirements dictated a Nova rocket for this strategy. Earth orbit rendezvous required two Saturn V rockets, with the payloads subsequently joined in Earth orbit and flown to the Moon. Finally, lunar orbit rendezvous envisioned a spacecraft and a two-stage lunar module that would detach itself from the spacecraft section in lunar orbit, descend to the lunar surface, and lift off again to rejoin the orbiting section for a

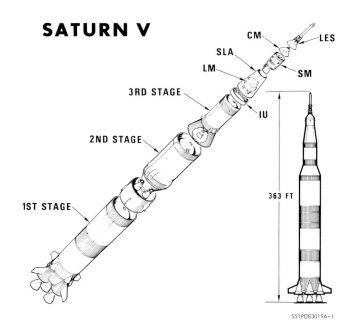

Saturn V, with the points of separation for each stage identified. NASA.

return to Earth. Though more complex, the latter mode possessed attractive features. Chief among them, perhaps, lunar orbit rendezvous could be launched with only one Saturn V, and in June 1962 NASA selected this course for Apollo.

The Marshall Center, meanwhile, completed contracting for the components of Saturn V. North American's Rocketdyne Division won the competition to build the second stage J-2 liquid oxygen–liquid hydrogen engines that would deliver 200,000 pounds of thrust. Five of them were to be clustered in Saturn V's second stage, and a single J-2 would power the third-stage rocket. Contracts for the rocket stages themselves went to the Boeing Company (first stage), North American Aviation (second stage), and Douglas Aircraft (third stage). To construct and test these stages, new facilities were acquired in Mississippi. To ship them between California, Mississippi, Alabama, and Florida, NASA would purchase and operate a small fleet of ships and barges.

With the decision for lunar orbit rendezvous, the Manned Spacecraft Center in Houston completed contracting for the Apollo spacecraft. Back in November 1961, North American Aviation had received contracts to design and build the three-man spacecraft and its associated command and service module, with a 20,500-pound-thrust engine to inject Apollo into lunar orbit and later bring it home. In November 1962, NASA selected Grumman Aircraft to build the two-stage lunar module that contained a 10,500-pound-thrust engine for descent and a 3,500-pound-thrust engine for ascent from the Moon's surface. All of these crucial parts had to work, or Apollo's astronauts would be stranded on the Moon or in lunar orbit.

Beginning in 1962, while the contracting was under way, the Office of Space Science and Applications at NASA headquarters pressed the Office of Manned Space Flight to include scientific instruments on Apollo that might help explain the Moon's origin and evolution. Engineers in Houston, intent on ensuring the safety of the astronauts, were reluctant to allocate the space, weight, and power needed for a scientific package. By early 1963, however, Maxime Faget, director of engineering and development in Houston, among others, realized that "it wouldn't look very good if we went to the moon and didn't have something to do when we got there."[2] In the months that followed, the center

staffed and contracted for an Apollo science component, and, in addition to test pilots, selected as astronauts a handful of scientists. American scientists in general, however, viewed the entire enterprise with ill-disguised disdain. Project Apollo was, after all, the first major national effort since World War II in which scientists were all but frozen out of positions of authority. An "engineering spectacular," they sniffed; or, as the editor of Science declared mordantly, Apollo as a public program simply represented "technological leaf raking."

But scientists had other reasons to complain. NASA's lunar program in the 1960s consisted of Apollo and three unmanned spaceflight projects: Ranger hard landers, Surveyor soft landers, and Lunar Orbiter vehicles that assayed and photographed the lunar surface. By 1964, however, these latter three spacecraft were redirected on missions in support of Apollo's engineering goals—locating landing sites and testing the bearing strength of the lunar surface. NASA deleted scientific instruments that interfered with this mission. At least to those scientists who had invested time and effort in the unmanned projects only to lose promised flight opportunities, the Apollo-project tail clearly wagged the lunar-program dog. Adding insult to injury, engineers in Houston insisted on calling Apollo a "program," not a project within a lunar program. The engineers were nonetheless correct; Project Apollo clearly drove NASA's lunar program—indeed, it dominated all activities of the space agency.

In September 1963, D. Brainerd Holmes, who directed Apollo in its formative period, clashed with Webb over funding of the project and left NASA to return to industry. He was succeeded by George E. Mueller, an electrical engineer who had guided air force missile and space projects for a major aerospace contractor, TRW. At NASA headquarters, Mueller reorganized the Office of Manned Space Flight and brought in a number of air force officers acquainted with his style of systems engineering management. First among them was Major General Samuel Phillips, named Apollo director at headquarters, who remained throughout the 1960s. Mueller and his staff evaluated the project and determined that the flight test program, methodically designed to evaluate each rocket stage and propulsion system in sequence before testing the entire Saturn ensemble including the spacecraft, would not succeed in time to meet President Kennedy's deadline for a manned lunar landing. He boldly ordered Saturn V to be tested "all up," that is, with all three stages *and* the spacecraft functioning on the first flight.

Lunar Flights Under Way

By the mid-1960s, Apollo contractors had completed spacecraft designs and mockups. After a design review on 23 November 1964, NASA officials authorized North American to begin manufacture of the command and service modules. But in the months that followed, manufacturing proceeded slowly. In a letter to North American's president in December 1965, Phillips expressed displeasure with the firm's progress, criticizing its attention to detail and quality control. Grumman's two-stage lunar module, in the meantime, passed a critical design review, but manufacture of this component also lagged behind schedule, threatening to delay Apollo flight tests.

At Cape Canaveral, workers completed Apollo's launch facilities on Merritt Island, which comprised a major part of the Kennedy Space Center. The director of launch operations, Rocco Petrone, oversaw construction of a 52-story Vertical (later, Vehicle) Assembly Building, or VAB, that dominated its flat, sandy surroundings. Essentially a giant shell containing overhead cranes and other equipment to stack and test the Saturn V indoors, it possessed an interior volume greater than that of the Empire State Building. A short distance away, Launch Complex 39, composed of two launching pads, stood ready to receive the first Moon rocket. To move the 363-foot-high Saturn V and its mobile launch platform from the VAB to Launch Complex 39, NASA contracted for immense, tracked crawlers. Each featured eight separate tanklike tracks; the cleats on these treads each weighed one ton. A hydraulic leveling system kept the Saturn V within one degree of absolute vertical atop the platform as the crawler made its way slowly from the VAB to its launch pad at a speed of one mile per hour. On 25 May 1966, a crawler successfully moved a Saturn V mockup, complete except for engines and spacecraft, over the prescribed route. The first complete Saturn V moved from the VAB to Launch Complex 39 on 20 August 1967.

Meanwhile, at nearby Launch Complex 34, an electrical short circuit occurred in an Apollo spacecraft atop a smaller Saturn IB during routine tests on 27 January 1967. In the resulting fire, three astronauts died. Design of the Apollo spacecraft, based on high-altitude aeronautical cockpits, featured a pure oxygen cabin environment. The cabin pressure on the ground, at sixteen pounds per square inch (psi), slightly greater than the air pressure outside, was to be reduced in space to five psi. Soaked in pure oxygen at sixteen psi, however, virtually any nonmetallic substance will burn. Indeed, in that environment a match flame could ignite the flesh of a man's hand. George M. Low, who succeeded Shea as Apollo spacecraft director at Houston in April 1967 after the fire investigation, later conceded: "Incredible as it may sound, we had all been blind to the problem . . . we had overlooked the [fire] hazard on the launching pad."[3]

At North American, redesign of the Apollo command and service modules ensured electrical integrity, and reliability and quality assurance efforts intensified. Engineers at Houston led by Faget corrected the cabin environment oversight by altering the cabin atmosphere on the ground to a mix of sixty percent oxygen and forty percent nitrogen at sixteen psi, slowly converting to pure oxygen in space at five psi. A compromise between the demands of fire retardance and those of medicine (too much nitrogen would cause "the bends" as pressure decreased), it would succeed admirably. Nonetheless, the fire at Launch Complex 34 delayed Project Apollo many months, again threatening a lunar landing by decade's end. NASA leaders began to speak of 1970 as the tenth year in the Apollo decade.

The first major test of the complete system, known as Apollo 4, took place on 9 November 1967 when an "all up" Saturn V propelled an unmanned command and service module 10,000 miles into space. Subsequently, rocket engines drove the spacecraft back into the atmosphere at a lunar return velocity of 25,000 miles per hour. The heat shield, subjected to half the surface temperature of the Sun during reentry, performed perfectly. Apollo 5, launched atop a Saturn IB on 22 January 1968, flew an unmanned two-stage lunar module for the first time. Computers on board shut down the descent engine prematurely during its test, however, and Grumman officials asked for another qualification flight in Earth orbit. After a technical evaluation, Low demurred; the next flight of the lunar module would be manned.

Other test flights followed in rapid succession. A Saturn V launched Apollo 6 a few months later, on 4 April 1968. This flight, supposed to be a simple repeat of Apollo 4, failed to accomplish its objectives when the giant booster malfunctioned during ascent. The unmanned spacecraft entered Earth orbit, nevertheless, and was later retrieved in the Pacific Ocean. Launch of the first manned flight, Apollo 7, occurred on 11 October using another Saturn IB. During the eleven-day, Earth-orbiting mission, three astronauts completed all of the spacecraft test objectives. Back in August, Low had proposed that the first manned Saturn V mission, Apollo 8, scheduled in December, be flown around the Moon instead of into Earth orbit. With the success of Apollo 7, his daring plan was adopted.

At the close of 1968, social and political turmoil gripped the United States. The 12-month death toll of American servicemen in a growing Southeast Asian war reached 15,000, and President Lyndon B. Johnson, principal architect of the nation's costly commitment in Vietnam, had declined to seek re-election. The assassinations of Robert Kennedy and Martin Luther King, riots near the Democratic national convention in Chicago, and the torching of city neighborhoods underscored tensions across the land. These unhappy events seemed hardly the mileposts of an economic and political system that slain President John F. Kennedy believed would eclipse Soviet attempts to establish a rigid, communist world order. But at year's end, Americans found reason to hope.

On 21 December 1968, Apollo 8 carried three astronauts to the Moon. They orbited the Earth's celestial neighbor for twenty hours before returning safely to a splashdown in the Pacific on 27 December. During this Christmastime mission, the first men to circle the Moon read from Genesis and photographed this barren, lifeless satellite, and its beautiful blue planet swathed in clouds, suspended in a black void. A U.S. postage stamp of one picture subsequently appeared in May 1969 and circulated widely. About this time Buckminster Fuller coined the term "spaceship earth," drawing attention to our fragile world where all peoples, for better or worse, had somehow to share its soil, water, and air.

The triumph of Apollo 8 set the stage for the first attempt at a manned lunar landing in 1969. Among project officials in Houston, Huntsville, and Washington, D.C., however, knowledge of the dangers

■

This view of rising Earth greeted Apollo 8 astronauts on 24 December 1968 as their spacecraft appeared from be- *hind the Moon after the lunar orbit insertion burn. NASA.*

that attended that endeavor tempered the worldwide praise that greeted the circumlunar flight. Moreover, the lunar landing module had still to be proven in space. On 3 March 1969, Apollo 9 astronauts entered Earth orbit for ten days and completed all phases of docking and maneuvers with the delicate lander. To confirm these operations, on 18 May, Apollo 10 carried another three astronauts and the lander into lunar orbit. On the fifth day, with two men on board, the lunar module separated and descended to a lower orbit, only 10 miles above the Moon, confirming proper operation of the descent engine and landing radar. After ascending once more, the lunar lander rejoined the command and service module piloted by the third astronaut, and all three men returned to a safe recovery in the Pacific Ocean on 26 May. The nearly flawless performance of Apollo 10's uncounted thousands of components paved the way for a manned lunar landing attempt in 1969.

At space agency headquarters in Washington, key leaders who had brought Apollo to the lunar landing attempt had already begun to depart. NASA

Deputy Administrator Seamans left in January 1968 and was succeeded by Thomas O. Paine, a General Electric executive and committed proponent of manned spaceflight. NASA Administrator James Webb resigned in October 1968 to establish a law practice in Washington, D.C., and Paine took over as Acting Administrator. In April 1969, President Richard M. Nixon formally named Paine NASA Administrator. If President Kennedy's 1961 challenge were to be met, a new NASA administrator and a Republican president would preside.

On a warm, clear Florida morning, at 9:32 A.M. Eastern Daylight Time on 16 July 1969, Apollo 11 rose from Launch Complex 39 on a roaring column of flame. Spectators at the scene and television viewers around the world watched the Saturn V ascend skyward until it disappeared from view. Four days later, the lunar lander separated from the Moon-orbiting command module and descended to the lunar surface in an area known since the eighteenth century as the Sea of Tranquility, touching down successfully at 4:18 P.M. EDT on 20 July. A short time later Neil Armstrong, clad in a bulky space suit, emerged from the lander, clambered down a ladder, and became the first human to set foot on the Moon. Armstrong and his colleague Edwin Aldrin inspected the lunar module, spoke briefly with President Nixon, and, in a genuflection to nationalist sentiment expressed in Congress, erected an American flag. Thereafter they placed scientific instruments on the surface and began collecting rock and soil

samples. Altogether, the two men spent 21½ hours on the Moon. Then, on 21 July while the world waited, the lunar module ascended from the Moon and rendezvoused with the orbiting command module piloted by Michael Collins for a return flight to Earth. On 24 July 1969, the three astronauts landed safely in the Pacific Ocean amid world-wide acclaim. Apollo had succeeded.

The remaining Apollo flights followed afterward at approximately six-month intervals, as can be seen in the accompanying table, concluding with Apollo 17 in December 1972. All save one proved successful, and in the one failed attempt no astronauts were lost. Each mission increased the time spent on the Moon, and later flights carried small electric vehicles used by the astronauts to travel over the lunar surface. The scientific instruments emplaced and the soil samples returned to Earth added considerably to our understanding of our satellite's composition and evolution, though they did not conclusively answer the question of the Moon's origin. Only the last mission carried a geologist-astronaut to the Moon, and many American scientists judged this a belated concession, even a slight, on the part of NASA's leaders. To be sure, having courted scientists' participation in Apollo, NASA Administrator Paine canceled the last three planned missions (Apollo flights 18–20) in 1970 after Congress significantly reduced funding of the space agency. That decision, whatever its justification, Cornell University astronomer Thomas Gold, among others, judged grievously short-sighted. It was, he snapped, akin to "buying a Rolls Royce and then not using it because you claim you can't afford the gas!"

In truth, Project Apollo's early termination resulted as much or more from its remarkable success as it did from any anti–space science bias within the Office of Manned Space Flight. After the first lunar landing, public enthusiasm waned precipitously. Although the one aborted flight, Apollo 13, momentarily revived attention, each successive Apollo mission demonstrated the remarkable to be routine. For many Americans, Apollo 11 clearly bested the

■

Apollo 11 lifts off on 16 July 1969 from Launch Complex 39, Kennedy Space Center, on the first manned lunar landing mission. NASA.

Mission	Crewmen[1]	Landing Data			Extravehicular Activity			Samples Collected (kg)	Surface Stay Time (hr:min:sec)
		Area	Date	Time (GMT) (hr:min:sec)	Traverse Vehicle	Distance Traveled (km)	Duration (hr:min:sec)		
Apollo 11	Armstrong Aldrin	Sea of Tranquility	7/20/69	20:17:40	None	~1	02:31:40[2]	21.0	21:36:21
Apollo 12	Conrad Bean	Ocean of Storms	11/19/69	06:54:36	None	1st: ~1 2nd: 1.3	1st: 03:56:03[3] 2nd: 03:49:15[3]	1st: 16.7 2nd: 17.6	31:31:12
Apollo 14	Shepard Mitchell	Fra Mauro	2/5/71	09:18:11	Modular equipment transporter	1st: ~1 2nd: 3.0	1st: 04:47:50[4] 2nd: 04:34:41[4]	1st: 20.5 2nd: 22.3	33:30:31
Apollo 15	Scott Irwin	Hadley-Apennine	7/30/71	22:16:29	LRV-1	1st: 10.3 2nd: 12.5 3rd: 5.1	1st: 06:32:42[4] 2nd: 07:12:14[4] 3rd: 04:49:50[4]	1st: 14.5 2nd: 34.9 3rd: 27.3	66:54:53
Apollo 16	Young Duke	Descartes	4/21/72	02:23:35	LRV-2	1st: 4.2 2nd: 11.1 3rd: 11.4	1st: 07:11:02[4] 2nd: 07:23:11[4] 3rd: 05:40:03[4]	1st: 29.9 2nd: 29.0 3rd: 35.4	71:02:13
Apollo 17	Cernan Schmitt	Taurus-Littrow	12/11/72	19:54:57	LRV-3	1st: 3.3 2nd: 18.9 3rd: 11.6	1st: 07:11:53[4] 2nd: 07:36:56[4] 3rd: 07:15:08[4]	1st: 14.3 2nd: 34.1 3rd: 62.0	74:59:40

[1] Commander listed first, Lunar Module Pilot, second.
[2] Based on times of hatch opening and closing.
[3] Based on times of egress and ingress.
[4] Based on times at which cabin pressure reached 3.0 psi during depressurization and repressurization.

Soviets in space and it was time, as it was at the end of World War II, "to bring the boys home." The nation's attention quickly turned to other, pressing domestic and international concerns. Congressmen recognized the change, and NASA's appropriation for fiscal year 1970 amounted to $3.7 billion, almost 10 percent less than for fiscal 1969, 25 percent less than for the space agency's peak year, fiscal 1965. At NASA headquarters, Paine and his new team of managers had little choice but to cancel some major civil space efforts—especially if they wished to undertake other manned spaceflight projects.

Apollo: The End of the Beginning?

When the Apollo 17 spacecraft landed in the Pacific Ocean on 19 December 1972, it rang down the curtain on America's manned lunar landing project. A few weeks later on 22 January 1973, 1,100 NASA officials, astronauts, scientists, and representatives of industry convened to celebrate the event in Washington, D.C., at what the *Washington Post* termed "the last splashdown party." Unable to attend, former president Lyndon Johnson penned them a

note earlier that day, a few hours before he died, hailing Apollo as "one of the real wonders of the world." Johnson's death unquestionably tempered festivities that evening, though partygoers uniformly looked forward to a bright space future. Apollo's director at NASA headquarters, Rocco Petrone, whom Paine had selected back in August 1969 to succeed General Phillips, informed reporters that the end of Apollo was by no means the end of the play. "It's the curtain at the end of the first act," he asserted. "It's just the beginning."

Petrone's remarks referred obliquely to NASA plans for a new manned spaceflight effort. One year earlier in January 1972, President Nixon had approved the design and manufacture of a manned launch vehicle called the space shuttle. The orbiting section of this launcher, which resembled a small airliner with delta wings, could be flown into space and back to a landing on Earth—and be reused for as many as fifty flights. The cost savings, NASA officials advised Congress, would make numerous space missions economical and render obsolete the larger, more costly expendable launch vehicles such as Saturn V. Indeed, to save more funds back in January 1970, before the space shuttle was authorized, Paine had also canceled further production of the Saturn V. During the next few years at contractor plants around the country, Saturn jigs and dies were broken up and, along with most engineering drawings, thrown out. The United States no longer possessed a replicable heavy-lift launch vehicle.

Although Congress approved the space shuttle, its representatives insisted that NASA build the vehicle at an unrealistically low cost, a misguided bargain to which NASA leaders agreed. The unhappy consequences became all too apparent in the years that followed Apollo. Beset with technical and managerial difficulties, the space shuttle lagged far behind schedule and its costs more than doubled. Worse for NASA and the air force, which also supported its development, the new manned launch vehicle would prove uneconomical to maintain and operate. To make it more economical, subsequent NASA and defense department leaders sought to employ four space shuttles as the *only* launch vehicles for all American space missions, civil and military, but these hopes exploded in January 1986 along with space shuttle *Challenger*. America's aerospace industry was hurriedly called upon to reopen production lines and again provide expendable, midsize launch vehicles. Ironically, almost twenty years after Apollo 11 landed on the Moon, NASA and the defense department petitioned Congress for funds to build another expendable heavy-lift launch vehicle equivalent to Saturn V, called the Advanced Launch System, or ALS.

NASA Administrator James Webb's 1961 Apollo reorganization that divided the space agency between manned and unmanned spaceflight offices prefigured the skewing of astronautical priorities. Though Webb himself may have viewed this focusing of talent and resources as a temporary expedient, proponents of manned spaceflight dominated NASA's leadership after 1969. In the years that followed, they assiduously preserved his separation of the two spaceflight constituencies, selected for executive and legislative approval new manned flight objectives first, and claimed for them the lion's

■

Apollo 11 astronaut Edwin E. Aldrin, Jr., descends the ladder on Apollo's Lunar Module as he prepares to take his first steps on the Moon, 20 July 1969. NASA.

■

On the Sea of Tranquility, Aldrin deploys the passive seismic experiments package. The Apollo Lunar Module is in the center background. Already deployed nearby is the laser ranging retro-reflector, and, in the far left background, the black and white lunar surface television camera. NASA.

share of the space agency budget. The unmanned space science and applications missions that were sanctioned would be designed to launch on, and eventually wait for, the manned space shuttle. Ultimately, NASA launches of automatic vehicles to investigate the solar system temporarily ceased between 1977 and 1989—hardly the index of a vibrant American space exploration program.

Besides the pronounced effects it had on the space agency and future direction of American civil and military spacefaring, what of Project Apollo itself? Two decades later, what can be said of its significance? Apollo unquestionably demonstrated before the world the vitality and ingenuity of American industry, extraordinary skills in organization, and consummate technical prowess. And the landing of humans on the Moon in 1969 undeniably marked a turning point in world history—though the event hardly matched the hyperbole generated in the news media. Many observers compared this first manned voyage to another world with Columbus's discovery of America. Instead of rich new lands and peoples to be conquered, however, the astronauts trod an inhospitable, airless landscape composed of inorganic matter. But however formidable the Moon may be for future colonists, the 1969 lunar landing clearly fulfilled President Kennedy's cold war challenge.

Indeed, Apollo surpassed contemporary Soviet space efforts by a wider margin and influenced them in more ways than the young president might have imagined. The Soviet Union did accept the challenge of a manned lunar landing, but abandoned that effort in 1972 after the Russian equivalent of the Saturn V failed in four consecutive flight tests. Thereafter, the Soviet space program increasingly emphasized manned spaceflight, albeit with small space stations in earth orbit, even imitating NASA's uneconomic space shuttle with a copy of its own. Furthermore, to reassert influence in world events after the 1962 Cuban missile crisis, the Soviet Union also competed with the United States in military armaments and military assistance to the Third World. By the autumn of 1989 the Soviet economy was bankrupt, and, in the USSR and eastern Europe, the centrally planned world of communism began to unravel. To the extent that Project Apollo contributed to these later events, too, it succeeded.

One other, unforeseen effect of this project may yet prove to be its most enduring contribution. The real legacy of Apollo, NASA's space science chief Homer Newell later observed, was not in directing man's imagination and attention outward, but, instead, focusing them inward toward our own "spaceship earth." If the photographs returned by Apollo impressed on our minds the validity of the Copernican view, they also made plain "earth's insignificance in the cosmic scale" and its "uniqueness and overwhelming significance on the human scale."[4] To be sure, the environmental movement, which noticeably began to stir in 1962 after publication of Rachel Carson's *Silent Spring,* was galvanized in 1969; in 1970 President Nixon established the Environmental Protection Agency, Yale University students formed what became the Natural Resource Defense Council, the U.S. issued a four-stamp antipollution commemorative that featured a view of the entire Earth from space, and the first "Earth Day" was held in the United States.

When Project Apollo ended, a backwater political and social issue became mainstream, not just in America, but in succeeding years throughout all of the world's industrialized nations. Apollo's role in this change, it is reasonable to believe, was far greater than any coincidence in timing. People saw their world more clearly than ever before, a lovely "blue marble" in the vastness of space, and agreed that its environment should be preserved and protected. If pollution of the Earth's air, soil, and water is eventually controlled, thereby ensuring for future generations at least the quality of life we know today, it will be owed in part to those who planned, designed, built, and guided this twentieth-century astronautical adventure.

Notes

1. William Compton, *Where No Man Has Gone Before: A History of Apollo Lunar Exploration Missions* (Washington, D.C., 1989: National Aeronautics and Space Administration Special Publication 4214).

2. Ibid.

3. George M. Low, "The Spaceships," in Edgar M. Cortright, ed., *Apollo Expeditions to the Moon* (Washington, D.C., 1975: National Aeronautics and Space Administration Special Publication 350).

4. Homer E. Newell, "The Legacy of Apollo," in ibid.

For further reading

Air and Space 4, no. 2 (June/July 1989) (special Apollo anniversary edition).

Aldrin, Edwin. *Return to Earth*. New York, 1973: Random House.

Armstrong, Neil, Michael Collins, and Edwin Aldrin. *First on the Moon*. Boston, 1970: Little, Brown and Company.

Borman, Frank. *Countdown*. New York, 1988: William Morrow.

Collins, Michael. *Carrying the Fire*. New York, 1974: Farrar, Straus and Giroux.

Compton, William. *Where No Man Has Gone Before: A History of Apollo Lunar Exploration Missions*. Washington, D.C., 1989: National Aeronautics and Space Administration Special Publication 4214.

Cortright, Edgar, ed. *Apollo Expeditions to the Moon*. Washington, D.C., 1975: National Aeronautics and Space Administration Special Publication 350.

Hallion, Richard, and Tom Crouch, eds. *Apollo: Ten Years Since Tranquility Base*. Washington, D.C., 1979: Smithsonian Institution Press.

Logsdon, John. *The Decision to Go to the Moon: Project Apollo and the National Interest*. Cambridge, 1970: MIT Press.

Murray, Charles, and Catherine Cox. *Apollo: The Race to the Moon*. New York, 1989: Simon and Schuster.

O'Leary, Brian. *The Making of an Ex-Astronaut*. Boston, 1970: Houghton Mifflin Company.

Schirra, Walter. *Schirra's Space*. Boston, 1988: Quinlan Press.

Space Policy Institute. *Apollo in Its Historical Context*. Washington, D.C., 1990: George Washington University.

Now That Man Has Reached the Moon, What Next?

WERNHER VON BRAUN
Introduction by Ron Miller

Wernher von Braun stands alone in the history of rocketry and space travel. Influenced in his youth by the space travel science fiction of Jules Verne, Kurd Lasswitz, and others, young von Braun went on to play a key role in the design and development of the V-2, the world's first successful large-scale rocket system. At the end of World War II he and over 100 key members of his team moved to the United States, where he was quickly acknowledged as the world's most experienced rocket engineer. In the decades that followed, he was responsible for designing many military and civilian rocket systems, culminating in the giant Saturn V launch vehicle that carried Apollo astronauts to the Moon.

In addition to his work as an engineer and designer, von Braun also devoted much time and energy to the popularization of spaceflight. The golden age of spaceflight—that period during the 1950s and 1960s when the subject was probably at its peak of interest with the American public—was created almost single-handedly by him. Spaceflight had never before had—and perhaps may never have again—such a charismatic spokesman. Von Braun seemed to be everywhere, speaking and writing about the exploration of space in passionate, convincing terms. Unlike other proselytizers, such as G. Edward Pendray, David Lasser, Arthur C. Clarke, and Willy Ley, von Braun never spoke of the manned exploration of space as a matter for the distant future. He told the postwar American public that spaceflight was quite literally around the corner, that the technology and know-how already existed; all that was lacking was the money

and the will. In magazine articles such as the now-classic *Collier's* series and *First Men on the Moon*, and television programs such as the Disney *Man in Space* series, von Braun relentlessly and convincingly preached the gospel of astronautics.

The following article in which he attempts to foresee the near future of spaceflight from the perspective of the Apollo 11 Moon landing, is a rare example of late von Braunian optimism, written just before something occurred that he probably would have considered unthinkable: Americans turned their back on their commitment to spaceflight.

Serious attempts to predict the future are almost as foredoomed to failure as their more flamboyant counterparts in the supermarket tabloids, although for quite different reasons. There is no question that von Braun, especially when he discussed the future of space travel, was far more knowledgeable and authoritative than, say, W. A. Criswell or Jeanne Dixon are about anything. Yet he could be just as wrong, or so it would seem—such as when he predicted in the following article that "completely reusable orbital space shuttle vehicles" would eventually reduce the cost of carrying payloads into orbit to $50 a pound or less. Our current partially recoverable shuttles cost from $200 to $250 million to launch, delivering 40,000 to 50,000 pounds into orbit. This is about $5,000 a pound—ten times what von Braun said 1969 expendable vehicle costs were and a hundred times what he hoped they would be for his fully recoverable shuttles in the future!

Von Braun also expected the Apollo program to continue until all of its available Saturn V rockets were expended—nine more lunar landings after Apollo 11. In reality, the program was abruptly canceled after Apollo 17, leaving three of the giant boosters—still the largest, most powerful ever constructed—to go unused. The United States put its fleet of space vehicles, its teams of technicians, and its astronauts "on ice." The result was that even if we could assemble one of the giant boosters today, the highly specialized industrial teams with the expertise needed to carry out a launch have all long ago been scattered throughout the private sector. The remaining Saturn Vs have literally become museum pieces. Or how could von Braun have foreseen that once we had erected his "Saturn Workshop"—which manifested itself as Skylab—we would abandon it after scarcely six months of active use, allowing it to fall back into the Earth's atmosphere, to burn up?

If von Braun failed anywhere, it was not in his technical knowledge of what *could* have been done. Virtually everything he predicts in the following article was well within the realm of reasonable possibility at the time he was writing (and to give him full credit, he was dead-on in his expectations for the potentials of weather, communications, and Earth resource satellites). He is careful to remind us repeatedly that it is not so much technical obstacles that we need concern ourselves with as ones of finance and determination. If he suffered from anything, it was an almost naïve optimism—surprisingly so considering his vast and all too often painful experience with bureaucracies, from the Third Reich to the Nixon administration. However, I do not believe that without his almost childlike sense of wonder, and that all too rare ability to look toward higher and more glorious goals beyond the petty lack of imagination, blindness, and boondoggery that ties most of the human race to the surface of the Earth, Wernher von Braun would have been the inspiration and driving force that he was.

Von Braun's failure was not that of incorrectly predicting the events of future space exploration, but rather of incorrectly predicting continued—and increasing—enthusiasm and financial support.

All in all, it does not matter that, looking from the triumphal success of the Apollo 11 landing, von Braun understandably saw only a future of continued progress in space. It is not terribly important, perhaps, that we only had one spacecraft orbiting Mars in 1971, as opposed to the pair that he envisaged, or that we did not have landers on Mars until 1976. We would only be quibbling about timing. What *is* important is that von Braun was certain that it could be done at all, and that it should be done. Was he being overly optimistic? Perhaps; but on the other hand, it may have been that very optimism that helped these events take place at all.

At the end of his article, von Braun discusses a manned mission to Mars, a subject always dear to his heart. There is little question that any future expedition to that planet will bear little resemblance to his scenario—his earliest foreseeable date for its launch is already half a decade behind us—yet that is of no more real importance than it was that the history of spaceflight did not follow the outline presented in the *Collier's* series.

Von Braun's article is like the alternate histories of science fiction, in that it shows us a 1990s that *might have been*. How can we read the following chapter and not wonder what happened to Apollos 18, 19, and 20, or to the cheap, daily flights of the space shuttle, or the Martian expeditions of the 1980s? In truth, the failure of many of von Braun's expectations seems to lie not in his overconfidence, but in our lack of confidence; not in his inability to grasp reality, but in our refusal to face it.

In late January 1969, von Braun received a letter from his old *Collier's* buddy, Cornelius Ryan. Ryan asked von Braun to write an article for *Reader's Digest* about his ideas on America's future in space.

After a few revisions, the article was finished and sent to Ryan in early October. Ryan felt that von Braun's writing style was unsuitable for *Reader's Digest*. During the next few months, NASA's William J. Bolce, Director of Special Staff for Manned Space Flight Field Center Development, rewrote the article. At the end of January 1970 Bolce submitted his version of the von Braun article to Ryan.

One month later, Ryan wrote a letter to Hobart Lewis, the editor-in-chief at *Reader's Digest*, agreeing with Lewis's decision to shelve von Braun's article. In his letter, Ryan articulated his true feelings about von Braun and the space program:

Seriously, cynical as that may be, the truth is that the tone of this country right now, in my honest opinion, is not very conducive to large expenditures on the space program. Von Braun, in spite of all his protestations, would like to keep on spending like a drunken sailor because, after all, space and its exploration is his life-time dedication.

I am glad, however, to get your note [about canceling von Braun's article] because both von Braun and the NASA chief, Bill Bolce, have been bugging me for weeks. I'll let them down gently and at the earliest moment take von Braun to "21" [a noted New York restaurant], gaze into his deep, blue Teutonic eyes, put a drink in his fist, and blast him off to Aquarius![1]

Ryan realized that the Apollo era was, in effect, over after only two lunar landings. Hence the article was canceled.

Here, printed for the first time, in slightly edited form, is von Braun's post-Apollo blueprint.

The landing on the Moon was a beginning, not an end. With the successful flight of Apollo 11, mankind took its first step on another heavenly body. We also demonstrated our capability to accomplish today what seemed impossible yesterday. It is now clear that we can seriously consider unmanned spaceflight missions to the farthest corners of our solar system; manned stations in Earth orbit or on the Moon; reusable space vehicles that can shuttle passengers, scientific gear, and supplies to an orbital base at a tiny fraction of today's cost; nuclear space vehicles for logistics supply of a lunar base or for other deep space operations; a manned expedition to the planet Mars; large astronomical observations in Earth orbit; and the application of our new space capability to a great variety of services of benefit to mankind here on Earth.

Space Task Group

To make the best possible selection from this broad spectrum of choices available to him, on 13 February 1969, President Nixon appointed a Space Task Group chaired by Vice-President Spiro T. Agnew. By 1 September of that year, it was to submit a coordinated space program for the future, along with an attendant budget proposal. Members of this Space Task Group were the Science Adviser to the President, Lee A. Dubridge; the Administrator of NASA, Thomas O. Paine; and, as representative for the Defense Department, Secretary of the Air Force Robert C. Seamans, Jr. The Space Task Group also included as "observers" Under Secretary of State for Political Affairs U. Alexis Johnson; the Chairman of the Atomic Energy Commission, Glenn T. Seaborg;

and the Director of the Bureau of the Budget, Robert P. Mayo.

The Space Task Group listened to numerous presentations and finally submitted to the President a recommendation for a future, balanced, integrated national space program, with the emphasis on the word "balanced." Unlike a single-minded objective such as President John F. Kennedy's famous "Man-on-the-Moon-in-this-decade," the post-Apollo program was to pursue a balanced rate of progress over the entire spectrum of space potentials. Specifically, the Space Task Group recommended emphasis on the following program objectives:

1. Increase utilization of space capabilities for services to mankind, through an expanded space applications program
2. Enhance the defense posture of the United States and thereby support the broader objective of peace and security for the world through a program that exploits space techniques for the accomplishment of military missions
3. Increase mankind's knowledge of the universe by conduct of a continuing strong program of lunar and planetary exploration, astronomy, physics, Earth and life sciences
4. Develop new systems and technology for space operations with emphasis upon the critical factors of: *(a)* commonality, *(b)* reusability, and *(c)* economy, through a program directed initially toward development of a new space transportation capability and space station modules that utilize this new capability
5. Promote a sense of world community through a program that provides opportunity for broad international participation and cooperation

As a focus for the development of new capability, we suggested that the United States accept the long-range option or goal of manned planetary exploration with a manned Mars mission before the end of this century as the first target.

This set of recommendations reflected not only the views of the Space Task Group itself, but those held by virtually all groups favoring a continuous, vigorous space program. If the President concurs with the Task Group's findings, the only remaining question then seems to be the pace at which these objectives are to be pursued in the coming years. That pace, of course, depends primarily on the space budget levels that will be available and can only be set, therefore, by the President himself and by the Congress.

To get a realistic glimpse of the future, any list of new space objectives must, of course, be viewed in the light of previously made decisions, our present space hardware posture, and the more immediate flight mission capabilities resulting therefrom.

Missions for the Remaining Apollo Fleet

For instance, the first successful manned lunar landing was accomplished before even one-half of the space vehicles originally approved for this program had been used in flight tests. In 1962, based on the state of rocketry at that time, it was thought that the first manned flight on a Saturn V rocket would be attempted only after eight or ten unmanned flights. Yet Frank Borman's unforgettable Christmas 1968 flight around the Moon was launched with the third Saturn V ever flown, and the sixth has carried Neil Armstrong's Apollo 11 to its successful lunar landing. Since a total of 15 Saturn Vs have been built and paid for, we now have a fleet of nine Saturn Vs left over for follow-on missions. With the smaller Saturn IB and the Apollo spacecraft, the situation is similar. The highly specialized industrial teams needed to operate this fleet of space vehicles cannot be put on ice, and neither can the dedicated and well-trained teams of astronauts who are ready to fly them.

The National Academy of Sciences, on request by NASA, has identified a number of important scientific objectives for lunar surface research, and it now looks as if in the wake of Apollo 11 there may be nine more manned flights to the Moon. These flights will take astronauts to landing sites of particular scientific interest, and each subsequent mission will offer an extended scientific capability and a longer stay time on the lunar surface. The last few flights of this series will even provide the astronauts with a lunar jeep that will enable them to explore areas of particular scientific interest several miles distant from the landing site but unsuited for touchdown.

NASA will also continue with the work on the so-called Saturn Workshop [later to be named Skylab], a rudimentary space station built by converting the spacious liquid hydrogen tank of a Saturn stage into an orbital "hotel." The purpose of this Workshop will be to gather practical experience, with

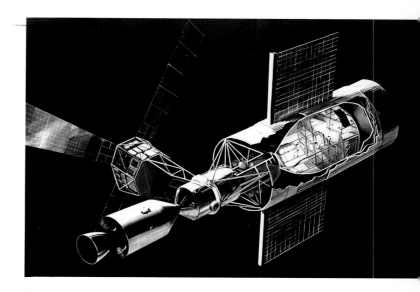

Part of the Apollo Applications Program, the Saturn Workshop later evolved into the Skylab space station. NASA.

astronaut-scientists staying in orbit for periods of up to two months. Attached to the Workshop will be a manned solar observatory designed to study the Sun in the light of ultraviolet and X rays that cannot reach the surface since the Earth's atmosphere is opaque to them. The heavy work schedule prepared for this observatory will also furnish valuable lessons about human proficiency for difficult scientific work performed under zero-gravity conditions over an extended period of time. The Workshop will be revisited several times to exchange crews and replenish supplies. These flights will be performed with leftover Apollo spacecraft boosted into orbit by Saturn IB rockets.

Unmanned Space Science

In the field of unmanned exploration of other heavenly bodies, the Mariner spacecraft, with their highly informative close-up photos of the planet Mars, have found wide acclaim and publicity. NASA has firm follow-on plans for two Mars-orbiting flights in 1971 and two unmanned soft landings on Mars in 1973.

Fixed stars outside of our solar system are still

beyond the reach of space vehicles (and most of them will forever remain so). But we can still study them with the help of unmanned (and later possibly with manned) astronomical telescopes, orbiting the Earth in airless space. Such telescopes need not view the stars through what Harvard astronomer Fred L. Whipple calls the "dirty basement window of our atmosphere," and, just like the manned solar telescope attached to the Saturn Workshop, they can also view the stars in types of radiation to which our atmosphere is completely opaque. The fabulously successful OAO II (Orbiting Astronomical Observatory), for instance, has made new star maps taken with special ultraviolet-sensitive equipment. These maps have already profoundly altered long-held views on the life cycle of stars.

Space Applications

In accordance with the Space Task Group's first recommendation, NASA will henceforth place greater emphasis on space applications for services to mankind. Some practical space applications have already attained a true "bread-and-butter" status where taxpayers' help is no longer required. U.S. commercial communications interests, pooled in the COMSAT Corporation, have now for several years ordered their own custom-made communications satellites and have even refunded NASA for launch services. The further growth of the communications satellite industry is not even determined by the rate of possible technological progress, but rather by the way certain "roles-and-missions" disputes between COMSAT, the traditional communications carriers (telephone companies), and the FCC (as regulatory agency) will be settled. In other words, today's communications satellite business has matured to the status of a typical public service industry with the baton passed from the engineers to the lawyers. But as we shall see later, the concept of communications satellites has a far greater potential than the more obvious applications originally foreseen for them— things such as relaying transatlantic telephone calls in lieu of carrying them via submarine cables, or world-wide television programs.

Probably the most promising task for Earth-oriented satellites deals with the question of natural resources. As the National Academy of Sciences put it: "The Earth is now recognized as one large space-craft whose self-contained environment must be maintained by wise management of its food, fiber, water, air, and other natural resource systems. To do so requires near real-time knowledge of man's interaction with many of these factors."

It has been estimated that in the year 2000, a mere 30 years from now, the Earth will be populated by 7½ billion people, as compared to 3½ billion today. The problem of food and other resources caused by this population explosion is further aggravated by the fact that the birth rate is highest in those parts of the world that even today cannot provide enough food and have not enough of the other natural resources needed to support jobs for the food providers. To replace our present freewheeling "Mother-Nature-will-take-care-of-her-children" system by a global Earth resources survey and management system is, therefore, one of the most pressing requirements of our time. Nor is it a task that can wait. If our generation cannot lay the groundwork for an orderly world-wide resource management system, our own children will be condemned to live in a world where vast segments of mankind will be engaged in a struggle for sheer survival.

What can space satellites contribute to solving this problem? Very much, indeed.

Imagine a satellite, manned or unmanned, that is equipped with a bank of, say, twelve ordinary photographic cameras, all pointing down toward the Earth and viewing an area the size of a typical U.S. county. Each of the twelve cameras is loaded with a different, special type of color film as well as a particular color filter. At a given instant all twelve camera shutters are opened simultaneously. The result is twelve pictures of that county, all in "false colors." One picture may be predominantly blue, another yellow, another red, again another green. But each picture will show the same outlines of fields, towns, rivers, and roads. One can now scan each film with a light beam (in the fashion a TV picture is generated) and convert the image into a string of numbers that express the relative brightness of the respective color at a given spot. The remarkable part is this: a pasture will create a "signature" distinctly different from that of a rye field, and a corn patch can be clearly distinguished from a rice paddy. Moreover, by setting up "calibration fields" on the ground and overflying them with the camera-equipped satellite, it is possible to refine this technique by comparing the collected data with the "ground truth." In this manner it will be possible to distinguish a poorly fertilized (and therefore poorly growing) cotton patch from a well-fertilized one, or a second-rate corn field from one bearing high-yielding hybrid corn.

This technique offers the key to world-wide crop prediction and an agricultural educational television service to advise farmers all over the world, in their own language, on vital and profitable things such as choice of suitable seed material, irrigation, fertilization, and the like. Inasmuch as a low-altitude satellite orbits the Earth in 90 minutes while the Earth slowly rotates on its axis, a few satellites suffice to render this service to every farmer on Earth.

The same satellites can also be used for the updating of maps (which, world-wide, is a $2 billion-a-year business) and to keep track of the rapid urbanization of mankind.

Thus, satellites can furnish us the two pieces of information crucial for a world-wide starvation prevention system: what amount of food is available, where is it, what kind is it, and what can be done to grow more? And, secondly, how many mouths must be fed and where are they?

But mankind does not live by bread alone. The factory that employs him depends on wood, metals, and fuel. Satellites have already detected forest fires and timber plagues caused by insects and infections that, in thinly populated areas such as northern Canada, cause timber damage of many tens of millions of dollars every year. Petroleum was found in Australia with the help of a single photograph taken by a Gemini astronaut using a simple hand-held camera. False-color photographs and so-called "side-looking" radar images are powerful tools to detect minerals and oil below the surface, because in combination they bring out features of particular geological significance. By correlating these pictures with comparable conditions in other locations where petroleum or certain minerals were actually found, effective prospecting from orbit becomes possible.

Hydrology is another field that is bound to benefit from these new orbital techniques. The job of hydrologists is to provide enough water of sufficient quality, at low cost, to the places of need, and to minimize the detrimental effects of such natural events as floods and such man-made effects as pollution. Here is an excerpt of what the Science Academy thinks NASA and its orbiting satellites can do for hydrology: "Get data on snow cover and ice occurrence in rivers and glaciers; get near-shore underwater detail in coastal waters, estuaries, large lakes, and major reservoirs; get details of saline intrusion, circulation patterns and pollution distribution in coastal waters, estuaries and lakes."

Observations from space will, in the opinion of most experts, enable us to extend to a whole week our present limited ability of predicting weather for one or two days in advance. In terms of dollars and cents this will mean: more efficient management of the routing and scheduling of air, highway, and water traffic; decreased spoilage of perishable commodities in transit or at terminal facilities; improved planning of recreational activities and sporting events; savings from unnecessary seeding, fertilizing, and spraying operations in agriculture; improved timing of hay, grain, or fruit harvest; optimum scheduling of construction work forces and assignment of material and equipment to construction sites; hurricane warnings; water management (advanced flood warnings); saving unnecessary irrigation when rain can be expected, etc.

The key to a reliable one-week weather forecast lies in duplicating, on large electronic computers, the complex interplay of physical forces that produce the ever-changing weather pattern all over the globe. Since a minor disturbance in one location can have grave consequences for a large area, a computer model of the Earth's atmosphere can spew out good weather predictions only if we keep updating it with a minimum of delay with the latest actual weather data collected from all over the Earth. Collecting and relaying the data to the ground computer center can be done most effectively by a limited number of satellites. Some of the information will be gathered directly from orbit. Such data will include television pictures of hurricanes, cloud formations, and jet streams. Satellite-borne infrared and microwave sensors can also measure the vertical temperature stratification of the atmosphere. But a satellite, as it circles the Earth in 90 minutes, can also collect meteorological data radioed up from a great number of manned and unmanned meteorological ground stations. Such stations may include radio-equipped weather monitoring buoys anchored or drifting in the oceans, which in turn can release radio-equipped meteorological balloons whenever the satellite appears overhead.

Another beneficiary of systematic Earth observation from orbit will be oceanography. The oceans affect the life of all mankind in three important ways: through weather, transportation, and food. Nearly all the moisture in rain clouds and the energy of tropical storms originates in the sea. More than 95 percent of the tonnage of commerce transported abroad goes by ship. And the oceans are a significant source of food protein.

The state of the oceans all over the world can be reduced to seven sets of data, all of which can be acquired by satellite observation: the sea surface temperature can be measured by its infrared and microwave radiation; the visual appearance can be photographed; local currents can be measured by the drift rate of floating objects such as radio-equipped buoys interrogated and located by the satellite passing overhead; icebergs and sea ice can be detected by radar imagery; sea state is shown by radar roughness; tidal waves and seaquakes can be tracked by radar and laser altimeters; and, finally, the plankton or chlorophyll content can be determined by an analysis of the water coloration with spectrographic methods. Correlation of all these data with the migration habits of fish may someday even enable us to direct fishing fleets to herring and tuna schools.

All of these Earth-related satellite observations have one feature in common. They require the satellites to serve as carriers of all sorts of photographic and other sensors, and they must also be able to communicate continuously with the ground. As they rise above a local horizon, they must instruct an unmanned station on the ground or a buoy in the ocean to turn on its data transmitter or to release a radio-equipped sounding balloon. And when passing over the continental U.S., the satellites must be capable of dumping the tape-stored data collected by their own sensors and those acquired from several thousand ground stations into the vast electronic memory of a central data-processing station on the ground that will ultimately disseminate the desired information to its respective customers.

Thus, communication by satellite is bound to break the narrow concept for which COMSAT was originally chartered, namely as a "carrier's carrier," which merely substituted satellite relays for the conventional wires, cables, or microwave links. As we are establishing what virtually amounts to a central nervous system for all mankind, imaginative new legislation is required to make full use of the potential of this new technology. In fact, today, the most serious problem with Earth resources satellites is not whether all of these things are technically possible. It is, rather, how to collect the dollars needed to operate the system from the multitude of its potential beneficiaries.

Suppose, for instance, satellites discover an area likely to contain rich oil and natural gas deposits: how do we use that newly won knowledge? Do we tell all the competing oil companies in the world that we have found indications of a potentially rich deposit in, say, one of the young developing countries in Africa, causing confusion and havoc in that completely unprepared land? Or suppose we find a vast tract of copper deposits in Mao Tse-tung's China. Should we tell him? Obviously, even politically this field of Earth resources surveys is loaded with questions.

Even if we limit our attention to the world this side of the Bamboo Curtain, the question still remains: how to assemble a group of potential beneficiaries of a space applications program so we can effectively tax it for its fair share of the development and operational costs. If we are to finance these programs in any other way than by direct taxpayer support, we must learn to assemble a "critical mass" of beneficiaries. Nor is it very attractive to concentrate on a few of these space applications and neglect the rest for the time being. The cost of an Earth resources system, after the satellites have been launched, lies in the continuous extraction, processing, and dissemination of the data they transmit to the ground. The more beneficiaries serviced by such a system, the more cost-effective it is bound to be. The oil, mineral, forestry, agricultural, and fishing industries and also disaster warning services (hurricanes, floods, etc.) could certainly benefit by billions of dollars per year from a broad, multifaceted space applications program.

Manned Space Flight

Some of these operational systems will undoubtedly be operated without being manned, but researchers in orbital space stations will contribute greatly to the development of the new techniques of "sensing from above." For this reason, a modularized space station, gradually evolving from a modest six-man station to a space base accommodating between 50 and 100 people, has been proposed by NASA and strongly endorsed by the President's Space Task Group.

Along with the space station, the Space Task Group also emphasized the need for a new space transportation system, designed to drastically slash today's high cost of carrying people and equipment into an Earth orbit. The present cost of orbiting one pound of payload is approximately $500. Completely reusable orbital space shuttle vehicles will slash this cost to about $50. Like an airliner, such a reusable vehicle will make a strict distinction between the astronaut flight crew up in the cockpit and the non-astronaut scientists and technicians in the rear passenger compartment. Detailed and highly promising studies of such vehicles are well on the way and contracts for their development will be let as soon as Congress will have appropriated the requested funds. Because of its potential cost saving, the reusable space shuttle will in due time replace most of the expendable launch vehicles presently utilized to launch unmanned spacecraft into orbit. Presently, there are occasionally disappointments whenever a multi-million-dollar spacecraft fails to deploy its solar cell arrays or refuses to accept ground commands during its critical activation phase. This could easily be avoided by having a reusable space shuttle standing by.

Space stations serviced by the reusable shuttle vehicles will be compartmented for astronomical, medical, physical, or Earth-related research. In due time they may be operated pretty much like our present research stations in Antarctica, with grants from the National Science Foundation. Professors and their graduate students will gather their scientific data in the station and return to their home institutions to evaluate their finds and prepare their final papers. Such research opportunities may well be offered to foreign scientists as well, thus fostering the broad international participation urged by the Space Task Group.

Beyond Earth orbit and the Moon, the red planet Mars still beckons. Mars is the obvious first target for a manned planetary expedition, and by 1973 when the first unmanned spacecraft will have soft-landed on Mars's surface and radioed back what they found there, we will know whether a detailed exploration by humans is warranted.

NASA has a complete blueprint for such a manned expedition to Mars. All elements, propellants, and crews will be carried into Earth orbit by a series of flights of the reusable shuttle vehicle and two Saturn V flights that will deliver extra-large payload units. The interplanetary expedition will consist of 12 men traveling in two ships flying in formation.

Departing from Earth orbit, the two ships will be thrust into a circumsolar orbit by twin nuclear-powered booster rockets that will subsequently be returned to their original Earth orbit for reuse. Two-hundred seventy days later the two ships will deboost, by their own nuclear rocket engines, into an orbit around Mars. They will remain in orbit for a period of 80 days. During this time, manned surface excursions will be carried out using a chemical-powered two-stage rocket, a Martian equivalent of the LM (Lunar Module) that carried Armstrong and Aldrin from lunar orbit to the Moon's surface and back.

For the return flight to Earth, the interplanetary ships' nuclear engines will be turned on for a second time. The home-bound flight will pass close enough to the planet Venus to dispatch two unmanned radio-equipped probes into the Venusian atmosphere. At the same time, Venus's gravitational field will be strategically utilized to reduce the speed at

MARS EXCURSION MODULE CONFIGURATION

■

A proposed manned Mars mission to have been accomplished using adapted Apollo hardware. NASA.

■

One of the components of the Rover Program was the NERVA (Nuclear Energy for Rocket Vehicle Applications) engine project. The development of this nuclear-powered engine was canceled in the early 1970s for lack of an approved planetary mission. NASA/AEC.

which the ships reenter the gravitational field of Earth. The ships will finally settle, with the help of another blast from their nuclear rocket engines, into an orbit around the Earth. Total round-trip time is 640 days or nearly two years. After refueling, restocking with supplies, and a thorough checkout, the ships will be used again for another voyage to Mars.

A heavy prototype of the nuclear engine required for such a voyage has already performed a number of highly successful static tests. The spacecraft in which the astronauts will live for most of their journey is nothing more than a single module that has been developed as one of the building blocks for the Earth-orbital space station.

Economy, commonality, and reusability are the highlights for NASA's space program for the next two decades. The plan for a manned Mars expedition embraces all three of these principles. Whether it will come to pass in the early 1980s (the earliest date technological development could support) or whether it will be later depends solely on the budget.

Farther out, there are the other planets of our solar system. Unlike Alexander the Great, who wept when he reached the Indian Ocean because there were no new worlds for him to conquer, our astronauts can go on and on with their peaceful conquest.

Conclusion

During the Renaissance, Prince Henry the Navigator of Portugal established in his seaside castle of Sagres the closest precedent to what NASA is trying to accomplish in our time. He systematically collected maps, ship designs, and navigational instruments from all over the world. He attracted Portugal's most experienced mariners. He laid out a step-by-step program aimed at the exploration of Africa's Atlantic coast and the discovery of Africa's southernmost tip, which he knew had to be circumnavigated if India were to be reached by the sea. With equal determination he pushed for the possibly shorter west-bound route to the Far East. Prince Henry trained the astronauts of his time, men like Ferdinand Magellan and Vasco da Gama, and he created the exploratory environment that launched Columbus from neighboring Spain on his historic voyage.

Self-centered medieval Europe was subsequently turned into an outgoing, exploring, and expanding continent. England became a different place after men like Sir Francis Drake or Sir Walter Raleigh followed in the footsteps of the Portuguese and Spanish navigators. As a direct result of an age of exploration that opened their eyes and revamped their standards, Europeans and their American offspring have ever since led the world in intellectual dynamism.

Henry the Navigator would have been hard put had he been requested to justify his actions on a rational basis, or to predict the pay-off or cost-effectiveness of his program of exploration. He committed an act of faith and the world became richer and more beautiful as a result of his program. Exploration of space is the challenge of our day. If we continue to put our faith in it and pursue it, it will reward us handsomely.

Note

1. Unpublished letter from Cornelius Ryan to Hobart Lewis, 27 February 1970, Frederick I. Ordway III collection.

For further reading

Clarke, Arthur C. *The Promise of Space*. New York, 1968: Harper & Row.

National Aeronautics and Space Administration. *America's Next Decades in Space: The Report for the Space Task Group*. Washington, D.C., September 1969: National Aeronautics and Space Administration.

President's Science Advisory Committee. *The Space Program in the Post-Apollo Period*. Washington, D.C., 1967: Government Printing Office.

U.S. Space Task Group. *The Post-Apollo Space Program: Directions for the Future*. Report to the President. Washington, D.C., September 1969: U.S. Space Task Group.

Von Braun, Wernher. *Space Frontier*. Rev. ed. New York, 1967: Holt, Rinehart and Winston, Inc.

Von Braun, Wernher, and Frederick I. Ordway III. *History of Rocketry and Space Travel*. New York, 1966 and later editions: Thomas Y. Crowell Co.

PIONEERING THE SPACE FRONTIER

*An Exciting
Vision of Our Next Fifty
Years in Space*

Part Four

Where Do We Go from Here?

Saturn viewed from its satellite, Rhea. Arthur C. Clarke
lamented that this stunning
view had only been repro-
duced in black and white in
the Bonestell-Ley book The
Conquest of Space *(see Epilogue)*. At a visual angle

of 30 degrees, we see 328,000-
mile (531,000-kilometer)-distant
Saturn and the four inner moons,
Mimas, Enceladus, Tethys, and
Dione. The rings are seen edge on.
Ordway Collection/Space & Rocket
Center.

Blueprint for Leadership

SALLY K. RIDE

ALAN LADWIG

Since the early 1950s, there has been general agreement on what the United States should do to hold a leading edge in space exploration. The following list, for example, was offered back in 1962:

1. Establish a low-Earth-orbit space station
2. Increase research on orbital rendezvous techniques
3. Construct a permanent lunar base
4. Speed up research on nuclear rocket engines
5. Accelerate ion-electric rocket research
6. Accelerate life science research
7. Develop a more ambitious plan to send humans to Mars
8. Increase funding for education to interest students in science and mathematics
9. Develop a 40-year space plan[1]

These recommendations could have come from any of the numerous national commissions and task forces that have been convened over the last 40 years in the name of space leadership. They might have been found in the first NASA long-range plan offered in 1959, or in the 1986 report of the National Commission on Space. The suggested course of action normally relies heavily on human exploration, usually includes an aggressive timetable, and is never inexpensive.

That wish list from 1962 was not implemented, and officials in charge also ignored this advice from the author: "We should, and can, plan for our space world in the year 2000 A.D. The planning must begin now—not in 1990."[2] What is the prognosis for America's space leadership in the 1990s? What kind of role will we play in the space world in the rapidly approaching year 2000?

There are those who look at the broad range of activities in today's space program and conclude that America is and has been the undisputed world leader in space exploration for the past 30 years. Others see a U.S. space program of "high velocity with no direction,"[3] which has, as a result, forfeited its leadership claim. Before we offer our diagnosis, let's look at the historical roots of leadership in space.

We're Number One

The importance of leadership emerged early in the space movement. The founders of America's space program were acutely aware that other countries were "seriously engaged in the business of rocketry."[4] This recognition quickly turned space research efforts into a race. Being a leader in this new frontier was defined as reaching strategic milestones ahead of the competition, of getting there first. Dire consequences, it was said, awaited those who came in second.

In October 1957, just a few weeks after Sputnik scored the first points in the space race, a *Life* magazine cover story asked space experts to describe what was needed to capture the leadership flag from the Soviets. Illustrations depicted a winning space program of recoverable piloted gliders, space platforms and stations, telescope satellites, colonies on the Moon, and nuclear rockets for journeys to Venus and Mars. Space enthusiasts believed that a commitment to such long-range goals would quickly propel the U.S. ahead of the Russians. One tongue-in-cheek researcher, the article noted, had proposed a sure-fire project to establish America's leadership:

This waggish scientist suggested that we fire a man on a one-way rocket flight to the Moon and send with him only a one-year supply of oxygen and food. The traditionally softhearted American public, he theorized, would instantly call upon all its world-renowned organizational talent, backed by stupendous expenditures of money and effort, to bring the lunar hermit safely home. By the time he was back with his wife and children, US space research would be in a position of leadership from which it could never be dislodged.[5]

America did not go to quite the lengths suggested by the "waggish scientist," but less than a year later, the National Aeronautics and Space Administration (NASA) was created to organize the nation's talent for a program of space exploration. The Space Act of 1958 directed the new space agency to preserve "the role of the United States as a leader in aeronautical and space science and technology"[6]—a driving obsession of the civilian space program ever since.

During the first two decades of the space program, our accomplishments were somewhat more modest than had been predicted by the early visionaries. Nonetheless, the deployment of remote-sensing Earth probes, the fly-bys and reconnaissance of our planetary neighbors, the landing of robotic spacecraft on Mars, and the stunning achievement of landing the first humans on the Moon clearly established America as a world leader in space exploration. As the decade of the 1960s drew to a close, this status provided the nation with the benefits of pride, international prestige, scientific advances, and technological progress. However, it became clear that even stupendous expenditures of money and effort could not guarantee that we would not be dislodged from a position of leadership.

Even before Neil Armstrong set foot on the Moon, space officials tried to gain presidential approval for missions beyond Apollo. In the 1969

report *America's Next Decades in Space,* a NASA planning committee cautioned that "decisions made this year will affect the course of space activity for decades to come. At stake is America's position of world leadership in technological and scientific progress."[7] Barely a year after the Apollo 11 mission, NASA's acting administrator, George M. Low, warned that America was in danger of losing its vanguard position. In a speech in Chicago, Low told members of a press association: "I am going to speak about the danger that exists today that we will soon lose the capability that gave us this achievement and leadership. . . . In today's environment, when national prestige is equated to national power, and when science and technology are a measure of national leadership, this is most important."[8]

In hindsight, the short-lived leadership glow from Apollo should have sent a signal to space officials. The benefits of getting somewhere first did not necessarily provide the basis for long-lasting leadership. To beat the Soviets to the Moon, the nation spent considerable resources (4 percent of the Federal budget at its peak) and employed as many as 450,000 people in industry and government. When Low gave his speech in 1970, the number of employees had dropped to 180,000 and NASA's budget was decreased by almost half.

But President Kennedy's challenge to send men to the Moon was not developed with long-term leadership in mind. In committing the nation to Apollo, he had been more interested in short-term political concerns than in establishing a lasting foundation of capabilities in space. There were those at the time who recognized that this approach was flawed if we really wanted to think of space as an operational area for a broad range of activities. Walter Dornberger addressed this topic in an interview on the eve of his retirement as vice-president of Bell Aerospace: "We must use a completely different approach. We must get away from this launching from pads, which costs millions and billions of dollars, to the more conventional way of taking off from a runway. . . . After we have gone to the Moon, we will start over again. . . . We must create an environment in space that can be used . . . not only for research, but for commercial and military purposes."[9]

The bold ideas advanced in 1969 for the post-Apollo program failed to rally political and public enthusiasm. Emotionally and financially drained from the experience of the Vietnam war, the nation turned inward and registered scant interest in NASA's vision. Unable to gain support from the Nixon administration for a program of space stations, lunar bases, and human expeditions to Mars in the early 1980s, space advocates had to settle for the development of a space transportation system—the space shuttle. Space leadership was now to be demonstrated through the operational capabilities of a fleet of space vehicles rather than astronauts beating the competition to planetary bodies.

A Loss of Vision?

Throughout the early 1980s, NASA tried to develop an operational ability, but again the vision had run ahead of the reality. The advertised capabilities of 40-plus launches a year with $100-per-pound payloads proved to be highly optimistic. The missions did, however, demonstrate the shuttle's capacity to deploy satellites and platforms, gather data from scientific experiments, perform life science research, retrieve and repair satellites, and enhance our ability to live and work in space. The development and operation of the space transportation system also advanced the ability of the nation to create and manage a highly complex, large-scale technological project.

Despite the success and benefits derived from shuttle missions, they did not satisfy those who had their minds set on visions of a bolder scale. The years of effort spent on the research and development of the shuttle had left little funding for other programs of NASA. While America had been known for its robotic exploration of the solar system, it was now almost 10 years since a probe was dispatched to another planet. Shuttle flights took us *around* Earth, but not far enough *beyond* Earth. To some critics, NASA was again running a program of high velocity but with no direction.

In this environment, Congress established the National Commission on Space in 1984. With members appointed by President Ronald Reagan, the Commission was charted to:

1. Define the long-range needs of the nation that may be fulfilled through the peaceful uses of outer space
2. Maintain the nation's preeminence in space science, technology, and application

3. Promote the peaceful exploration and utilization of the space environment
4. Articulate goals and develop options for the future direction of the nation's civilian space program[10]

The Commission interpreted this charge to mean that they were to present bold goals and options. In the introductory remarks of their final report, Commission members modified their charge to read: "Formulate a bold agenda to carry America's civilian space enterprise into the twenty-first century."[11] The Commission established a framework to consider aspirations that went beyond space shuttle missions. It proposed "a sustained step-by-step program to open the inner solar system for exploration, basic and applied research, resource development, and human operations. . . . U.S. leadership will be based upon a reliable, affordable transportation system and a network of outposts in space."[12]

Unfortunately, as the Commission was preparing its report, the available space transportation systems for the U.S. suffered major setbacks. A tragic accident occurred in January 1986 during the launch of the space shuttle *Challenger*. This was followed by launch failures of both Delta and Titan expendable vehicles. Suddenly, "building institutions and systems that make accessible vast new resources and support human settlements beyond Earth orbit, from the highlands of the Moon to the plains of Mars," seemed like an unlikely dream, and the report did not receive the discussion it may have deserved.[13]

While the U.S. regrouped after the accident, other nations entered the leadership contest and demonstrated concrete achievements. The Soviet Union had long ago adopted an approach that was systematic and evolutionary. After they had dropped out of the race to the Moon, the Soviets had turned to a strategy that incrementally developed operational capabilities and relied on proven technology. The primary focus of their program had been to gain operational experience in long-duration living and working in space. They had established endurance records in a series of space stations, culminating in a one-year stay by a cosmonaut in their Mir space station. With launch capability beyond their needs, they began to venture cautiously into the commercial world of space. There was even talk of sending cosmonaut pioneers to the planet Mars.

There were also fears that countries with space

budgets a fraction of that of the United States would somehow run away with the leadership garland. The capabilities of the Europeans and Japanese had significantly expanded beyond the days when space was a two-country arena. Both the Japanese and member countries of the European Space Agency had developed independent launch capabilities and were pursuing strategies that sought to advance science in selected areas and to achieve commercial viability in others.

Program at the Crossroads

The post-*Challenger* hiatus had again brought concerns of space leadership to center stage. Despite the recommendations of the National Commission on Space, critics felt the nation lacked a concrete plan. Editorials proclaimed that the American space program lacked direction and vision. What was needed, it was said, was a single overarching goal with a timetable, just like Kennedy had established for the Apollo expeditions to the Moon.

Did the situation warrant so much concern? Was the civilian space program really guilty of this alleged loss of vision? What was perceived as a loss of direction may actually have been an appropriate response to the new conditions and circumstances. In the wake of the *Challenger* accident, the priority was to return the shuttle to flight. The restricted budget, brought on by the Gramm-Rudman budget legislation, also created an environment that made it difficult to focus on long-term aspirations.

In the fall of 1986, NASA responded to the criticism by adopting a revised set of goals and objectives and creating a Long Range Planning Task Force (on which the authors served). The goals set out were to:

1. Advance scientific knowledge of the planet Earth, the solar system, and the universe beyond
2. Expand human presence beyond the Earth into the solar system
3. Strengthen aeronautics research and develop technology toward promoting U.S. leadership in civil and military aviation[14]

The Task Force selected four initiatives for study, definition, and evaluation as elements of a leadership program:

1. Mission to Planet Earth would use the perspective afforded from space to study and characterize our home planet on a global scale.
2. Exploration of the Solar System would retain leadership in exploring both the inner and the outer solar system.
3. Outpost on the Moon would build on the legacy of Apollo and return to the Moon to establish a permanent scientific base.
4. Humans to Mars would send expeditions to the surface of the red planet, leading to a permanent base.

The intent was not to choose one initiative over the others, but to use these candidate programs as a basis for discussion and understanding. For this reason, initiatives were chosen that spanned a broad spectrum of content and complexity. In evaluating the initiatives, the space shuttle program and the plans at that time for the space station were assumed as givens for planning purposes.

The Task Force concluded that the objective of leadership did not require that the U.S. be preeminent in all areas and disciplines of space enterprise: "The broad spectrum of space activities and the increasing number of players make it virtually impossible for any nation to dominate in this way. Being an effective leader does mandate, however, that this country have capabilities which enable it to act independently and impressively when and where it chooses, and that its goals be capable of inspiring others—at home and abroad—to support them."[15] Thus two distinct attributes are required for a space leadership program. First, it must build the nation's capabilities to explore and operate in space. This requires launch capability that guarantees our access to space. Second, the program must feature visible and periodic accomplishments to sustain the necessary long-term commitment and support.

The Task Force believed that before the nation could commit to a specific space goal, it was necessary to develop a comprehensive strategy for the civilian space program. As a tool to evaluate potential strategies, the Task Force developed a "space leadership matrix." Four stages of space leadership were identified:

1. The pioneer stage, where innovation is displayed or a significant "first" is achieved
2. The complex second stage, where a pioneering program is broadened or expanded

Region of Space	Pioneer Stage	Complex Second Stage	Operational Stage	Commercially Viable Stage
Deep space	Star probe	Lunar observatory		
Outer solar system	Neptune fly-by–probe	Cassini		
Inner solar system	Mars sample return	Automated rovers	Lunar base	
	Human expedition to Mars	Lunar outpost		
High Earth orbit	Large space structures	Robotic servicing	Space transfer vehicle	Solar power satellites
Low Earth orbit	Variable-G facility	Earth-observing platforms	On-orbit assembly	Materials processing
Supporting technologies and transportation	National aerospace plane	Shuttle II	Assured access and return	Commercial launch vehicles

3. The operational stage, where mature and routine capabilities are demonstrated
4. The commercially viable stage, where the private sector takes over operations with the goal of making a profit

These leadership stages were then applied to physical regions of space: deep space; the outer solar system (the planets beyond the asteroid belt); the inner solar system, from Mars in toward the Sun; high Earth orbit; and low Earth orbit. The leadership stages were also applied to supporting technologies, such as launch capabilities, orbital facilities, etc., that would be required to undertake all programs. Each square within the matrix defines a particular target for leadership.

The matrix analysis provided a means to conceptualize alternative courses for action. It was intended to demonstrate that because the range of activities and opportunities has expanded so enormously since the early days of the space program, a more thorough analysis of how and where we want to demonstrate leadership was required.

Who should determine a space leadership strategy? According to the Task Force, a national strategy should be enunciated by the President with the support of Congress. NASA's role should be to investigate and recommend options and then implement those aspects of a leadership program for which it is responsible.

National Space Strategy under President Bush

Ever since President Kennedy set the standard, it has been recognized that support from the Oval Office is indispensable for national space leadership. Thus it was unfortunate that President Reagan was not available when Thomas O. Paine delivered the report of the National Commission on Space to the White House in 1986. Reagan's failure to embrace the recommendations of *Pioneering the Space Frontier* turned the report into another exercise in rhetoric.

The administration of President Bush seems interested in moving beyond rhetoric. National Space Policy was revised in November 1989 and recognized "that leadership requires U.S. preeminence in key areas of space activity critical to achieving our national security, scientific, technical, economic, and foreign policy goals."[16] However, the policy concurred with one of the conclusions of the Leadership Task Force in stating that it was not necessary to achieve preeminence in all space disciplines. Bush offered the power and prestige of the White House in additional ways. He reconvened the National Space Council, with the charter to provide a coordinated process for developing a national policy and implementation strategy. The Council provides a visible means to focus high-level attention on the space agenda. Additionally, the president requested a 24 percent increase to NASA's fiscal year 1991 budget, the largest increase for any major agency.

In the spring of 1990, President Bush approved a National Space Strategy as recommended by the National Space Council.[17] Its top priority is maintaining a national launch capability that will ensure reliable, affordable, and routine access to space. Success in achieving this aspect of the strategy is essential if the nation is to achieve current missions, let alone future ventures beyond Earth's orbit.

NASA's responsibility for this part of the strategy is to manage the shuttle program and provide a reliable launch capability moving toward the operational stage. The agency also has a responsibility to develop launch capabilities for the future. Without

Artist's conception of advanced space station in low Earth orbit. In-space assembly and construction and autonomous rendezvous and docking procedures are some of its features. NASA.

major advances in propulsion and vehicle technology, there is little chance of reducing launch costs. To achieve a U.S. "heavy lift" capability, NASA and the Department of Defense are funding research on the Advanced Launch System (ALS). The goal for ALS is to produce a new family of launch vehicles capable of placing up to 200,000 pounds into low Earth orbit. Such vehicles are envisaged as reducing launch costs to $300 per pound. Another joint NASA/DOD effort is supporting development of the National Aerospace Plane. Here the goal is to develop and demonstrate technologies for hypersonic flight, including the long-coveted objective of a single-stage-to-orbit spacecraft.

The private sector's responsibility in this area is to develop the market for expendable launch vehicles. Faced with competition from established and emerging firms abroad, more than half a dozen American companies have invested $600 million to gain a share of this market. To earn a position of leadership in this sector, American companies will have to meet the challenge from their international competitors and be perceived as the suppliers of high-quality, low-cost commercial launch services.

The Space Exploration Initiative

In commemorating the 20th anniversary of Apollo 11 on 20 July 1989, President Bush outlined the second feature of his space strategy: to expand the space frontier through robotic and human exploration of the solar system. Unlike the 10-year plan for Apollo, this program will require a decades-spanning commitment of resources. The objective of this new Space Exploration Initiative is to magnify our knowledge of the solar system and to establish a permanent presence on the Moon and Mars.

America's preeminence in the field of robotic exploration has been revitalized. NASA's space science chief, Leonard Fisk, considers us poised to "expand our knowledge of the universe in which we live more rapidly than at any time in human history."[18] Our leadership in space science has been demonstrated through the pioneering accomplishments of programs such as the fly-by of Neptune by Voyager 2, when it completed its 4.4 billion mile "grand tour" of the outer planets. The November 1989 launch of the Cosmic Background Explorer has challenged our understanding of the Big Bang and the early universe. Magellan is now in orbit around Venus on a major mapping mission. Building on the success of Voyager, Galileo was launched toward a 1995 encounter with Jupiter, and Ulysses was sent on its way in early October 1990 to study the polar regions of the Sun. The Hubble Space Telescope, the highly visible cooperative program between the United States and the European Space Agency, is now in orbit and acquiring the long-awaited penetrating view of the universe. Despite the focusing problem with Hubble's mirrors, its instruments are expected to provide significant scientific return.

An additional 36 science missions are scheduled to be launched before the end of the decade. Several of the upcoming robotic missions will provide precursor information to assist the design and development of eventual human missions. Both the 1992 Mars Observer and the planned 1996 flight of the Lunar Observer will return data on surface and atmospheric conditions that will enable human missions to be carried out more efficiently and safely.

An essential step toward accomplishing the Space Exploration Initiative is the construction of a space station in low Earth orbit. A space station is required to perform the life science research that must precede any expedition to Mars.

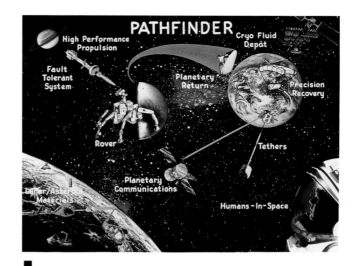

■

Project Pathfinder, later called the Exploration Technology Program, was designed to provide advanced technologies required for an ambitious, long-term space program. NASA.

All aspects of further space exploration will rely on advanced technology to enhance mission efficiency and lower the costs and risks of exploration. Technology development is required in the areas of surface exploration, in-space operations, propulsion, nuclear power systems, aerobraking, automation and robotics, life support, and flexible structures. Formerly known as Project Pathfinder, this research program has not achieved meaningful support through the budget process. Born again in the fiscal year 1991 budget as the Exploration Technology Program, its final allocation will serve as an important barometer to gauge Congressional support for the leadership strategy.

Mission to Planet Earth

A third element of the National Space Strategy stresses the vantage point that space provides for advancing the understanding of Earth. A multi-agency research effort known as the U.S. Global Research Program offers a timely opportunity to demonstrate U.S. leadership in the areas of remote sensing, environmental monitoring, and Earth science.

NASA's contribution to the Global Research Program is the Mission to Planet Earth initiative. It will integrate results from space observatories, an advanced data and information system, a ground-based research program, and international and interagency programs. A series of instruments and satellites will be deployed, designed to gather information on the atmosphere, oceans, weather, and surface characteristics. Dubbed the Earth Observation System (EOS), it currently includes two polar-orbiting observatories from NASA, a series of environmental satellites to be operated by the National Oceanic and Atmospheric Administration, and polar-orbiting platforms developed by the European Space Agency and Japan. To maximize the tremendous amount of information to be generated by EOS, new information systems and computational capabilities are required. An EOS Data and Information System will be developed through competitive studies by industry and will be available in the early 1990s. This system is intended to optimize the scientific utility of the data, as well as provide easy access to the international scientific community. Smaller satellites and instruments are to continue to be launched every few years to provide near-term results and help validate EOS systems and data retrieval.

Commercial Potential of Space

The long-term view of many space advocates has included thriving commercial markets. The last element of the National Space Strategy addresses the nation's ability to establish a leadership position in the area of space commerce.

A recent study by the American Institute of Aeronautics and Astronautics (AIAA) identified opportunities for commercial space operations in satellite communications, Earth observations, space processing and research applicable to ground-based manufacturing, life sciences, transportation, and ground and orbital services. To realize the full potential of these opportunities, the AIAA study concluded that the U.S. government must "reorient its present adversarial relationship with industry and institute major policy changes aimed at helping industry and academia."[19] To address this concern, the National Space Council is conducting a review of these relationships and intends to issue revised regulations and policies.

■

A lunar base sustaining mining operations may one day be commercially viable. NASA.

A Balanced Program for America

A more recent task force that was established to develop an agenda for the civil space program was led by Norman R. Augustine. Formed in mid-1990 at the request of Vice-President Dan Quayle, the Advisory Committee on the Future of the U.S. Space Program concluded that in determining a space agenda, it is not sufficient to merely list a collection of projects to undertake. According to the Committee, "It is essential to provide a logical basis for the structure of the program, including a sense of priorities."[20]

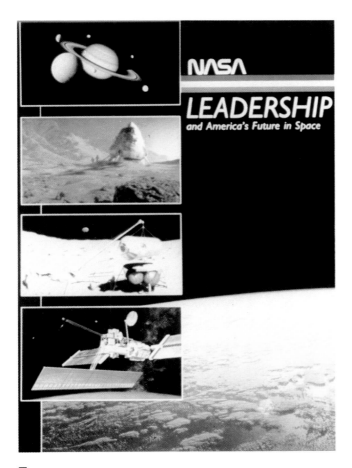

By developing and implementing a National Space Strategy, the United States can remain a leader in space research and exploration. NASA.

In concluding that science merits the highest priority for funding, the Committee's final report recommended that the "mission-oriented" portion of NASA be designed to support two major undertakings: a Mission *to* Earth and a Mission *from* Earth. As described earlier, the Mission to Earth will focus on an enhanced understanding of the planet's global climate change. The Mission from Earth directly supports the goals of President Bush's Space Exploration Initiative. Justified largely on the basis of intangible benefits, the Committee believes that human activities in space should be directed toward the long-term magnet—the exploration of Mars.

To ensure that these missions are achieved, the Augustine Committee echoed recommendations that have appeared in previous reports. It is mandatory that NASA's budget for advanced technology be augmented and stabilized. A two- to three-fold enhancement of the current budget seemed reasonable to the Committee. Also as stated in the past, the Administration should fully support the development of an evolutionary, heavy-lift launch vehicle.

The Augustine Committee report was followed in June 1991 by the Report of the Synthesis Group on America's Space Exploration Initiative.[21] Created by NASA administrator Richard H. Truly and placed under the chairmanship of retired Air Force lieutenant general and former astronaut Thomas P. Stafford, the Synthesis Group was tasked to examine new and innovative approaches and technologies for returning to the Moon and sending humans to Mars within President Bush's Space Exploration Initiative. After synthesizing ideas submitted by individuals and organizations (universities, federal research centers, technical societies, and aerospace and nonaerospace industries), the Group came up with several exploration options and ten recommendations. These latter are as follows:

1. Establish within NASA a long-range strategic plan for the nation's civil space program with SEI as its centerpiece
2. Establish a national program office by executive order
3. Appoint NASA's associate administrator for exploration as the program director for the national program office
4. Establish a new, aggressive SEI acquisition strategy

5. Incorporate SEI requirements into the joint NASA–Department of Defense heavy-lift launch vehicle program
6. Initiate a nuclear thermal rocket technology development program
7. Initiate a space nuclear power technology development program based on SEI requirements
8. Conduct focused life sciences experiments (on space station Freedom)
9. Establish education as a principal SEI theme
10. Continue and expand an outreach program (to include all entities in addition to the aerospace industry that are affected by SEI)

Some critics feel the National Space Strategy falls short because it does not expedite a human trip to Mars. If we were undertaking the challenge only for national prestige, the concern might be justified. But as we should have learned, one-time expeditions for national prestige do not sustain long-term support. Neither do they provide the lasting capabilities required to take advantage of the full range of benefits that the resources of space may provide.

The implementation of the National Space Strategy will be difficult because of competing demands for Federal resources. Congress and the public have indicated a natural concern for where the revenues will come from to sustain such an ambitious strategy. Without the necessary revenues, the strategy will become yet another rhetorical exercise.

Philosopher Eric Hoffer once observed that a leader "has to be practical and a realist, yet talk the language of the visionary and the idealist."[22] America's space strategy must maintain a balance between realism and idealism if it is to make meaningful advances toward leadership goals. The current National Space Strategy begins to strike this balance. The strategy is built on measurable objectives for near-term programs, as well as a long-range direction for human expansion into the solar system.

Notes

1. Donald Cox, *The Space Race* (Philadelphia, 1962: Chilton Books), pp. 258-270.
2. Ibid, p. 271.
3. This phrase is from "Moon Age: New Dawn?" *Newsweek*, 7 July 1969, p. 40.
4. "The Feat That Shook the Earth," *Life*, 21 October 1957.
5. Don Schanche, "Space beyond Sputnik Lies within Our Grasp," *Life*, 21 October 1957, p. 29.
6. National Aeronautics and Space Act of 1958, p. 2.
7. *America's Next Decades in Space* (Washington, D.C., 1969: National Aeronautics and Space Administration), p. 1.
8. Speech by George M. Low, "Our Future in Space: A Challenge in Leadership," Inland Daily Press Association, Chicago, Illinois, 19 October 1970.
9. Interview of Walter Dornberger by Claude Witze, *Air Force and Space Digest*, October 1965, pp. 80–88.
10. Public Law 98–361, Title II—National Commission on Space, Section 201, 16 July 1984.
11. National Commission on Space, *Pioneering the Space Frontier: Final Report of the National Commission on Space* (New York, 1986: Bantam Books), p. 1.
12. Ibid, p. 5.
13. Ibid, p. 2.
14. *NASA: Agenda for Tomorrow* (Washington, D.C., 1988: National Aeronautics and Space Administration), p. 3.
15. Sally Ride, *Leadership and America's Future in Space* (Washington, D.C., 1987: National Aeronautics and Space Administration), p. 12.
16. "National Space Policy" (The White House, Office of the Press Secretary, 2 November 1989).
17. Prepared remarks of Vice-President Dan Quayle to the American Institute of Aeronautics and Astronautics, Crystal City, Virginia, 1 May 1990.
18. Statement on NASA's Office of Space Science and Application FY 1991 Budget by Leonard Fisk before the Committee on Science, Space and Technology, U.S. House of Representatives, February 1990.
19. "Issues in Strategic Planning for Space: Commercial Space Growth" (American Institute of Aeronautics and Astronautics, May 1989).
20. *Report of the Advisory Committee on the Future of the U.S. Space Program* (Washington, D.C., 1990: U.S. Government Printing Office).
21. *Report of the Synthesis Group on America's Space Exploration Initiative.* (Washington, D.C., 1991: U.S. Government Printing Office).
22. Eric Hoffer, *The True Believer* (New York, 1951: Harper & Row), p. 107.

For further reading

Cox, Donald. *The Space Race*. Philadelphia, 1962: Chilton Books.

Hoffer, Eric. *The True Believer*. New York, 1951: Harper & Row.

National Space Council. *1990 Report to the President*. Washington, D.C., 1991: National Space Council.

Report of the Advisory Committee on the Future of the U.S. Space Program. Washington, D.C., 1990: U.S. Government Printing Office.

Report of the Synthesis Group on America's Space Exploration Initiative. Washington, D.C., 1991: U.S. Government Printing Office.

Ride, Sally. *Leadership and America's Future in Space*. Washington, D.C., 1987: NASA.

U.S. National Commission on Space. *Pioneering the Space Frontier: Final Report of the National Commission on Space*. New York, 1986: Bantam Books.

Spaceflight and the Public Mind

EDWARD O. BUCKBEE

CHARLES WALKER

Space Science Centers

Is space a thing to be conquered "just because it's there," or can a genuine public good be realized through the establishment of an aggressive space program? What is the usefulness of spaceflight other than curing the curiosity of children, dreamers, and science fiction writers?

Questions such as these have been asked since spaceflight first wavered between fiction and reality. Public reactions to it have ranged from innate fear of the unknown and resistance to change to a renewed inquisitiveness toward what exists beyond our world. The value of addressing a public that was information-poor was not overlooked by those leading the race to space during the 1950s and 1960s. Many recognized that knowledge would create a public that not only was more receptive to and at ease with the concept of spaceflight, but that actively promoted its cause. NASA visitor centers, science and technology centers, space theaters and museums, and multidisciplinary museums were organized to satisfy the hunger for information and foster the excitement of discovery. Such facilities continue to grow in the wake of today's advancing technology.

An exemplary leader among those who sought to excite and motivate the public was the late Dr. Wernher von Braun. He envisioned a public showcase of space technology that would address the public's questions and fears as well as stimulate positive public opinion. Throughout the early 1960s, while he was director of the NASA Marshall Space Flight Center in Huntsville, Alabama, von Braun joined with other dynamic individuals to push for the creation of a space technology museum. The Al-abama legislature approved construction of what became the U.S. Space & Rocket Center in 1965. Since its opening in 1970, the Center has brought space and its opportunities closer to the people of Alabama, the nation, and the world.

Von Braun felt strongly that a motivational public presentation should incorporate interactive, hands-on exhibits. Due to his influence, the U.S. Space & Rocket Center provides an innovative approach to public education. A small-scale, live rocket engine firing, a gyro chair, a centrifuge, and a wide variety of other interactive exhibitry welcome the public. The Center's museum collection currently possesses the most complete array of spacecraft and launch vehicles in the world. These include the Saturn V that powered the Apollo astronauts to the Moon, the Saturn I, and such early Huntsville-developed rockets as the Redstone and Jupiter. In 1989, a complete space shuttle launch vehicle was assembled for exhibit. It features the orbiter with an external tank and two solid rocket boosters that were NASA prototypes. Rocket Park is also a showcase for military missile systems created at the nearby Redstone Arsenal, including the Jupiter, Redstone, Pershing, Chaparral, Hawk, and Lance. Additionally, in cooperation with NASA, the U.S. Space & Rocket Center operates bus tours through the Marshall Space Flight Center. (Though unrelated to the Alabama operation, NASA's Kennedy Center in Florida has a similar cooperative agreement for tours.) The Omnimax film system, with its 67-foot hemispherical screen, transports visitors to the Center on a startling real space journey and gives man unprecedented

■

Ground-breaking ceremonies for the Alabama Space and Rocket Center (now, U.S. Space & Rocket Center), 5 August 1968. Left to right: Edward O. Buckbee, director; Jack Giles, commissioner; Wernher von Braun, director of the NASA Marshall Space Flight Center; Martin Dor- *ity, representing Alabama Governor George Wallace; Lieutenant Governor James Allen; Major General Charles Eifler, commander, Army Ordnance Missile Command; and Huntsville Mayor Glenn Hearn. U.S. Space & Rocket Center.*

perspective of the magnitude of the universe. The offerings at the Huntsville and other space centers aim to keep the drama of spaceflight alive in the public mind.

For some, the mystery of space research adds a certain romance to space science careers. Von Braun realized that such an appeal was particularly strong among the young and the young at heart. This appeal, he reasoned, could be used to develop increasingly greater interest and participation by generations that would continue the quest for space. Besides space science centers and multidisci-

plinary museums, the forward-thinking von Braun felt there was a need for a more intense program that would encourage and motivate young people to select and master a curriculum strong in math and science studies. This would, in turn, build a strong foundation for a high-technology work force. Von Braun's influence was felt when, in 1982, the Space & Rocket Center hosted the first session of the U.S. Space Camp.

Though a number of youth programs currently exist to achieve the goals von Braun sought in youth education, the Space Camp program set a precedent that many aerospace professionals feel is yet unrivaled. Each day at Space Camp begins with an interactive computer lesson in the topic for the day, such as rockets, propulsion, or microgravity. Exercises in actual NASA astronaut microgravity and disorientation simulators, underwater assembly of space hard-

■

Overview of part of the Space Camp/Space Academy training area. U.S. Space & Rocket Center.

Space Camp trainees trying out the Manned Maneuvering Unit. U.S. Space & Rocket Center.

A Space Academy student on a gyro chair, which simulates zero gravity. U.S. Space & Rocket Center.

ware, model rocket launch, and mission training are among activities that spur Space Camp trainees to consider a career in the aerospace industry.

The Space Camp program has grown dramatically. Its participants now range from youngsters aged 10 to primary and secondary school mathematics and science educators. (The programs for junior high school, high school, and adult trainees are referred to as Space Academy.) The programs and curriculum are prepared by an education committee, which includes NASA representatives, classroom teachers, and veteran astronauts. These programs, recognized by the Alabama State Board of Education as academically sound experiences for school students, provide professional equivalency credit to attending teachers.

U.S. Space Academy Level II programs for high school students are accredited by the University of Alabama in Huntsville. Students can receive up to 3 hours of undergraduate credit for successfully completing all three "tracks" of the Level II program. A survey has shown that 91 percent of all Space Camp and Space Academy attendees have become more interested in mathematics, science, and technology than before their space training experience; 63 percent have taken an additional course in mathematics or science that they would not have taken before. Through the formation of the U.S. Space Camp Foundation, the motivational camp and academy curricula continue to expand, with facilities near NASA's Kennedy Center in Titusville, Florida; at Kitakyushu, Japan; and at Rudu, Belgium. A Space Camp facility in Madrid, Spain, is expected to open in the spring of 1993.

■

The U.S. Astronaut Hall of Fame in Titusville, Florida, tells the story of each of the Mercury 7 astronauts. The capsule shown is Sygma 7, *which was flown by Walter M. Schirra on 3 October 1962. U.S. Astronaut Hall of Fame.*

An effort is under way to promote cooperative learning experiences between the young people of the U.S. and the Soviet Union. The program has included a computer linkup between Soviet young people and Space Camp trainees and a visit made by a Space Camp delegation to the Moscow City Pioneer and Schoolchildren Palace (the closest Soviet equivalent of Space Camp). During a visit by a Soviet delegation, an award bestowed primarily on Soviet cosmonauts was given to Space & Rocket Center management. Center managers visited the Soviet Union in 1989 at the request of the Soviet Academy of Sciences for a meeting on the history of aviation and astronautics. It is planned to continue exchange programs and visits between U.S. and Soviet youth.

With the advent of space science centers, motivational youth programs, and increased opportunities for media attention, America's space program has gained public favor. This popularity has become a catalyst for the creation of even more educational opportunities. Public demand, coupled with the maturity of the space program, has widened the truly interested audience, suggesting continuing public favor and ever-increasing popularity. Evidence of this is the 600,000 visitors at the U.S. Space & Rocket Center in 1990, with 8,200 attending the 20th birthday celebrations. A record 26,000 youngsters went through the Huntsville and Titusville Space Camps in that year, and, by the spring of 1991, the 100,000th attendee had been registered.

Contemporary Space Societies

According to Jon Miller, professor of political science at Northern Illinois University, one in four Americans possesses a high level of interest in space travel.[1] But only about 10 percent of adult Americans are what Miller calls the "de facto" or "attentive" public in day-to-day space issue politics. These citizens are very interested in spaceflight and consider themselves well informed, following the news on the subject of space and willing to inform Congress and the White House of their opinions.

In the aftermath of the successful Apollo lunar landings, as space launchings dwindled and program goals were perceived as a reduced national priority, the pattern of public attitudes about space seemed to change too. In 1974, some pivotal events occurred.

The last crew occupied the Skylab. This first-generation U.S. space station was NASA's effort to apply the space technology of the Apollo program to broad scientific and industrial use. NASA was also appropriated an initial low level of funding for the design and development of the reusable space shuttle. The White House, Congress, and the press were increasingly critical. Faced with these shifting priorities, some members of the public, especially students who had caught the bug of space exploration, were feeling disenfranchised. Even the technical professional societies, such as the American Institute of Aeronautics and Astronautics (AIAA), sometimes despaired. All the space program's constituents soon recognized that public interest was the necessary force to drive renewed spaceflight programs. The question was how to stimulate sufficient public interest.

Between 1973 and 1975, two differing approaches were taken that gave rise to two quite distinct organizations. In 1973, NASA and aerospace industry officials determined that grass-roots support for their plans was necessary. Officers of the National Space Club, an industry association founded as the National Rocket Club the day Sputnik 1 was launched in 1957, decided that they should go public. Their objective was to create a new organization, a membership association dedicated to the public support of NASA. To do this effectively they needed an individual with a big name to attract public attention. There was general agreement among the organizers that Wernher von Braun was the person for the job. To millions of people, he had become the first really well-known and understandable space scientist.

In 1974, shortly after his retirement from NASA, von Braun agreed to become the first president of the newly formed National Space Association. While it was seeking start-up funds from the aerospace industry, the organization encountered resistance from some who perceived it as just another association. So in early 1975 its name was changed to the National Space Institute.[2] Von Braun described the purpose of the NSI as "to generate broad public support for the many direct contributions our national space program can render."[3]

The NSI was to reach out to the public through celebrity recognition. Board members included Isaac Asimov, Hugh Downs, Bob Hope, and Jacques Cousteau. Various mechanisms for membership development and communication were considered.

These included a newsletter, *Insight,* later to become a self-sustaining publication, first called *Space World* and now *Ad Astra;* high visibility conferences; tours to space shuttle launches; and Dial-a-Shuttle, a phone-in service allowing people to listen to live space shuttle communications. Because of its NASA connections, the NSI was originally tapped by the Reagan administration to start the Young Astronauts Program. The NSI connected the public with the political process through testimony to Congress. It was the first widely representative space interest organization to tell Congress what its members thought.

During the same period that the space establishment was organizing the NSI to interface with grass-roots American public support, some elements of that public were coalescing and reaching up from the grass roots. Several space-attentive individuals, only a few of whom had technical training, and none with public name recognition, were inspired to act in support of a renewed space effort. What fired their imaginations was an old idea modernized by a Princeton University physics professor.

In the fall of 1969 Professor Gerard O'Neill sought to inspire a first-year class of Princeton physics students to become more interested in their technical subjects. He saw a challenge in demonstrating to these prospective scientists and engineers that their professions were "relevant" to human problems. The question that he posed to his students came out of his interest in space (two years earlier, he had been a finalist in the first group of Apollo scientist-astronauts) and his concern over the then-current paradigm of a human steady-state future of limited growth. O'Neill asked, "Is a planetary sur-

face the right place for an expanding technological society?"[4] The rudimentary results of that class exercise stimulated him to expand on the idea of large space habitats fabricated from extraterrestrial resources. Space colonies! A concept expressed previously by Konstantin E. Tsiolkovsky, J. D. Bernal, Arthur C. Clarke, and Dandridge M. Cole had found a new apostle.[5]

Publishing an elaboration of the idea in the magazine *Physics Today,* along with a letter in *Nature* and a small conference in 1974, began a popular movement.[6] The public saw an idea that held hope for the solution of some global problems—and it would take lots of people into space! To many who despaired over diminished U.S. space activity, and who had earthly concerns focused by the energy crisis, it was a great idea on an absolutely grand scale.

Young engineers, scientists, students, and concerned citizens rallied around this idea of large-scale space development. In Tucson, Arizona, "the first large organization stimulated by O'Neill's vision appeared" with the incorporation in August 1975 of the L5 Society.[7] The name came from O'Neill's proposition that large human settlements should be located in orbits around gravitationally stable points in the Earth-Moon system. One such location follows the Moon in its orbit of the Earth by 60 degrees. It is termed Lagrange point five, or L5. The first president of the L5 Society was a young entrepreneurial engineer, Keith Henson. He and his wife, Carolyn, began this organization with an intense sense of purpose. From them came the unofficial ultimate goal of the society: to disband in a mass membership meeting in a space colony.

L5ers began making political contacts even before they began seeking memberships. They worked out of the Henson home with borrowed equipment and an all-volunteer staff; those who became members were mostly fellow activists, many with a strongly independent and even libertarian bent. The L5 Society formed a chapter system that expanded to over 90 officially recognized local groups, although most were relatively small and inactive. It also created a

Professor Gerard O'Neill, center, *spiritual father of the L5 Society. Carolyn Henson,* left, *and her husband, Keith,* right, *founded the society in* 1975. *This photo was taken on 6 November 1980 after a lecture by O'Neill at the University of Arizona. National Space Society.*

National Space Society's office in Washington, D.C. National Space Society.

phone tree network of volunteers that alerted members to take action concerning relevant national space issues. Some individuals within the organization were also good at sloganeering. One notable example was "Decentralize: get off the planet!"

During the late 1970s and early 1980s, many things changed for both organizations. Von Braun died in June 1977. The occasional radicalism of the L5 Society polarized its membership and closed doors to growth. Neither it nor the National Space Institute achieved for very long the public stature that was needed. In many ways the two groups gave the appearance of representing opposite ends of pro-space opinion. Many saw the NSI as being just the public relations arm of NASA and the aerospace industry; to many people the L5 Society was the anti–space establishment. Science fiction author and L5 board member Jerry Pournelle told its annual conference in 1984 that this group of "kooks" was the "advanced planning department of the human race."

In 1985, even as the division seemed to be increasingly evident between those who wanted to explore space and those who wanted to stop along the way and develop it, these two groups found themselves coming together out of an economic necessity. Guided most visibly by L5 officers Gordon Woodcock and Mark Hopkins and NSI's Glen Wilson, a merger of the two was hammered out. In 1986 the combined membership voted to name the new organization the National Space Society. Today the NSS is growing with the L5 Society chapter system and the national phone tree network. It publishes a glossy magazine *(Ad Astra)* and is involved in educational programs around America. It still conducts the NSI's space shuttle launch tours and holds regional and national meetings for membership and the public.

As the concept of space travel and its meaning to America and the world are still evolving, so are its public and private institutions. Many groups have sprung forth to present spaceflight to the public. As with the environmental movement, diversity of interest will probably prevent complete coalescence of public-interest space groups. But that is not important. Among the public, active interest in promoting space travel is now organized; and the public appreciates the importance of space. At the end of the 1980s more than three out of every four Americans polled believed that the Apollo Moon landings were worth the expense and effort.[8] Ten years earlier less than half those polled felt that way. The vision shared by von Braun, O'Neill, and many others is now common. As von Braun put it, "Earth does not pose a limit for man. Our limit is the sky."[9]

Notes

1. Jon D. Miller, *The Impact of the Challenger Accident on Public Attitudes toward the Space Program: A Report to the National Science Foundation* (Public Opinion Laboratory, Northern Illinois University, 25 January 1987).

2. Michael A. G. Michaud, *Reaching for the High Frontier* (New York, 1986: Praeger Publishers).

3. Wernher von Braun, "Space and America's Most Pressing Problems" (undated paper).

4. Gerard O'Neill, *The High Frontier: Human Colonies in Space* (New York, 1976: William Morrow).

5. See Konstantin Tsiolkovsky, *Beyond the Planet Earth*, translated by Kenneth Syers (New York, 1960: Pergamon Press); J. D. Bernal, *The World, the Flesh and the Devil* (London, 1929: Methuen); Arthur C. Clarke, *Islands in the Sky* (New York, 1954: Holt, Rinehart & Winston); and Dandridge M. Cole and Donald W. Cox, *Islands in Space* (New York, 1964: Chilton).

6. Gerard K. O'Neill, "The Colonization of Space," *Physics Today*, September 1974, pp. 32–40; Gerard K. O'Neill, Letter to the Editor, *Nature*, August 1974.

7. Michaud, *Reaching for the High Frontier*, p. 83.

8. *USA Today* poll, conducted by Gordon S. Black Corp., 14 July 1989.

9. Wernher von Braun, document quoted in the *Rosslyn Review*, 22 January 1976.

Sampling of Space-Related Centers and Museums

Chicago Museum of Science and Industry, Henry Crown Space Center
57th Street and Lake Shore Drive, Chicago, Illinois

Kansas Cosmosphere and Space Center
1100 N. Plum St., Hutchinson, Kansas

The Space Center
Alamogordo, New Mexico

National Air and Space Museum
Washington, D.C.

Reuben H. Fleet Space Theater and Science Center
Balboa Park, San Diego, California

San Diego Aerospace Museum
2001 Pan American Plaza, San Diego, California

U.S. Space & Rocket Center
Huntsville, Alabama

Other Space and Aeronautical Information Centers

Air Force Space Museum
Cape Canaveral Air Force Station, Florida

Hugh L. Dryden Flight Research Center
Edwards, California

Goddard Space Flight Center
Greenbelt, Maryland

Lyndon B. Johnson Space Center
Houston, Texas

John F. Kennedy Space Center
Cape Canaveral, Florida

Langley Research Center
Hampton, Virginia

Lewis Research Center
Cleveland, Ohio

George C. Marshall Space Flight Center
Huntsville, Alabama

John C. Stennis National Space Technology Laboratories
NSTL, Mississippi

U.S. Army White Sands Missile Range Museum
White Sands, New Mexico

Vandenberg Air Force Base
Titan Missile Museum
Vandenberg, California

Principal Public-Interest Space Organizations

National Space Society
922 Pennsylvania Avenue, S.E.
Washington, D.C. 20003
202/543–1900

Purpose

Information, education, and activity-oriented organization. Concerned with all aspects of civilian space exploration and development leading to the creation of a spacefaring civilization. Over 30,000 members with some 130 chapters world-wide.

National Space Club
655 15th Street, N.W., #300
Washington, D.C. 20005
202/639–4210

Purpose

Organized to promote U.S. leadership in rocketry and astronautics through scholarships and public education. Membership of 1,500.

The Planetary Society
65 North Catalina Avenue
Pasadena, CA 91106
818/793–5100

Purpose

Promotes space exploration, planetary research, and the search for extraterrestrial intelligence. Sponsors public events and offers educational materials. Over 100,000 members around the globe.

Spacecause
International Space Center
922 Pennsylvania Avenue, S.E.
Washington, D.C. 20003

Purpose

Lobby for all aspects of the U.S. civil space program.

Spacepac
International Space Center
922 Pennsylvania Avenue, S.E.
Washington, D.C. 20003

Purpose

Independent pro-space political action committee. Supports candidates on the basis of their willingness to work for the exploration and economic development of space.

Space Studies Institute
P. O. Box 82
Princeton, NJ 08542
609/921–0389

Purpose

Scientific, research, and educational organization. Dedicated to opening the high frontier of space through technology development and the use of space resources for human benefit. Membership numbers more than 4,000.

Spaceweek National Headquarters
1110 NASA Road One, Suite 100
Houston, TX 77058
713/333–3627

Purpose

Promotes the public celebration of space. Assists organizations in developing public space-related activities during July each year.

Students for the Exploration and Development of Space
M.I.T. W20–440
77 Massachusetts Avenue
Cambridge, MA 02139
617/253–8897

Purpose

Education-oriented campus-based organization of high school and college students. Publishes newsletter and career information. Sponsors national and international conferences, and scholarship program. More than 4,000 members.

United States Space Foundation
P. O. Box 1838
Colorado Springs, CO 80901
719/550–1000

Purpose

Educational organization serving as a national resource for all aspects of civil, commercial, defense, and international space activities. Conducts teachers' workshops and an annual public symposium. More than 1,250 members.

Young Astronaut Council
1211 Connecticut Avenue, N.W., Suite 800
Washington, D.C. 20036
202/682–1985

Purpose

Administers the Young Astronaut Program for elementary and junior high school students promoting the study of math, science, and space-related subjects. Over 26,500 chapters and 650,000 members world-wide.

For further reading

Cobun, Peter. "A Camp for Space Science." *Science Year 1991, World Book Annual Science Supplement*. Chicago, 1990: World Book.

Cobun, Peter. "U.S. Space and Rocket Center." *Science Year 1991, World Book Annual Science Supplement*. Chicago, 1990: World Book.

Cole, Dandridge M., and Donald W. Cox. *Islands in Space*. New York, 1964: Chilton.

Hiller, B. B., and Neil W. Hiller, *SpaceCamp*. New York, 1986: Scholastic. (A novelization for young readers of the ABC Motion Pictures film release "SpaceCamp," produced by Patrick Bailey and Walter Coblenz and directed by Harry Winer.)

Michaud, Michael A. G. *Reaching for the High Frontier*. New York, 1986: Praeger Publishers.

Miller, Jon D. *The Impact of the Challenger Accident on Public Attitudes toward the Space Program: A Report to the National Science Foundation*. 25 January 1987: Public Opinion Laboratory, Northern Illinois University.

O'Neill, Gerard K. *The High Frontier: Human Colonies in Space*. New York, 1976: William Morrow.

Schulke, Flip and Debra, and Penelope and Raymond McPhee. *Your Future in Space: The U.S. Space Camp Training Program*. New York, 1986: Crown Publishers.

U.S. Space & Rocket Center. Huntsville, 1990: U.S. Space & Rocket Center.

United States Space Camp. Huntsville, 1990: U.S. Space & Rocket Center.

Toward the Moon, Asteroids, and Mars

WILLIAM K. HARTMANN

Over the last three decades, we have seen destructive arguments between the proponents of unmanned and manned exploration. The strictest-minded researchers, interested only in obtaining new measurements from instruments, argue that the next space program should consist only of unmanned black boxes sailing off to various planets, moons, asteroids, comets, and plasmas. To most of us—to most of the public, many scientists, and all space buffs—this is unsatisfying. Space exploration has been a human adventure as well as a mechanical means of data gathering. Data gathering is the rational side of space exploration and human adventure is the less rational side. Is there any way to make a rational defense of human spaceflight? Twenty to forty billion dollars per planet is a lot to pay just for the thrill of witnessing the first footsteps on virgin regolith (the unconsolidated residual surface material covering the solid rock of a planet or moon). And personally, I'd like space exploration to amount to more than the thrill that dune-buggy drivers get when they despoil the wilderness. It's a question of what kind of civilization we want to build. Space exploration ought to do *something* for our civilization. Does it?

I propose to evaluate our coming space opportunities in this context. In my view, the future exploration of the Moon, asteroids, and Mars—robotic and human—ought to be an integrated program that reflects the kind of civilization we want to build. I think we should want, and actually do need, a program that involves a base on the Moon; ongoing robotic reconnaissance of asteroids, Phobos, Deimos, and Mars; testing of asteroid resources; and probable eventual human exploration of Mars. Such a program would be driven not only by interesting intellectual challenges, like the origins of the solar system and of life itself, but also by practical concerns about what is happening on Earth: changes in our climate, impending exhaustion of mineral and fossil fuel reserves, and pollution by heavy industry. The program that we can choose to shape would be designed not only to give us science facts, but to see if we can demonstrate human capabilities in space: to gain knowledge about how climate changes work; to discover metals and other resources in asteroids and to utilize them; and to demonstrate the potential for utilizing solar energy in space. The program would be a blend of data gathering and exploration, research and adventure, robotic and human activity.

Where We Stand: Current Plans

Every year in March, NASA's Johnson Space Center in Texas is the site of an annual Lunar and Planetary Science Conference. Each year, one night, "NASA Night," is devoted to presentations about the current state of the American program, and foreign visitors often present the latest plans of other space agencies as well. In recent years, the dismembered Saturn V booster from the Apollo program, lying on its side in the grass at the entry to the Johnson Space Center, often seemed to represent the air of gloom that hung over NASA Night. Always the NASA officials were upbeat:

several missions were in the works; last year's cuts were awful, it was true, but this year there was a good chance that . . . , etc. Often, however, researchers were cynical. Grant increases didn't materialize. Problems with the shuttle ate up dollars that might have gone into smaller, cheaper mission launches with expendable boosters. Arguments ensued between the black box researchers and the advocates of the shuttle and space stations.

One change in recent years was the tone of the Soviet presentations. In the 1970s and early 1980s, the Soviets were tight-lipped about their future plans. But from the mid-1980s on, with glasnost, the Soviets presented each year a more and more amazing program aimed at the Moon and Mars. In March 1989, the upbeat Soviets outdid even their earlier performances. Their fresh new slides from the Phobos-2 probe showed the black Martian moon, Phobos, hanging in front of Mars. The Russian speaker who showed these was interrupted by a spontaneous ovation from the audience. Phobos-2 was even then closing in on Phobos to get even more impressive results.

The confident Soviet scientists went on to describe with slides and films the most ambitious program they had ever presented. A possible 1992 lunar orbiter would map lunar mineralogy. The Mars '94 twin probes would deploy Soviet-French balloons to drift over Mars for 10 to 12 days, covering several thousand kilometers, photographing surface features and touching down at night to gather ground data. In 1996, they planned two probes that would each fly by three or four asteroids and one comet, approaching one final asteroid close-up to deploy penetrators onto the asteroid's surface (this would be based on the design of the Phobos mission). A 1998 launch using the Energia booster would send a Viking-class lander and/or rover to the red planet to return with samples. At the end of the century might come a Mercury rover. Cosmonauts might reach the Moon soon after 2000, with a lunar base established by 2010.

The Soviets emphasized the value of international cooperation on all these missions, especially the Mars sample return mission. Academician Valery Barsukov reported that during a November 1988 conference in Washington, the Soviets had invited Americans to participate in all their missions, so that there would be "no question of who is behind or who is ahead. We will both be ahead." Asked about the lunar base, he went on to remark, "I hope there are two flags flying on the lunar base." There was more applause.

Within weeks, events dampened this optimism. Phobos-2 was lost, apparently due to mechanical malfunction, before it could accomplish its most challenging goals. (Contrary to impressions from Western press reports, however, Phobos-2 was not a total failure. It did get exciting new data, such as an improved measurement of Phobos's puzzlingly low density—similar to that of certain water-rich carbonaceous meteorites.) Severe criticism from Soviet journalists, scientists, and ordinary citizens was now leveled at the Soviet space program. The bold perestroika program at home was still meeting delays in improving the Soviet domestic economy. Letters to the editors of the newly opened editorial pages in the USSR became ever more critical: "We need groceries here; Mars can wait."

The upshot is that the future of the Soviet Moon, asteroid, and Mars program is uncertain. Surely there has been a shift from the successful Soviet Venus lander program of the past to a new first-priority emphasis on Mars. Almost surely there will be an ambitious attempted mission in 1994, possibly slipping to 1996, with an orbiter and balloon or surface probes. Probably there will be follow-up robotic Mars probes in the later 1990s. One of the big questions is whether an international mission will emerge, such as a Soviet-American robotic sample return mission.

In the U.S., on 20 July 1989 President Bush used the 20th anniversary of the first footsteps on the Moon to declare that Americans should return to the Moon, establish a permanent presence there, and go on to Mars. At the March 1990 Lunar and Planetary Science Conference in Houston, there was therefore quite a new mood on the American side. NASA managers were clearly taking this as a mandate to begin planning with a scale and mood not seen since the Apollo days. Suddenly NASA Night featured slides of new, improved lunar landing modules and designs for piloted Mars landers.

The most encouraging thing from my perspective, however, was that all the NASA speakers stressed a vision of a coordinated program blending robotic and manned exploration, clearly intending to head off the kinds of arguments we had during the 1970s, when black box scientists blasted the shuttle and space station so vehemently and so publicly that it arguably hurt the whole program instead of improving it.

As for missions on the American side, the Galileo probe was already on the way to Jupiter, the Magellan radar mapper already en route to Venus, and the robotic Mars Observer probe was awaiting launch for its 1992 mission. It is planned to go into orbit to observe the atmosphere chemistry and some soil properties of Mars. So things seemed upbeat.

Recently, however, the American program has also suffered a setback. Incredibly, the Hubble Space Telescope, which had been expected to be the greatest advance in astronomy since Galileo, and which had awaited its launch in storage and test facility for several years due to the Challenger-induced delay in shuttle launches, turned out to have a serious design or manufacturing flaw in one or more of its main mirrors, and had never been adequately tested optically in final assembled form on the ground. Once it got into orbit, researchers discovered that it did not focus sharply. This was a stunning blow. Such a basic flaw in American design and engineering throws doubt on America's ability to design and fly challenging missions at the turn of the century. To add delay to injury, the complete shuttle fleet was grounded for many weeks at the same time due to an elusive leak in the fuel system.

So we are left with a real question about the future of space exploration. Europe and Japan are rapidly emerging as centers of space exploration. A consortium of European countries successfully built the Giotto probe that stared into the eye of Halley's comet without blinking; Japan has sent less sophisticated probes past Halley's comet and the Moon. Yet of the leading spacefaring nations, the United States and the Soviet Union, we face questions about the competence of their design, manufacturing, and/or quality control processes; and all major projected missions, from the European-American Cassini mission to Titan to the projected U.S. space station, are being questioned. In short, these are questions about the nature of our global technological civilization. Do we still have the will, funding, and ability to explore space? Will we decide that other activities are more important?

A Practical Program for the Moon, Asteroids, and Mars

Scientific as well as practical considerations favor a vigorous program in the coming decade that will focus on the Moon, asteroids, and Mars. A number of forces are converging on this multi-pronged program, although these forces have not been widely recognized. They are as follows:

1. The general evolution of pure research questions in planetary science, particularly questions about the early history of planets and evolution of their surface environment
2. The need to understand environmental influences that may cause climate change and ecological degradation of Earth
3. The depletion of fossil fuel and mineral resources of Earth, including petroleum, coal, and metal
4. The degradation of Earth's environment by dumping of industrial waste products into the ecosphere—a process that will increase as Third World countries try to emulate the consumer economies of developed countries
5. The general political desire to apply space research to terrestrial problems

Space research may have answers to all five problems. In brief:

1. Exploration of the Moon and asteroids provides access to rocks that reveal processes from 3.5 billion years ago, back to the beginning of the solar system 4.5 billion years ago; most Earth rocks are much younger than 3.5 billion years, because of Earth's active erosion processes.
2. Mars gives us a chance to study the most Earth-like planet, on which (to our surprise) a dramatic climate change happened that apparently ended a period of liquid water flow in rivers, causing a change to frozen, arid conditions.
3. Asteroids contain abundant metals and other resources.
4. If we can demonstrate the ability to process and refine the resources of asteroids *in space,* and utilize the 24-hour-per-day solar energy in space, we may be able to reverse the tide of industrial degradation of Earth.
5. All of these steps are dramatic examples of understanding the Earth better and applying our knowledge to exciting problems.

I will describe specific projects that I believe should be important elements in space exploration. Some of these diverge somewhat from the themes proposed by advisory committees of NASA and foreign space agencies, because they include more than purely scientific problems; they spill over into problems of practical application. There are four steps in the program.

1. *Establish a lunar base.* A lunar base, in addition to being a site for repairable radio and optical observatories, low-gravity physiology experiments, etc., would have a unique opportunity to study a problem of interest to a broad range of sciences: the problem of obliteration of many terrestrial species 65 million years ago, apparently as a result of the impact of one or more asteroids. A concentration of asteroidal elements, together with soot and tsunami deposits, exactly in the soil stratum that marks the end of the Cretaceous period 65 million years ago has convinced many scientists that a 10-kilometer-diameter asteroid impacted at that time, causing global forest fires and sending "tidal waves" rolling over parts of continents. Dust was thrown into the stratosphere, blocking sunlight for months, and climate changes wrought havoc in the food chain, eventually causing the extinction of dinosaurs and many species of animals and plants.

An important question for this theory is whether there was one random asteroid impact or a whole shower of asteroids (or comets). Some scientists have claimed that the few ancient impact craters on Earth are clustered in age, indicating periodic episodes of impact every 30 million years or so. Others go further and speculate that a distant, small, undiscovered star orbits around the Sun in this interval of time, disturbing the comet swarm that surrounds the solar system, causing waves of comets to crash into the planets every 32 million years or so. Still other scientists dispute this. A number of other unexplained episodes of extinction occur in Earth's fossil record, for example 32 and 240 million years ago. A high percentage of species died in each of these. But little firm evidence has been found to correlate these extinction catastrophes with an asteroid impact.

The cause of these extinction episodes is crucial to understanding the evolution of life on Earth. Biologist and historian of science Stephen Jay Gould has gone so far as to say that confirmed asteroid-impact extinctions would create a revolution in Darwinian evolution theory, because Darwin pictured evolution

Return to the Moon. Painting by William K. Hartmann.

as fueled only by competition among species and individuals against a background of very slow geologic evolution; asteroid impacts would imply catastrophic changes caused by external forces from beyond Earth's ecosphere.

Interestingly enough, if we had a lunar base, we could test these ideas. We could send astronauts out to collect rock samples from, say, 4,000 modest-sized impact craters nearby. Dating techniques would establish the age of each crater. We could

■

Lunar base during an eclipse
of the Sun. Painting by
William K. Hartmann.

then plot the frequency of impact during Earth's and
Moon's history, with a resolution of about 1 million
years. The results would indicate whether Earth has
really been subjected to periodic waves of impacts or
only random blasts. Such results, in turn, would be
of high interest not only to lunar scientists but to
planetologists, astronomers, paleontologists, biolo-
gists, and others.

2. *Conduct asteroid reconnaissance.* We already
know from telescopic spectral observations and com-
parisons to meteorite samples that different spectral
classes of asteroids exist, of different compositions.
Some contain rich metal resources. Most of us recall
seeing pure nickel-iron alloy meteorites in museums.
These are broken pieces of asteroids that have
melted and differentiated into metal portions and
stony portions, like the iron and slag components in
a smelter. Apparently the nickel-iron is exposed in
many asteroids, and there may be several-kilometer

■

Looking homeward from the
Moon. Painting by William
K. Hartmann.

Exploring the lunar crater
Tycho. Painting by William
K. Hartmann.

chunks of pure metal on Earth-approaching orbits, as well as in the more populous asteroid belt. Other types of stony asteroids, as we know from meteorite samples, contain concentrations of other resources, such as the platinum-group metals. Still other asteroids contain water of hydration, or possibly ice, that may be a valuable resource for astronauts. Already at the University of Arizona and elsewhere, programs are under way to develop ways of utilizing these resources.

What we need to do is fly missions to a dozen asteroids and find out which spectral classes correspond to which compositions. In particular, which ones have high metal concentrations? And, are any of these among the group that approach close to Earth? These missions would be an extraordinarily important exploratory investment in our future. The reason is that nearly all projections of resource utili-

zation call for exhausting the easily accessible reserves of metal ores and fossil fuels during the next century. We can be fairly sure that significant economic and environmental change will result from this, possibly of grave discomfort to society. But if we can spend the next 10 years finding new resources in space, we have a way out. Evaluations of the total resource base in asteroid materials are remarkable. Individual modest-sized Earth-approaching asteroids, easier to visit than Mars, could supply Earth's total consumption of certain minerals for decades.

At this point, many readers object that such a program is a great mistake: a "disposable planet philosophy" that calls for exhausting Earth and then polluting space. I view it the other way. Pollution of interplanetary space is a relative non-problem, since the entire mass of Earth is hardly enough to cause

*Asteroid reconnaissance.
Painting by William K.
Hartmann.*

*Reconnaissance ship firing
exploding penetrator at asteroid to create seismic signals.
Painting by William K.
Hartmann.*

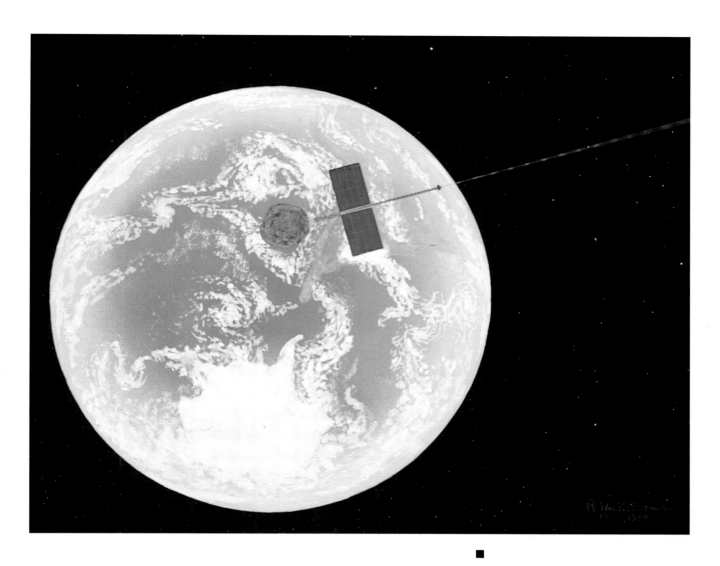

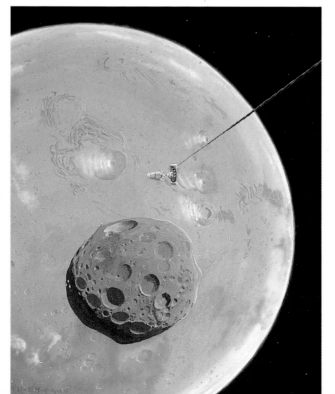

Mass driver bringing home an asteroid. Painting by William K. Hartmann.

Phobos base with attached transportation tether. Painting by William K. Hartmann.

Exploring volcanic crater on Mars. Painting by William K. Hartmann.

Astronaut in dune field on Mars. Painting by William K. Hartmann.

noticeable debris in the space from Venus to Mars; and, if processed into dust or smoke, it would be soon swept out of the solar system by the solar wind. The real problem to us as a species is continuing to dump our waste into our planet's ecosphere. Today, we are digging ever deeper, getting ever lower grade ores and fuels, and dumping the industrial by-products (from carbon dioxide to plutonium, from ozone-destroying gases to plastic debris) into our ecosystem. If we could find metal resources in space and demonstrate the technology to use solar energy to refine them, also in space, then we could begin to let our planet relax back toward its natural state, while we transfer our heavy industry into space.

This scheme to save the Earth is not yet economically viable. But every year, total costs of materials go up as ore gets poorer and harder to get and we pay for the environmental costs of processing them, while the costs of operating in space go down. Some day the curves will cross. We in this generation need to lay the groundwork, so that our grandchildren will know what opportunities are available in space.

3. *Reach Mars orbit and visit Phobos.* Tied into the asteroid program, and beginning our Mars program, will be the effort to reach Mars orbit and to study the satellites of Mars, Phobos and Deimos. This will be done first by robotic probes (as has already begun) and then by humans.

Phobos and Deimos are both small, black objects that appear to be the same as a class of black asteroids found in the outer half of the asteroid belt. They may have originated as asteroids and been captured by Mars. As such, they give us a chance to study a remote, strange type of asteroid on the way to Mars.

Two benefits result. First, we learn more about origins of asteroids and satellites. Second, we could use Phobos as a ready-made space station and supply base for Martian exploration. The black type of material on Phobos is believed by some researchers (including the writer) to contain water beneath its dehydrated surface, either in molecular form chemically bound in hydrated minerals or as ice. Thus, it may have resources valuable to Mars astronauts.

Some visionaries have even suggested establishing "Phobos University." The first human expeditions to Mars, instead of being quick round-trip dashes, might instead plan to colonize Phobos as a study

base for several years, with crews rotating through a permanent facility. It would basically be a case of shipping space station modules to Mars.

4. *Explore the surface of Mars.* Here the goal would be to solve the greatest mystery of Mars: how it went from a planet with running rivers (2 or 3 billion years ago) to a frigid, extremely dry planet today. Do not misunderstand the word "dry." It means that there is no liquid water on Mars today. But the water is there, in three forms: ice in the polar cap, ice in underground permafrost layers, and water hydration in various minerals.

Strangely enough, Mars has many ancient-looking dry riverbeds. If liquid water were exposed on Mars today, it would rapidly boil away or freeze. The atmosphere is too thin to allow liquid water to be stable. Apparently, in the past, the atmosphere was thicker. Where did the air go? How did the atmospheric density and chemistry change? Why? How long ago did the river channels splash with swirling currents? If we could answer these questions, we could perhaps understand better the processes of climate change that are affecting Earth today.

This fourfold program of space research would make an integrated scientific and practical program, easily understood by the public. It would not only have benefits for academic scientists in many fields but could have direct pay-offs to society. It would be a gamble, but an exciting gamble in which all residents of Earth could share vicariously. During any stage of our exploration, if we began to find that the asteroids or Mars did not live up to our expectations, we could pare back our efforts. On the other hand, the program might lead to an interplanetary economy matching the dreams of science fiction writers.

For further reading

Hargrove, Eugene C., ed. *Beyond Spaceship Earth.* San Francisco, 1986: Sierra Club Books.

Hartmann, William K. *Moons and Planets.* Belmont, California, 1983: Wadsworth.

Hartmann, William K., Ron Miller, and Pamela Lee. *Out of the Cradle.* New York, 1984: Workman Publishing.

Joint Working Group of the National Academy of Sciences and the European Science Foundation. *A Strategy for U.S./European Cooperation in Planetary Exploration.* Washington, D.C., 1986: National Academy of Sciences.

U.S. National Commission on Space. *Pioneering the Space Frontier: Final Report of the National Commission on Space.* New York, 1986: Bantam Books.

The Next 25 Years in Space

THOMAS O. PAINE

After the development of space station Freedom in this decade, the twenty-first century will see "Sons of Freedom" throughout the inner solar system. But to optimize the contribution of new space station technology to President Bush's Space Exploration Initiative, NASA needs to begin with a longer-range perspective on Martian exploration. The real question is not how Freedom's evolution leads to Martian exploration, but rather what space station program we need in the 1990s to initiate a Mars base by 2015.

At the first meeting of the National Commission on Space in 1985, we decided to look 50 years into the future, estimate the probable economic and technological environment, and recommend the appropriate space program for twenty-first-century America. We did not try to judge what might be salable in 1986 Washington—second-guessing the temper of the White House and Capitol Hill was not our assignment. When we had finished our work, we thought that our long-range vision would probably be considered too far-out in the first decade, about right in the second, and too pedestrian by the third. So far, I'd say it's about on track.

To respond to President Bush's Space Exploration Initiative, NASA, in my view, must develop six challenging new technology bases and program elements. Such a program will cost $300 to $400 billion dollars (three to five Apollo programs), probably requiring NASA manned spaceflight budgets of $9 billion to $15 billion through 2015, depending upon international participation.

1. *A highway to space,* using economical joint NASA–U.S. Air Force man-rated, heavy-lift launch vehicles to provide regular, automated, low-cost access to Earth orbit for massive cargoes and passengers. Two challenging programs are required: America's builders of missiles and bombers must retool to turn out post-Titan, post-shuttle, twenty-first-century heavy-lift launch vehicles in economical serial production, and NASA and the Air Force must work together with industry to construct and operate on a commercial basis a new state-of-the-art international spaceport on a Pacific atoll near the equator, with excellent year-round weather.

Kennedy and Vandenberg in the U.S., Kagoshima in Japan, Baikonur in the USSR, Taiyuan and Xichang in China, and Kouru in French Guiana cannot handle the future volume, cannot process large international payloads, cannot provide access to both equatorial and polar orbits, cannot safely launch nuclear reactors, cannot guarantee reusable stage recovery, and, most important, cannot achieve low cost through high productivity. The president's Space Exploration Initiative will require a highly automated launch complex meeting all these requirements by about 2001. NASA and the Air Force should organize a major project involving Japanese partners, architects, engineers, the State of Hawaii, Pacific Island authorities, and launch vehicle builders. We need an early decision on the best safe site for this essential twenty-first-century spaceport; Palmyra Island provides a good reference standard.

2. *Orbital spaceports* evolved from international space station Freedom technology, circling the Earth, Moon, and Mars, to support remote human operations and the assembly, storage, repair, refueling, checkout, launch, and recovery of robotic and

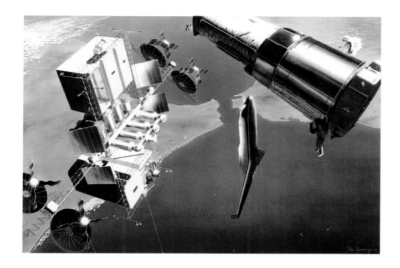

A concept of an Earth-orbiting transportation depot to provide assembly and storage of satellites, orbital transfer vehicles, and upper stages. Painting by Pat Rawlings. NASA.

piloted spacecraft. NASA is working hard to maintain space station Freedom's technology base, systems designs, microgravity research program, and international partnerships in the face of severe budget pressures. Questions being asked by the U.S. Office of Management and Budget and the Congress about the future are highly relevant and deserve to be answered. I believe that the best response is to work backward from large spaceports in orbit around three worlds.

From the outset, NASA should concentrate on the eventual requirements of Spaceport Mars, with lunar and Earth spaceports providing prototype testing and operating experience. These heavily shielded orbital bases must be able to keep men and women secure and healthy for years millions of miles from Earth, while serving as rescue centers, communication and transportation nodes, and fuel farms capable of converting water into hydrogen and oxygen.

3. *A bridge between worlds* to open regular transport to the Moon and to extend spaceflight to Mars (perhaps using automated electric propulsion/aerobraking cargo carriers and heavily shielded, artificial-gravity-equipped, international passenger spaceships cycling in permanent orbits between Earth and Mars). Reusable modular space-based transfer vehicles with hydrogen-oxygen engines and aerobraking shields will be required for flexible Earth-orbit transfer, and for Earth-Moon and Earth-Mars missions. Vehicles modified with landing legs will shuttle between orbital spaceports and the lunar and Martian surfaces.

Economical cargo transport beyond Earth orbit is in prospect using low-thrust, high-specific-impulse

solar or nuclear electric propulsion systems, with the propulsion electric generators adding to the useful delivered payloads. Large cycling spaceships swinging permanently between the orbits of Earth and Mars appear promising for twenty-first-century interplanetary passenger transport. Aerobraking transfer vehicles can ferry travelers between the cyclers and Spaceport Earth at one end of the long voyage, and the cyclers and Spaceport Mars at the other, eliminating the need to accelerate and decelerate the massive transports.

A cycling spaceship on the Mars run will probably resemble a 5,000-ton oceanographic vessel more than a Boeing 747 airliner. Large mass and volume will make possible redundant power and life support systems, well-equipped deep-space laboratories, comfortable living quarters, and closed-ecology biospheres. Safety features can include heavy shielding to protect crews from cosmic rays and solar flares, medical clinics, artificial gravity chambers, exercise gyms, and other health maintenance facilities.

Although the Apollo project demonstrated the feasibility of expendable spacecraft for flights to the Moon, the president's goal of bases on Mars suggests that NASA consider using prototype cycling spaceships on return trajectories in the Earth-Moon system to gain operational experience and confidence for Martian operations tens of millions of miles from Earth. Well-equipped lunar cyclers would also give scientists valuable research platforms for interferometry and other deep-space experiments, and allow engineers to check out robotic operations, artificial gravity chambers, and closed-ecology biospheres with 24-hour diel illumi-

The Wisconsin Center for Space Automation and Robotics designed this concept for mining helium on the Moon. NASA.

■

A lunar base concept depicting space nuclear power units and pilot plant for resource processing. NASA.

nation. During solar flares and passages through the Van Allen Radiation Belts, lunar travelers would welcome the massive shielding that will be essential aboard spaceships on the Mars run.

4. *Prospecting and resource utilization systems* to map and characterize the resources of the inner solar system, and to develop robotic processes for "living off the land" using indigenous materials on other worlds. Automated and piloted lunar orbiters, landers, and rovers have taught much about the Moon's resources, but we've literally only scratched the surface. Lunar soil for shielding, and oxygen for breathing and propulsion, may be the first resources developed.

The scarcity of hydrogen and other light elements on the Moon makes it less promising than Mars for self-sufficient settlements, since water will probably have to be imported. There's an outside chance that sunless craters at the lunar poles might contain trapped ice, so polar prospecting is planned in the next few years. Japanese lunar probes and NASA's reassembled Mars Observer spare parts might settle this question, but final proof may require geochemical penetrators. This is one of many robotic missions that must be planned to meet the requirements of the president's Space Exploration Initiative and to support the concurrent Mission to Planet Earth.

The Moon's proximity to Earth permits teleoperated systems, which are difficult to control on Mars due to communication time delays across 100 million miles. Robotic mapping, prospecting, and sample-return rover missions in the next decade must provide the engineering data needed to design Martian bases and their lunar prototypes, but more complex research should be postponed until scientists arrive.

5. *Closed-ecology biospheres* to recycle air and water and provide food and organic products within Earth-like habitats on other worlds. New systems will be required to support people living in bases tens of millions of miles from Earth. Air and water must be recycled and nourishing food produced within automated closed-cycle life support systems. We can probably recycle air and water, but little is known about constructing reliable biospheres that can be depended upon for food and organic products.

Closed-ecology experiments include the ambitious Biosphere II project outside Tucson, Arizona, NASA's compact but minimal Closed Ecology Life Support Systems (CELSS) project, and the Soviet Bios-3 project. Resolute Soviet test subjects have

One version of a transportation depot in Mars orbit. Illustrated are extravehicular activity; in-space habitats, which are tethered to and revolve around the depot, thus creating artificial gravity; and a docking port for excursion vehicles. Painting by Robert McCall, 1987. NASA.

been sealed within Bios-3 for 6 months, but some food was imported. The fare was reportedly terrible, but other enclosed agriculture in the Soviet Union has been successful. This is an excellent field for U.S.–USSR cooperative programs involving multidisciplinary government and university laboratories. Of all the critical elements, closed-ecology technology remains the least understood, the most challenging, and NASA's weakest field. Reliable CELSS designs with years of successful operating experience are essential for long-duration spaceflight and bases throughout the inner solar system.

6. *Lunar and Martian bases* to furnish advanced life support, habitats, power supplies, robotic systems, construction facilities, workshops, laboratories, transportation, and exploration infrastructure for sustained international operations on the Moon and Mars. By 2015, we must have in place the technology base and communication and transportation infrastructures needed to support a network of bases beyond Earth. By then all locations on the Moon should be accessible through surface or ballistic transport, and multidisciplinary international laboratories and workshops should be in operation, including broad-spectrum astronomical observatories operating on the far side. These should feature large infrared telescopes designed to detect planets orbiting other stars and check their atmospheres for traces of water vapor or life-generated oxygen.

The techniques perfected to build lunar bases will then be repeated on Mars. Men and women must "live off the land" with minimal dependence on the arrival of supplies every two years from distant Earth. This time scale obviously implies maternity wards from the outset. In addition to habitats and research laboratories, lunar and Martian bases both require better space suits, solar and nuclear electric generators in the 10–100 megawatt range, decentralized computers, automated plants to process indigenous materials, robotic construction machinery, general-purpose fabrication plants (with software links to twin factories on Earth), maintenance shops, transportation and communication facilities, etc.

Innovative architecture should take advantage of the Martian environment; for example, the use of on-site materials with ice binders to replace concrete in the subfreezing climate, and inflatable structures that take advantage of low atmospheric pressure. Japanese research institutes and corporations are displaying great interest in this field. With NASA's sights set on Mars, lunar base prototype systems

must be designed for adaptability to Martian conditions. The five previous elements all combine in this ultimate challenge.

As humanity moves outward from Earth, we must be prepared for alarms and excursions, breakthroughs and failures, triumphs and tragedies. Space exploration will remain a challenging enterprise, unsuited to the faint-hearted and irresolute. Success will require sustained U.S. commitment, while post–cold war advances in science, technology, and economic productivity effect profound changes on Earth. America will require bold leaders able to balance potential returns against losses to reach timely, informed decisions. Of course the next 25 years will not develop smoothly along the lines I've projected, so flexibility and back-up plans are prudent. But the time has come to commit major resources, as we are already doing in space station Freedom.

This leads me to a final recommendation of a step that should be taken immediately. NASA needs to organize a small high-level systems group (along the lines of BellComm in the Apollo program) to provide top-down oversight and overall integration of the above six elements essential to achieving the goals of the president's Space Exploration Initiative. This group must work backward and lay out the programs, budgets, and milestones that will support the first Martian baby in 2015.

For further reading

Allen, John, and Mark Nelson, with an introduction by Margaret Augustine. *Space Biospheres*. Revised edition. London and Tucson, Arizona, 1988: Synergetic Press.

Committee on Planetary and Lunar Exploration, Space Science Board. *A Strategy for Exploration of the Outer Planets*. Washington, D.C., 1986: National Academy of Sciences.

Oberg, James E., and R. Alcestis. *Pioneering Space: Living on the Next Frontier*. New York, 1986: McGraw-Hill.

Paine, Thomas O. "Humans in Space: Getting Them There, Supporting Them, and Enabling Them to Do Things." Paper presented at International Symposium on Technologies for Living on Frontiers at Australian Academy of Technological Sciences, Sydney, 8 September 1988.

U.S. National Commission on Space. *Pioneering the Space Frontier: Final Report of the National Commission on Space*. New York, 1986: Bantam Books.

Von Braun, Wernher. *The Mars Project*. Urbana, 1953: University of Illinois Press; rpt. 1991.

Visions of the Space Generation: Setting Sights on New Goals

ROBERT D. RICHARDS

TODD B. HAWLEY

PETER H. DIAMANDIS

Everywhere we look we find the building blocks of life. From the hearts of ancient meteorites to the vast interstellar nebulae, the tendency of the universe toward biological life is manifest. Among the greatest mysteries of the universe are that matter is capable of organizing itself into something that we call "life," that living things are capable of developing an interest in discovering their origins and destiny, and that the ability to do so exists within us humans.

The search for an understanding of our place in the universe has occupied our species since our ancestors first raised their furrowed brows to the heavens. The same search continues today, the fuel for all religion and all science, an inspiration for great art and philosophy. This fundamental urge toward exploration and discovery has led us forward, step after step, in our evolution as a sentient species. Few people are aware that one of the most pivotal evolutionary steps has happened only recently, despite the fact that an entire generation of people alive today has been fundamentally altered because of it. We humans have, in this generation, taken our first steps from our planetary cradle into the universe that surrounds us, and it has changed us forever.

The space generation was born on 4 October 1957, when the first instrument of humanity left the bounds of Earth. The flight of Sputnik I marked a clear division in humanity's evolution, a division that led to man's footprints on another world, the initial robotic reconnaissance of the solar system, and that will lead in the future to the establishment of humanity on other worlds of our solar system and, eventually, throughout the universe.

The space generation has been presented with opportunities that no other generation in human history has had. For two million years humanity has been two-dimensional—bound by gravity, physically and psychologically, to its mother Earth. But the space generation marks the beginning of three-dimensional man. The spirit and the vision of humanity are no longer constrained by gravity—they now extend beyond its reaches, into interplanetary space and all the universe beyond.

This new perception of our place in the universe was widely felt around the world in the 1960s when Apollo 8 returned the first pictures of our whole planet floating delicately in the vastness of space. That first photograph gave humanity a sudden sense of perspective; for the first time, the awareness dawned that the Earth is not eternal, but rather a fragile, finite place that requires careful stewardship.

The space generation came of age with the Apollo program, with motivations and expectations firmly implanted in their minds. By the mid-1980s, members of this generation had matured enough that they were able to begin to effect change. Now young professionals in a wide variety of areas the world over, the space generation is beginning to influence the commercial and political bodies responsible for the directions that humanity undertakes in space.

Historically, most large programs of exploration into new frontiers were motivated by the promise of commerce, and this will be the fundamental motivater in the exploration of space. But at the same time we find that the people who actually pioneered the new frontiers had different motivations. They were largely motivated by the promise of a new way of life, a chance to explore, to build a new society, or to escape the confines of an existing one. The space generation sees all these opportunities in humanity's future in space.

Leaving the Planetary Cradle

We have only now begun to recognize the fallacy that land, energy, raw materials, and other resources for human development must come from the Earth alone. Earth's reserves of energy and raw materials have been plundered at an alarming rate in the twentieth century—100 years of strip mining, dam building, waste heat and waste dumping that have taken their toll on Earth's fragile biosphere. By tapping into space energy and nonterrestrial materials for industrial use in space, we can stop our damage to Earth and move to a superior long-term paradigm for the protection of our home planet and parallel expansion of the industrial superstructure of our evolving technological civilization.

Scenarios for the development of solar power satellites (solarsats), asteroidal and lunar mining, and other likely space energy and materials sources are becoming well understood. Programs for their implementation will get under way in a few short years, leading to major new industries over the course of a single lifetime. These Space Age industries will have clear benefits for Earth by way of new products and energy. In the longer term, though, the capabilities of these new industries will be employed for even greater purposes.

While demand for space products and resources will be high on the Earth, a small but growing foothold will exist in space itself for emerging space industries. Manufacturing, processing, and entirely unexpected services and products will enable a growing number of organizations and individuals to be based in space on a full-time basis. Following the path laid out in the twentieth century by visionaries such as Konstantin Tsiolkovsky, J. D. Bernal, Dandridge M. Cole, Arthur C. Clarke, Gerard K. O'Neill, and Peter E. Glaser, these fledgling space industries will create a platform for a space-borne culture. The first children, the first schools, and the first retirement communities will arise at the fringes of space commerce and service industries, which will unfold in rapid succession as we enter the twenty-first century.

As we move out into space, human instinct and industry will lead us to reevaluate our notion of "the world." Just as the discovery of the American continents gave us a new world—our present global sense of Earth—we will begin to see the Moon, Mars, and ultimately free-space civilizations as part of our world in a very fundamental way. As inner solar system activity and settlement take place, new social freedoms and constraints will lead to opportunities to shape new—and perhaps ancient—forms of social contracts and interactions. Near-limitless energy and resources will drive early "artificial societies" toward experimentation and innovation in social structures, thus extending the human experiment beyond the generally inflexible matrix of current societal frameworks on Earth.

The Evolution of a New Species

Deep within the genetic code and ancestral instincts of our species is an insatiable urge to explore new frontiers. From the desert plains of Africa to the rivers and mountains of the Americas, from the origins of humanity to every region of this planet where we have existed, our species has risen to meet each terrestrial challenge. With each new frontier settled, we have sought another. And with every frontier passed, humanity has achieved a new vantage point. The challenge of Earth's deserts or mountains, of the depths of its oceans or the surface of the Moon, have presented humanity with opportunities to test and expand its limits and its capabilities.

Once the economic and sociological fruits of space are tasted, our expansion into it will be dramatic. This movement will be driven by the vast wealth of untapped materials and energy available within our solar system. Methods of travel approaching the speed of light will be achieved, allowing humans to cross the immense distances between the planets in mere hours—with much the same frequency and casualness with which humans have traversed the skies of Earth in the latter half of the twentieth century.

If we are to search for star systems to settle, other intelligent species with which to exchange knowledge, or venture into the universe to search for its ultimate mysteries, even high-technology and near-light speed will require decades, lifetimes, or generations to accomplish.

All life evolves in response to environmental stimuli. Changing environments and isolation are fundamental drivers of the evolutionary process. It should be no surprise therefore that the settlement of other star systems may lead to new evolutionary branches of *Homo sapiens*. We may in fact find that this happens with remarkable rapidity. Left to nature, the evolutionary process typically runs with agonizing slowness—millions of years are standard evolutionary calibrations. But with the help of microbiological sciences, these calibrations may be reduced to hundreds of years or even decades. What miracles lie ahead in genetic engineering we can only guess, but of certainty is the impact that human-engineered humans will have on the adaptability of our species to a variety of extraterrestrial environments, even those that would be lethal to human beings of the twentieth century.

By the time that our solar system has been settled and the majority of its mysteries identified, the human race will set forth across an uncharted and unknown void. With little expectation of ever again seeing the birthplace of humanity, the interstellar explorers will bring with them the most reliable commodity entrusted to them—the sum total of human knowledge from the sonnets of Shakespeare and the writings of Plato to the designs and technical drawings for fusion drives and power generators. In self-contained, traveling "worlds," humanity and its earthly habitats will be sown as fertile seeds tracing their lineage back to a brave group of hunter-gatherers on the plains of Africa.

With no new technology available to collapse a journey measured in light years, each new interstellar "world" will set forth as a totally self-sufficient biosphere. With the need to survive all but the most devastating of failures, as there are no guarantees of a destination, each "world" will set forth on a multi-lifetime—or multi-generation—mission to search out the unknown, to settle the regions of the galaxy, and perhaps most importantly to extend the outreach of Earth's life-forms, thus helping to ensure our long-term survival and presence in the universe.

Wild Cards

"Any technology sufficiently advanced will be indistinguishable from magic" (Arthur C. Clarke). Wild cards are those technologies, discoveries, or conceptual breakthroughs that fundamentally change the way we think and act, altering the course of human events. For the individual living in the year 1900, wild cards included such unimaginable or seemingly impossible developments as airplanes, the atom bomb, genetic engineering, space travel, artificial organs, and communications satellites, items that the next generation takes for granted.

What will be the wild cards during the next 50 to 100 years and how might they fundamentally alter the way we think and act? They might include:

1. Economical and practical fusion energy
2. Sentient, artificially intelligent computers
3. Indisputable evidence of extraterrestrial intelligence
4. Communication or contact with extraterrestrials
5. Discovery of gravity control
6. Indefinite extension of life
7. Nano-technology and molecular machines
8. De novo creation of new life-forms by humans
9. Near or even faster-than-light travel
10. Harnessing anti-matter as an energy source

These and other wild cards will all have the direct effect of accelerating the inevitable—helping the human race to settle and explore the cosmos. Imagine if the average human life span were extended 500 years—how many more wonderful discoveries would Einstein or any of humanity's great thinkers have made if their life had been ten times longer, in good or perfect health? But with every technological advance must come the wisdom with which to implement it. What is perhaps not obvious is the great danger that these same wild cards present to destroy or cripple our fragile existence. Since the discovery of fire, nearly every great technological tool has had the capacity to injure as well as improve the quality of life. Our progress toward the future envisioned in this chapter is not linear—it is an exponential growth in capability and expanding horizons. The space generation will see in its lifetime much more than is now thought possible or even conceived.

The Challenge

The most critical issue facing today's space visionaries is the one of changing our two-dimensional social structures to fit our new three-dimensional world. There are people in the world today who wish to turn space into a battlefield, in a sense transplanting old strategies of siege and conflict into the cosmos. The space generation must look at the

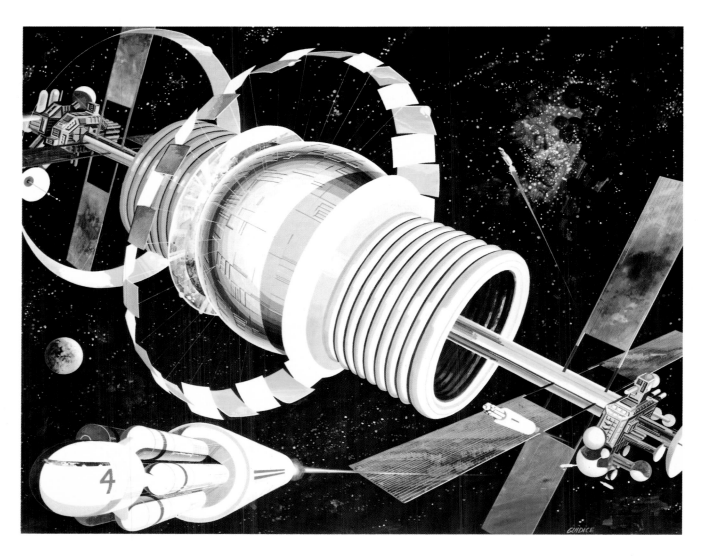

Solar power satellite (solar-sat) concepts have existed for decades. Grumman Aerospace Corporation, Bethpage, New York, designed this one in 1978. From its position in orbit, the satellite would transmit concentrated solar power as microwave beams to terrestrial rectifying antennas, "rectennas," where it would be converted into electricity and fed into the power grid. *NASA.*

Left: *Bernal Sphere, a con-* *space habitat housing as* *cept proposed by Gerard* *many as 10,000 people. Paint-* *O'Neill, is a design for a* *ing by Rick Guidice. NASA.*

world from the new perspective that it has gained. We must meet the challenge of the peaceful exploration and development of space, for if we don't, we may be destined to destroy ourselves, or at best descend into the shadows of our ancestral caves.

It may be that intelligence such as ours has flickered on a billion worlds, but has rarely survived annihilation by its own technology. It may be that every developing technological species has a window of opportunity—a time when a choice must be made whether to be self-destroying or self-creating. The technology for either choice is very similar; it is the intent that matters. The destiny of humanity will be determined by our ability to transcend catastrophe, whether natural or from our own devices. The universe cares not whether we are ready to safeguard our species; that is a local affair that is only of concern to us.

Vast and all but insurmountable, we know that the universe will confront us with an endless succession of challenges. But with every plateau reached, we will achieve a new vantage point. Today the space generation can call upon the wisdom of a thousand generations of human will and knowledge to overcome the forces of nature and the more formidable, darker forces of human nature. We have the enabling tools of science and technology, and the promise of infinite energy and resources among the stars. With all this, and new knowledge yet to be gained, we, like those who came before us, will search for the weaknesses in the walls that constrain us, and finding them will set our sights on what lies beyond.

■

View of Earth taken by the *Apollo 11 spacecraft en route* *to the Moon. The Earth is* *about 98,000 miles in the dis-* *tance. Will living beyond the* *border of planet Earth assist* *in erasing self-imposed terres-* *trial borders? Will this still* *unfamiliar vantage point* *reinforce the interdependence* *of mankind? NASA.*

For further reading

Heinlein, Robert A. *Stranger in a Strange Land.* New York, 1961: G. P. Putnam.

O'Neill, Gerard K. *The High Frontier: Human Colonies in Space.* Revised edition. Princeton, New Jersey, 1989: Space Studies Institute Press.

Ride, Sally K. *Leadership and America's Future in Space: A Report to the Administrator.* Washington, D.C., 1987: National Aeronautics and Space Administration.

U.S. National Commission on Space. *Pioneering the Space Frontier: Final Report of the National Commission on Space.* New York, 1986: Bantam Books.

Epilogue

ARTHUR C. CLARKE

No contribution of mine to this volume could be more appropriate than the review I wrote in 1950 of the famous Bonestell-Ley book, *The Conquest of Space*. Here it is, exactly as it appeared in the *Journal of the British Interplanetary Society* (January 1950, pp. 41–42), followed by some comments to put it in today's perspective.

THE CONQUEST OF SPACE

(Paintings by Chesley Bonestell; Text by Willy Ley. pp 160, 18 fig., 48 plates, 16 in colour. $3.95; Viking Press, NY, 1949)

The eagerly-awaited Bonestell-Ley book has at last arrived, and it proves to have been well worth the waiting. Magnificently produced, it is extraordinary value for the money and the publishers are to be congratulated on their boldness and enterprise. It is a large book—11″ x 8 ¼″—and besides many line drawings, contains 48 plates, 16 of them four-colour reproductions. (It is pleasant to record, incidentally, that the colour plates were made in England, where apparently this sort of thing is done better than anywhere else. It is not so pleasant to record that the British Customs held up the original plates five weeks while the red tape slowly unwound. We also do this sort of thing better than anyone else!)

The book has a splendid cover jacket showing, on the front, the lunar rocket painting which has already been used as a cover of *Astounding Science Fiction,* and on the back, what is perhaps the finest of all Bonestell's works—the thin ring of Saturn, almost "new" and with the rings nearly edge on, against the deep blue of Titan's sky. (Titan, of course, being the only satellite which could have a blue sky.)

Of the interior illustrations, the black-and-whites would have been sufficiently impressive in themselves, but they inevitably lose by contrast with the colour plates. Is it too much to hope that when *The Conquest of Space* becomes the success it deserves to be, the proportion of colour to monochrome may be gradually increased? The reviewer would have given a good deal to see the "Great Wall," the Alpine Valley, Copernicus, Saturn from Rhea, and Jupiter from Satellite V in colour, and is only reconciled to the monochrome of the view over Theophilus, Saturn from Phoebe, and Saturn from Dione, by happening to possess coloured reproductions from other sources.

The colour plates are, going through the book, as follows: preparing the rocket for its trip to the Moon (in the reviewer's opinion, the least successful of the plates, since it somehow lacks the Bonestell touch, and might have been done by any merely competent artist); the Leibnitz Mountains during an eclipse of the Sun by the Earth; view from the South Pole of the Moon, with the Earth on the horizon; the rocket on the Moon, ready for the return; the surface of Mercury; the surface of Venus; Martian landscape seen from the polar cap; Mars seen from Deimos; Saturn from Japetus; Saturn from Titan; Saturn from Mimas; the double star Mira from a hypothetical planet; Martian landscape, green areas; Martian landscape, desert areas; surface of Jupiter; and Saturn's rings from the surface of the planet.

Willy Ley will no doubt be resigned to having his text overshadowed by the paintings, but he is by no means the junior partner in the enterprise. In a rather short space, he has given a remarkably detailed and thorough account of the subject, covering the theoretical principles of astronautics and, on the astronomical side, giving a clear account of the solar system and the characteristics of the planets. (Though it's a little surprising to find one of the four chapters devoted entirely to the asteroids.) Some of the statements in the astronomical section may be regarded as rather dogmatic, though probably Ley would defend this on the grounds of lack of space. In particular, it is somewhat surprising to find it stated more or less flatly that the lunar craters are meteoric in origin; there is no indication of the fact that a substantial proportion of astronomers—if not a majority—thinks that the meteoric theory is quite untenable.

The text is often dramatic—as in the opening passage, describing a typical White Sands launching—and frequently amusing. This sentence will appeal to many: "The layman may dream of a rocket which has a take-off weight of 33 tons for every ton of remaining weight, but the designing engineer would not touch the job and would indeed, gladly furnish the applicant with the addresses of his competitors."

It is much to be hoped that this fine book will become available in this country, despite present difficulties. No better introduction to astronautics could possibly be imagined, and many will echo Dr. Robert S. Richardson's remark, "I only wish that a book containing such illustrations could have fallen into my hands when I was a youngster." It is probably destined to fire many imaginations and to change many lives in the years to come.

On reading this review exactly 40 years later, my first reaction is astonishment at the price of this beautiful book—today, it would cost ten times as much!

I am also rather embarrassed by my comment on the meteoric origin of lunar craters. With the 20–20 vision of hindsight, it now seems incredible that anyone could ever have doubted that the majority of craters are meteoric. What confused the issue, of course, was the fact that there are signs of obvious volcanic activity on the Moon, so it seemed unnecessary to invoke *two* separate mechanisms.

I certainly never dreamed, when I was writing this review, that a couple of decades later, I should be working with Chesley on a joint volume, *Beyond Jupiter* (which I see cost only *three* times as much as *The Conquest of Space* when it was published in 1972!).

In the preface to *Beyond Jupiter,* I wrote:

The Conquest of Space *appeared in 1949, and probably did more than any book of its time to convey to a whole generation the wonder, romance and sheer beauty of space travel. Turning its pages today, almost a quarter of a century later, I can still recapture some of that initial excitement. About half of the book has already happened; the scenes which Bonestell painted, using the best contemporary knowledge, have now been photographed by robot space probes—and even more astonishing, by handheld cameras. On the whole, the pictures stand up very well; sometimes, indeed they are uncannily prescient, and future generations will hardly believe that they were so far in advance of the reality.*

And yet, that isn't the most amazing fact about Chesley's "visual forecasts." No one could have believed that in his own lifetime, he would be privileged to see the reality of the places he had depicted so long ago—thanks to the almost miraculous performance of the Voyager space probes.

Finally, I am quite sure that the last sentence of my review of *Conquest of Space* was amply fulfilled—and the work of Chesley and his colleagues will continue to inspire generations of astronauts to come.

Contributors

Ben Bova, formerly with the Martin and Avco-Everett Research Laboratory aerospace organizations, former editorial director of *Omni* magazine, president emeritus of the National Space Society and former president of the National Space Institute, is the author of some 75 science fiction and nonfiction books, including *The Voyagers Trilogy, The New Astronomies, The High Road, Assured Survival: Putting the Star Wars Defense in Perspective, First Contact: The Search for Extraterrestrial Intelligence, Welcome to Moonbase,* and *The Science Fiction Hall of Fame* (volumes IIA and IIB).

Edward O. Buckbee with Wernher von Braun and others helped guide the development of the U.S. Space & Rocket Center; since its opening in Huntsville, Alabama, in 1970 he has served as its director. Buckbee also spearheaded the development of the affiliated Space Camp and Space Academy, from which some 100,000 youngsters have graduated. More recently, he was closely involved in the creation of the U.S. Astronaut Hall of Fame in Florida and facilities in Japan, Belgium, and Spain based on the Huntsville center.

Arthur C. Clarke is a renowned and prolific author of science fiction and science fact, spaceflight visionary, and creator of the concept of communications satellites. Among his nonfiction works are *Ascent to Orbit, Astounding Days, The Challenge of the Spaceship, The Exploration of the Moon, The Exploration of Space, Interplanetary Flight, Profiles of the Future,* and *The Promise of Space.* His science fiction includes *Across the Sea of Stars, Childhood's End, Expedition to Earth, A Fall of Moondust, Imperial Earth, Prelude to Mars, Rendezvous with Rama, The Sands of Mars, The Sentinel, Tales from the "White Hart,"* and the three space odysseys: *2001* (on which the famed film was based), *2010,* and *2061.* With artist Chesley Bonestell, Clarke wrote *Beyond Jupiter.* He serves as chancellor of the International Space University and the University of Moratuwa.

Michael Collins joined the National Aeronautics and Space Administration in 1963, flying his first space mission as pilot of Gemini 10 in 1966. This was followed in 1969 as command module pilot on the historic Apollo 11 mission to the Moon. A retired major general in the U.S. Air Force Reserve, he left the space program in 1970 to become assistant secretary of state for public affairs; later he served as director of the National Air and Space Museum of the Smithsonian Institution. Collins is the author of *Carrying the Fire, Liftoff: The Story of America's Adventure in Space,* and other works.

Peter H. Diamandis is a founder and former CEO of the International Space University, the world's first university dedicated to international multidisciplinary graduate-level space studies; founder and first chairman of Students for the Exploration and Development of Space, the world's largest high school and college pro-space organization; cofounder and current director of the Space Generation Foundation; and founder, president, and CEO of MicroSat Launch Systems, a commercial space corporation dedicated to providing low-cost and reliable access to space. He holds B.S. and M.S. degrees from MIT in molecular biology and aerospace engineering and an M.D. from the Harvard Medical School.

R. Cargill Hall served as operations research analyst and historian for Lockheed Missiles & Space Company before moving to the California Institute of Technology's Jet Propulsion Laboratory as historian. He has served as a historian in several U.S. Air Force commands and is currently chief of the Contract Histories Program, Office of Air Force History. Hall is the author of *Lunar Impact: A History of Project Ranger* and numerous articles on space law and the history of aeronautics and astronautics appearing in *The American Journal of International Law, Technology and Culture, Aerospace Historian,* and others. He edits *Space Times.*

William K. Hartmann, internationally known as an astronomer, writer, and painter, discovered several of the giant multiringed basins on the Moon, coauthored the most widely accepted theory of lunar origin, and served as a coinvestigator on NASA's Mariner 9 Mars mapping mission. His research has shown relationships between comets and black-colored asteroids of the outer solar system, and he codiscovered the cometary outburst of "asteroid" 2060 Chiron in 1988. Asteroid number 3341 is named after him. Hartmann is author with Ron Miller of *The Grand Tour, Out of the Cradle,* and *Cycles of Fire.* With Miller and two Soviet artists, he edited *In the Stream of Stars,* a collection of Soviet and Western space art. Hartmann's paintings are found in national and international collections and were exhibited in Moscow and Yalta by the USSR Union of Artists. He served on the NASA Fine Arts Team to cover the Galileo launch to Jupiter in 1989. Hartmann holds a Ph.D. in astronomy, an M.S. in geology, and a B.S. in physics.

Gerald S. Hawkins obtained his Ph.D. in radio astronomy with Sir Bernard Lovell at Jodrell Bank, England, and a D.Sc. for astronomical research at the Harvard-Smithsonian Observatories. In 1963, he discovered that Stonehenge was built by neolithic people to mark the rising and setting of the Sun and Moon over an 18.6-year cycle, a discovery that stimulated the new field of archaeoastronomy. Formerly professor of astronomy at Boston University and Dean of the College at Dickinson College, he is the author of ten books (translated into nine foreign languages), including *Stonehenge Decoded, Beyond Stonehenge,* and *Mindsteps to the Cosmos.*

Todd B. Hawley is a founder and CEO of the International Space University, founding director of the Space Generation Foundation, and founding director of MicroSat Launch Systems. He completed undergraduate studies at George Washington University in 1983, and received his master's degree in Science, Technology and Public Policy there in 1988. Hawley earlier served on the White House–sponsored Young Astronaut Council and as the first international secretary general of the Students for the Exploration and Development of Space and was elected twice as national chairman. He is a distinguished colleague of the Space Studies Institute.

Alan Ladwig was formerly president of the Forum for the Advancement of Students in Science and Technology, manager of NASA's Shuttle Student Involvement Program, and manager of the Space Flight Participant ("teacher-in-space") program. He later joined NASA's Office of Exploration and finally the Office of Space Station. At NASA, Ladwig collaborated on the preparation of such long-range studies as *Leadership and America's Future in Space, Beyond Earth's Boundaries: Human Exploration of the Solar System in the 21st Century,* and *Exploration Studies Technical Report.* Since leaving the space agency, he has been an aerospace consultant.

Randy Liebermann is an art historian and collector in science and technology specializing in the history and evolution of space development. He is an authority on working relationships between scientists and artists.

John M. Logsdon is director of the Center for International Science and Technology Policy and of the Space Policy Institute of George Washington University's Elliott School of International Affairs. He is the author of *The Decision to Go to the Moon: Project Apollo and the National Interest* and editor of *The Research System in the 1980s: Public Policy Issues.* He has

been a Fellow at the Woodrow Wilson International Center for Scholars and was the first holder of the chair in space history of the National Air and Space Museum.

Ron Miller, a leading American illustrator of astronomical, astronautical, and science fiction topics, is the author or coauthor of some 20 books, including *The Grand Tour, Cycles of Fire, Out of the Cradle,* and *In the Stream of Stars* as well as a new translation of Verne's *20,000 Leagues Under the Sea,* which Miller also illustrated.

Sam Moskowitz is a leading historian of science fiction and author or editor of 60 books, including *The Immortal Storm, a History of Science Fiction Fandom; Explorers of the Infinite; Seekers of Tomorrow; Strange Horizons; Science Fiction by Gaslight; Science Fiction in Old San Francisco;* and *Under the Moons of Mars.* He was the director of The First World Science Fiction Convention in New York in 1939 and recipient of The Pilgrim Award from The Science Fiction Association for lifetime contributions to the field. He is a member of the Science Fiction Hall of Fame.

Frederick I. Ordway III formerly worked at America's first rocket engine enterprise, Reaction Motors, Inc., at the Guided Missiles Division of the Republic Aviation Corp., and with the von Braun team at the Army Ballistic Missile Agency and subsequently at NASA's Marshall Space Flight Center. Later, he became a professor at the University of Alabama in Huntsville's Research Institute and School of Graduate Studies and Research, where he remained until joining the Energy Research and Development Administration that subsequently merged into the Department of Energy. Ordway is the author or coauthor of such books as *International Missile and Spacecraft Guide, Basic Astronautics, Applied Astronautics, Conquering the Sun's Empire, Intelligence in the Universe, Space Travel: A History, The Rocket Team, New Worlds, Dividends from Space, The Rockets' Red Glare, Pictorial Guide to Planet Earth,* and *Life in Other Solar Systems* as well as some 250 articles; and, in addition, has edited a number of books including *Astronautical Engineering and Science* and *History of Rocketry and Astronautics.*

Thomas O. Paine, former deputy administrator and administrator of NASA, directed the space agency during the first seven Apollo expeditions to the Moon. He is a former president, chief operating officer, and director of the Northrop Corp.; a member of the National Academy of Engineering; and a director of the National Space Society and the Planetary Society. A leading advocate of an expanded space program, Dr. Paine directed NASA's *America's Next Decades in Space* report to the presidentially appointed Space Task Group and later served as chairman of the President's National Commission on Space, whose final report, *Pioneering the Space Frontier,* was both widely distributed and highly acclaimed.

Robert D. Richards is a cofounder and director of the International Space University; founder of the Canadian branch of Students for the Exploration and Development of Space International and of Young Astronauts Canada; cofounder of Space Generation Foundation; senior associate, Space Studies Institute; and president and chief operating officer of Canada Space Technologies, Inc., dedicated to providing international industrial and research communities with low-cost access to space.

Sally K. Ride holds a Ph.D. in physics from Stanford University, where she worked with a low-temperature research group on experimental general relativity, X-ray astrophysics, and free-electron laser physics. Ride was selected as an astronaut candidate by NASA in January 1978, completing her training and evaluation period in August 1979. She performed as an on-orbit capsule communicator during the STS-2 and STS-3 shuttle missions and served as a mission specialist on STS-7 launched from Kennedy Space Center, Florida, on 18 June 1983, the second flight of the *Challenger,* and on STS 41-G, launched on 5 October 1984. She served as a member of the Presidential Commission on the Space Shuttle Challenger Accident. Through the NASA Office of Exploration, she produced the report *Leadership and America's Future in Space.* In the autumn of 1987, Ride became Science Fellow at the Stanford University Center for International Security and Arms Control and later director of the California Space Studies Institute, University of California at San Diego.

Ernst Stuhlinger received his education at the University of Tübingen in Germany, where he studied physics under Professor Hans Geiger (cosmic rays and nuclear physics). In 1943, while serving in the German army in the Russian campaign, he was assigned to Wernher von Braun's rocket development center at Peenemünde, where he worked on guidance and control systems until 1945. After the war, he was invited by the U.S. government, along with 126 colleagues, to come to the United States to continue work in rocketry first in Fort Bliss, Texas, and White Sands, New Mexico, and, from 1950 on, in Huntsville, Alabama. His main areas of work included guidance and control, instrumentation for scientific investigations, electric space propulsion systems, and space project planning. Stuhlinger retired from NASA in 1976 and joined the University of Alabama in Huntsville. Recently he has served as a consultant for aerospace companies in projects including the shuttle, the space station, and manned Mars missions. He is the author of *Ion Propulsion for Space Flight* and many other works.

Wernher von Braun received his Ph.D. in physics from the University of Berlin in 1934, two years after beginning work with the German Army Ordnance Department on liquid-propellant rocket engines. Starting with a single mechanic, he soon built up a small rocket development station at the Army Proving Grounds, Kummersdorf, near Berlin. From April 1937 to the end of World War II he served as technical director of the Peenemünde rocket research center, where the A-4 (V-2) ballistic missile and other rockets were developed. With more than a hundred of his colleagues, von Braun was brought to Fort Bliss, Texas, by the U.S. Army in 1945; from the nearby White Sands Proving Ground some 70 modified V-2s were instrumented to undertake pioneering exploration of the upper atmosphere and borders of space. Von Braun and his team transferred to the Redstone Arsenal in Huntsville, Alabama, in 1950, where for 10 years he held key technical posts for the army. From 1960, he served as director of the NASA Marshall Space Flight Center. Particularly gratifying to von Braun during his army-NASA period at Redstone was the successful launch of America's first satellite in late January 1958 and the nearly faultless performance of the Saturn series of launch vehicles during the Apollo lunar exploration program that began in the late 1960s and ended in 1972. After retiring from NASA, he was named vice president for engineering at Fairchild Industries. Von Braun was the author or coauthor of many papers and books, the recipient of numerous honorary degrees, and a member of the U.S. National Academy of Engineering and the International Academy of Astronautics. He was founding president of the National Space Institute. He died in June 1977.

Charles Walker, now Senior Manager for Space Systems Development at the McDonnell Douglas Space Systems Company, was the first non-career, industry-sponsored astronaut, serving as payload specialist on three space shuttle missions during 1984 and 1985. On those flights, he operated equipment designed by McDonnell Douglas for its EOS biotechnology pharmaceutical program that accumulated 20 days and 7.1 million miles of spaceflight experience. Earlier, he served as test engineer on the aft propulsion subsystem for the space shuttle orbiters.

Fred L. Whipple is Phillips Professor of Astronomy Emeritus at Harvard University, and director emeritus of the Smithsonian Institution Astrophysical Observatory. He contributed to early spaceflight symposia in New York and in San Antonio, Texas, and participated in the *Collier's* series of articles on the possibilities of space exploration. He has served on many National Academy of Sciences, National Science Foundation, NASA, and U.S. Air Force advisory boards and panels and committees of the International Astronomical Union, and is the author of dozens of papers and the books *Earth, Moon and Planets; Survey of the Universe* with Menzel and de Vaucouleurs; *Orbiting the Sun;* and *The Mystery of Comets.*

Frank H. Winter, assistant curator in the Space Science and Exploration Department of the National Air and Space Museum, Smithsonian Institution, is the author of *Prelude to the Space Age: The Rocket Societies 1924–1940, Rockets into Space, The First Golden Age of Rocketry,* and many other works.

Index

Page numbers in italics refer to illustrations.